An Introduction to
Pastoral Care and Counseling

An Introduction to
Pastoral Care and Counseling

Ezamo Murry

2011

An Introduction to Pastoral Care and Counseling— *Published by* The Rev. Dr. Ashish Amos of the Indian Society for Promoting Christian Knowledge (ISPCK), Post Box 1585, 1654 Madarsa Road, Kashmere Gate, Delhi-110006.

 ISPCK Classic Series - 2

© Author, 2005
(Revised Edition - 2009, 2011)
Reprint - 2006

Cover picture credit: Internet Sources

ISBN: 978-81-8465-016-7

Laser typeset by **ISPCK,** Post Box, 1585,
1654, Madarsa Road, Kashmere Gate, Delhi-110006.
Tel: 23866323/22
e-mail– ashish@ispck.org.in • ella@ispck.org.in
website-www.ispck.org.in
Printed at Repro India Ltd, Mumbai.

CONTENTS

PART – TWO
Introduction   to Pastrol Counseling

Preface

Having taught introductory courses in Christian Ministry under the Senate of Serampore College for some years I felt the need of a comprehensive guide book on the subject. The contents show the topics introduced and many of them are from the papers I presented in seminars.

I am grateful to the authors and publishers whose materials I used in this book. No formal permission was taken from them as this book is not primarily for a wide commercial distribution. Proper acknowledgments are made in the text where others' works are referred to.

This book is intended to be a guide for both ministerial students and general readers. This will also be a great help to the students of English medium Bible Schools, Pastors as well as lay trainees for ministry. Suggestions for further corrections and improvement of the book are most welcome. Endnotes given instead of Bibliography.

Ezamo Murry

Part - One
Introduction to Christian Ministry

General Introduction
of the Subject

God is actively seeking to reconcile the fallen creation to Himself.[1] God's Eternal Son, Jesus Christ is the agent of this work of reconciliation ever since the fall of Adam. Jesus Christ was present in all redemptive work of God among the old Israel as the *type* of the later messiah manifested in the Incarnation (cf.Ex.17:6;1 Cor. 10:4).

God considered himself as the Shepherd of Israel in searching the lost Israel and considered all his servants, kings, prophets, priests, wise men and women, and the leaders of Israel as shepherds of God's people (Ezk. 34; Ps. 23; Jer. 23:1-4;Isa. 40:11 to cite a few). Jesus used this image of a caring and searching shepherd for himself (Mt. 18:12-14;Lk.15:3-7;Jn.10:1-18 cf. Heb.13:20;Rev.7:17). Thus, God is in his mission to search and care for the fallen creation. In so far as it is God condescending and searching the creation it is a ministry.

Jesus is the ideal shepherd who searches, cares, restores, guides, and sustains the creation. The final proof of an ideal shepherd or the self-giving minister of God is self sacrifice for the sheep. Shepherding task is not always calm, peaceful and comfortable. At times the shepherd's genuine love for the sheep requires confronting the enemies of truth, love and life. David the shepherd describes this task of the shepherd in 1 Samuel 17:31. This is to be taken seriously by all who want to be ministers of God.

Jesus the great Shepherd turned his twelve into shepherds. He wanted them to continue the ministry that he began to do even after he left them. Jesus spelled out to the future ministers that he was sending them as sheep among the wolves, that they would be persecuted and killed even as Jesus himself was to be killed. But he told them to go and serve in the world with courage, for he had conquered the world and that he will be with them always as they continue his work in the world. He made this task clear to all of them when he reinstated Peter as his trusted minister (Jn. 21:15-19).

The whole church is called to join this ministry. It is not only the disciples, the pastors, deacons, evangelist, teachers and prophets but the whole church (the *Laos* of God) is called to minister in the world. It is true there are some individuals called out for some specific tasks in the community and they are ordained to go further steps in obeying and following Christ for the benefit of the greater community. We should not forget the fact that the whole people of God is called to join God in God's continuing ministry in the world. St.Paul mentioned this fact in 1 Cor.12 and Eph.4, by which he spelled out the importance of each member of the church in ministry.

In today's world the needs of persons are so varied that many forms of ministry are developed to attend to these specific needs of the changing world. The church itself takes different shapes, as a large congregation, as smaller fellowship and house churches. Similarly the forms of ministry should also vary: ministry to the individuals, to the families, to the industries, to the prisons, to the rehabs, to the institutions, to the hospitals and to a pluriform community of culture, race, and creeds, for this ministry are also categorised to **office** (those appointed to serve a post for a longer period, like the pastors) and **charism** (those serving the people by virtue of their gifts even without an official appointment) and **task force..**

A very important fact for the ministers to remember is that Christian ministry is a service involving humility and self –sacrifice. Ministry is the continuations of the work of Christ the servant of God. Christian ministry was born when Jesus Christ declared, "I came not to be served, but to serve" (Mk.10:45). Jesus further told the would be ministers that Christian Ministry is a reversed order of the worldly order of rank- the greater serving the smaller, or the master serving the slaves (Lk.22:24-30). In that world of Jesus' time servanthood was a degrading concept but Jesus himself took up that servanthood and turned it into a glorified concept. The author of 1Peter Chapter 5:1-4 repeats this ideal. Looking back some twenty years how Jesus lived out his words, St.Paul eulogised the character of a servant of God, the obedience and humility of Christ in Phil.2:1-11.

Christian ministers are called to such a self-giving services without expecting immediate reward. However, Jesus would not leave his human followers curious as to what reward they have for following him. Here too Peter spearheaded to express the anxiety of the community and asked," Look, we have left everything and followed you. What then will we have?"

(Mt.19:27). Jesus replied Peter saying, all things considered, no one would lose anything by following him. In fact any loss will be compensated hundredfold (19:19). To Jesus life is to be found by losing it for God's sake.

The goals of Christian ministry is put forward precisely by Jesus in his Nazareth Manifesto, Lk.4:18-19,… to bring good news to the poor, to proclaim release to the captives, to bring recovery of sight to the blind, to let the oppressed go free, and to proclaim the year of the Lord's favor. It has also been pointed out that the text from which Jesus quoted this manifesto had more goals, thus, to bind up the brokenhearted, to comfort all who mourn… to give them a garland instead of ashes (Is 61:1-3).

This is in line with the traditional ministerial task of the church (pastor) stated by one of the pioneers of Pastoral care, Seward Hiltner. They are: Healing ministry, guiding ministry, sustaining ministry.[2] When healing is impossible or distant, sustaining ministry takes over to stand by the side of the sufferer. Pastoral guiding, Hiltner warns us, is not coercive or imposed guidance. It is rather an *eductive* guiding, by which the interest of the helpee is dug out and helped to proceed that direction. To this have been added few other tasks by the later researchers in the field as the content of the course shows, viz., Reconciling ministry, Nurturing ministry etc.

Foundations for Christian Ministry

Christian ministry should necessarily be based on the *Bible*, the source of information for faith and action. The written word which is also the account of the interaction between God and the world remains the source of direction and wisdom for the ministry of the church. Christian ministry is not just one of the acts of kindness which many other human groups do in the world. It is unique in that it has the mandate of the Lord Jesus Christ. It is also unique in the sense the mission is rooted in the word of God and in theological stand of the church. The church is a sent community and thus it is missional conveying the good news of Jesus Christ to the world. Jesus said his blood was poured out for many for the forgiveness of sins (Mt.26:28). The church in its missional existence is in search of those "many' for whom Christ died to save. The church teaches the word of God and the kingdom values to the disciples. Christian ministry is always contextual, applying the living word to the emerging human situations. If the given word is not made relevant to the human situations today the word of God is no more a living word but remains a message to a particular context of thousand of years ago. The following are the important foundations of Christian ministry.

A. Biblical/ Theological

B. Missiological

C. Educational

D. Contextual

Forms of Christian Ministry

A. *Worship: (See Chapter 3 for longer treatment)*

All kinds of Christian activity begin by adoring, praising, and worshiping Christ. It is the duty and pleasure of the Creation to pay homage to the Creator. The Creator is worthy of receiving the creation's response in praise and worship. One important function of the church is therefore, worship (leitouragia) a worthy service rendered to the Creator. The church in history has developed varieties of liturgical traditions for this purpose. In brief, liturgical tradition refer to the churches including, the Anglican, the Roman Catholics, the Orthodox Church, the Union Churches in India, following some set materials in their worship. Non-liturgical churches including the Presbyterians, the Baptists do not have any set liturgy to follow in their worship services. They are free churches with the liberty to frame and compose the worship order of the day as they find fitting for the moment. Whichever tradition is followed the worshippers mind should be genuinely dedicated to the divine in worship. Worship can be private or corporate. In either case no superficiality or nominalism will get through the heart of God. Worship is a moment of intensified intimacy with the Creator for a communion with the Creator and for the fellowship of the believers. The Lord's Supper signifies these two aspects of corporate worship. In worship we renew our dedication, we listen to the voice of God (objective factor in worship) and we express our gratitude and homage (subjective factor in worship). Our worship enacts what we are expected to live and do in the world. It is rightly said, when worship ends service begins. We live out in the world whatever we experience in worship continue with:

1. Definition of worship

2. Elements of worship (praise, adoration, confession, thanksgiving etc.)

3. Worship in the liturgical and non-liturgical traditions

4. Music in worship

B. *Preaching: (See also Chapter 4)*

The Church has also the task of proclamation (kerygma), communicating the divine truth through human personalities (Phillip Brooks), proclaiming the word through the administration of the sacraments, and more importantly, living out the word by life examples. Preaching often becomes the central part of worship. There are different types of sermons, like textual, exegetical, historical, Bible characters, life situation, topical, and expository types. Theses days the members of the congregations are well informed to inquire critically any subject the preacher takes up. Therefore the preacher should be accountable to the listeners too. Dr.Surya Prakash had suggested that the preachers discuss the sermon with the congregation or at least some members as the former frames the sermon before presentation. This is so because the preacher cannot simply deliver his/her goods to the congregation without relevance. The preacher should analyze the audience, the occasion and the context to be appropriate to the given context, occasions and the audience to which he/she speaks continue with:

1. Preaching and communication

2. Methods of study and interpretation of biblical texts

3. Different types of sermons.

4. Sermon accountability

5. Analysing the audience, the occasion, and the context

C. *Counseling* is a specialised ministry within the general ministry of the church. Most of the counseling situations are one to one caring conversation in an atmosphere of total trust, acceptance, and confidentiality between the two parties. Counseling can also be of group activities involving partners, family members. Even preaching is often considered an aspect of group counseling. Christian counseling is unique in that it recognizes the presence of the Spirit in all counseling situations. Christian counseling is different also by the fact that it includes God in the agenda when the counselee so desires and it uses religious resources. There is no chance of exploitations in Christian counseling relationships though it can happen in other secular counseling. There are different types of counseling, viz., short time counseling, long term-counseling, formal and informal counseling, depending on the need of the counselee. In every culture there are very many cultural and traditional teachings more and insights by which persons in need of attention can be helped. We need to use these cultural heritage that are helpful instead of following only the western and scientific insights. Sudhir Kakar, the well known Indian psychoanalyst had investigated the healing systems of India and enumerated various methods that are being used by the traditional Indian healers. (for this section see also the other course, Introduction to Counseling)

1. Functions of Care (healing, sustaining, guiding, nurturing, reconciling).

2. Principles and goals of Pastoral Counseling

3. Approaches to Counseling (Directive, Non –Directive)

4. Types of Counseling (Informal-formal; short-long term, Educational; Supportive; Crisis, Vocational, Referral).

5. Personality development. Self–Care of the Christian minister

6. Traditional methods and resources of counseling

D. Education: (See Chapter 4 for more on Education)

Martin Luther is quoted as saying, to the effect, 'even if there be no soul or heaven, we still have to educate the children for the affairs of our world'. Education is one important ministry of the church (didache). Educational Ministry concerns with the nurture of the members with the word of God, with the kingdom values, the right way of living a life that glorifies Christ. H.J.Clinebell, a renowned Pastoral educator and counselor considers nurturing as one vital part of the church's ministry. Unlike preaching that is often an emotional appeal to convince the hearers teaching is a more systematic, cognitive, and logical presentation of the word of God. The Gospel report that Jesus executed both the teaching task and the preaching task. At times the gospels require a critical study is not to and contextual, and comparative study as done in theological seminaries. Such a critical study is not to mitigate the truth of the gospel but to establish a reasoned foundation of what we believe.

1. Methods of Teaching:

    a. Oral (story telling, lecture, sermon, symposium, debate).

    b. Audio-Visual (flannelgragh; film strips; slides; TV; video; blackboard; chart and maps; computers).

    c. Action Oriented (Visits to places of importance; creating indigenous visual aids (e.g. Puppets); Involment in social works; projects; role play; skits).

2. Organisation and Administering the Educational Program of the Church

   a. Sunday School

   b. Youth groups

   c. Adults groups

   d. Bible Study groups

   e. Baptismal classes

   f. Confirmation classes

   g. Training leaders for Christian education program.

E. *Church Organisation and Administration:*

Ministry is possible if only the members of the church, their talents, their visions and goals are well organised and administered. An organisation attempts to bring people together intentionally to coordinate and maximize their afford for higher task accomplishment. The church is not a crowd but an organised group for a purpose. It requires staffing, coordinating, monitoring, reporting, budgeting and constant reviewing of the task performance. Its administration subject includes property management, time management, personal management, programs management, beside others. It is of no use debating whether or not Jesus organised the early church or whether the New Testament has any pattern of the church for us to follow today. We affirm that the church today, as a human group needs organising and administering properly for fulfilling its mission delegated by God. Of late the house church movement is a strong movement even in India. This does not have to be a large organisation needing a complex structure and administration. Church organisations should be seen as a gathering of believers in Christ and not as a trade union or a city corporation. Its head must be Christ and every policy, norms and guidelines should be framed keeping this fact in mind. The constitutions, the operation and the goal of this organisation, therefore, are to be an effective instrument of God. Continue with:

1. Patterns of Church organisation (Episcopal, Presbyterian, Congregational.

2. The functioning of the local Church (Church members, Church committee, Church records, Church finances, Church property, and Church discipline and legal Matters).

3. House Churches movement

Contemporary Issues in Christian Ministry

The initial ministry of the early church could have been more of maintaining fellowship, breaking bread together in prayers, proclaiming the word followed by certain acts of charity to those in need. Today the ever –expanding church coupled with the emerging new human situation requires different modes of ministry to meet these current needs. The societal organisation and re-organisation, the change in climate, the ecodepletion in the biospheres, the emerging new identities of people and nations, the shifts in economic and political powers, the reclaiming of human and animal rights, moral degradation and brokenness, sickness of the humanity – all these contextual issues call for attendance by the church. When the Church ceases to respond to the contemporary issue appropriately it has become a monument or a museum, not a dynamic, functioning body. Few of these agendas of ministry have been listed in the content of the course that follows. continue with:

A. Partnership of women and men in the church

B. Indigenisation of worship and life-style

C. Ministry to persons with HIV/AIDS and addiction behaviors; persons with disability

D. Christian witness in a pluralistic society (responsibility evangelism, compassionate social service, liberating social action, building communities of peace).

E. Challenges of fundamentalism, communalism, and violence in India.

F. Eco-justice and eco-theology.

Endnotes

1. God being beyond gender is the Mother and Father of all Creation. The use of *Him* here does not hold exclusivism.

2. Preface to Pastoral Theology, Adingdon, Nashville.

BIBLIOGRAPHY

NB: A lengthy-bibliography is given for this course in order to provide relevant materials for each section.

Abha, Raymond *Principles of Christian Worship.*

Adams Daniel J., *Biblical Hermeneutics: An Introduction*, Ser. ITL 1987.

Allmen, J.J.V.Von *Worship, its Theology and Practice*, London Lutterworth. 1965.

Amalopravadoss, *Towards Indigenisation in Liturgy*, NBCLC.

Anderson, Douglas, *New Approaches to Family Pastoral Care*, Philadelphia, 1980

Answorth-Smith, *Letting go: Caring for the Dying* Ian& Peter Speck & *and Bereaved*, SPCK 1987.

Autton Norman, *Pastoral Care of the Mentally Ill*, London SPCK 1982.

_______________.,Pastoral Care in Hospitals.

_______________.,*The Pastoral Care of the Dying*

Berne Eric, *Transactional Analysis in Psychotherapy.*

Butler Donald J, *Religious Education*, H& Row, 1980.

Boys, Mary C, *Biblical Interpretation in Religious Education*, Birmingham 1980.

Brenner, S.F., *The Art of Worship*, New York, Macmillan 1961.

Brister, S.F., *Pastoral Care in the Church*, NY H&Row, 1964.

Burkhart, John E., *Worship*, Philadelphia, Westminister, 1982.

Clinebell, H, J., *Basic Types of Pastoral Care and Counseling*, Abingdon 1067/ 1982.

_______________.,*Ecotherapy*, Fortress Press 2004.

Coleman R.J., *Gospel Telling: The Art of Theology of Children's Sermons;*

Cully I.V., *Imparting the Word: the Bible Xn. Educations*, Westerminster, 1962

_______________.,*Christian Child Development*, NY H & Row 1979.

Colston & Paul Johnson *Personality and Christian Faith*, Abingdon 1972.

Currie,Joe., *The Barefoot Counselor*, Bangalore 1976.

___________, *In the Path of the Barefoot Counselor*, Bangalore 1987.

Davies, J.G. *New Perspectives on Worship Today*, SCM Press 1972.

___________, (ed.) *A New Dictionary of Liturgy and Worship*, SCM London 1986.

Dure, M.H., *Understanding the Adolescent, London SPCK 1968*

Das Somen, *Confirmation Lessons*, Delhi ISPCK, 1996.

Davies, J.D., *West minster Dictionary of Worship*

Durrany, K.S., *The Women's Movement in Religious Communities in India* ISPCK, Delhi 2001.

Devadason,E.D.,*Christian Law in India*, Madras, DSI Publication.

___________, *Adulthood and Identity*, Philadelphia 1971.

Emerson, J.G, *The Effective Parish in the 21st Century*, ISPCK 2001.

___________, The Pastor   to Dalits.

Garrett,T.S.,*Worship in the Church of South India*, Lutterworth 1965.

Grose & Grose *Studies for Church Membership and Confirmation*, ISPCK 1997.

___________, Called to Serve, ISPCK 1997.

Groome, T.H. *Christian Religious Education H&Row,NY 1980*.

Hrangkhuma (Ed.). *Christian in India ISPCK reprint 2000*.

Hrangkhuma & Kim, *The Church in India, ISPCK, reprint 1999*.

Hollis, M.*Paternalism and the Church*

Hoefer Herbert *Gospel Preaching, Madras*, Gurukul, 1981.

Irwin, Paul b., *Care and Counseling of Youth in the Church*, Fortress 1985.

Jackson, E.N.,   *The Role of Faith in the Process of Healing, SCM* London, 1981.

Killinger, John, *Fundamentals of Preaching*, Fortress Press 1985.

Kakar, Sudhir & Chowdhury, *Conflicts and Choice: Indian Youth in a Changing Society*, Delhi Somaiya Publication 1970.

Kakar, Sudhir, *Identity and Adulthood*, Delhi, OUP 1979.

_______________, Indian Childhood – Cultural Ideals and Social *Reality*, Delhi OUP.

_______________, Mystics, doctors...

Krass, A.C., *Go... Make Disciples.* ISPCK Delhi, (reprint) 2001.

Le Bar, L.E., *Education that is Christian*, NY Flemming H.R.1968.

Little, Sara, *Learning Together in the Christian Fellowship*, J.Knox Press.

Lazareth, W.H., *Growing Together in Baptism, Eucharist Ministry*, Geneva 1982.

Maharajan, M., *Equipping Laity for Church Growth*, ISPCK Delhi 2001.

Massey, J, Carl *Designing the Sermon*, Abingdon 1980.

Mathew, C.V.& Corwin, *Area of Light*, ISPCK, Delhi 1098.

Maxwell, W.D., *An Outline of Christian Worship*, OUP London, 1961.

Murry, E., *An Introduction to Pastoral Care and Counseling*, ISPCK, 2005.

Neibuhr and Williams, *The Purpose of the Church.*

Oden, Thomas, *Pastoral Theology of Ministry*, San Francisco.

Paton, David, *New Forms of Ministry*, House Press Edinburgh, 1965.

Paqshantham, B.J., *Indian Case Studies in Therapeutic Counseling*, Bangalore 1984.

Paulus, Vimala, *Introduction to Christian Education*, Madras, CLS, 1965.

Roger, Carl, *Client Centered Therapy*, Houghton Miffin, 1965.

Rudge, P.F., *Ministry and Management.*

Rochelle, Jay C. *The Revolutionary Year*, Fortress, 1973.

Ryburn, W.M., *The Theory and Method of Christian Education*, Madras, CLS 1986.

Ramseuy, Michael, *The Christian Priest Today*, SPCK 1975.

Sangster, W.E. *The Craft of the Sermon*, Pickering & Inglis 1974.

Skoglund, J, *Worship in the Free Churches.*

Spivey, R.V, *Preaching the Word*, London SCM 1981.

Schillebecks, *Ministry: A Case for Change*, SCM 1981.

Sleeth, R.E.,*God's Word and Our Words*, John Knox 1986.

Swarup Paul, *Baptism,* Delhi ISPCK 1998.

Saunder, D.J., *Visual Aids for Village Workers, Jabalpur,* CARAVS 1968.

Stewart, W. *The Church and Ministry,* Madras CLS.

_______________, *The Nature and Calling of the Church*, Madras CLS.

Satir Virginia, et.al., *Helping Families to Change,* NY 1983.

Switzer, D.K., *The Ministry as Crisis Counselor,* NY Abingdon 1983.

Yaylor, H.(ed) *Tend My Sheep,* ISPCK, Delhi.

Wooton *Christian Worship of God,* CLS Madras.

Winter, Gibson (ed) *Social Ethics,* London SCM 1968.

Wise Caroll, *The Meaning of Pastoral Care,* NY Harper & Row.

Webster, J.C.B *The Pastor to Dalits,* ISPCK 1997.

Young & Meiburg, *Spiritual Therapy,* Hodd & Stoughton, London.

Wingate, Andrew, *The Church and Conversions,* ISPCK 1999.

CHAPTER 1

Ministry : Christ's and Ours

1:1 Christ's Ministry

> For the Son of Man also came not to be served but to serve, and to give His life as a ransom for many. (Mk. 10:45)

The above statement of Jesus our Lord forms the basis of Christian ministry. Ministry is basically a service to the others without calculating the reward. Jesus Christ came to the world in obedience to God and in the form of a servant to the will of the Father who sent him. His life was given in doing the will of God and in serving the people.For us, the living followers of Christ, we give our lives daily in doing good works as living sacrifices which is a reasonable service or worship to God (Rom. 12:1). Our service to God is done through our service to fellow humans (Mt. 25:31-46). For, it is impossible to love God without loving our fellow humans (1 Jn. 4:11, 20; Mt. 5:23). Jesus' love for humans and his death for them was a ministry to God.

Jesus' ministry was to uplift humanity. He recognised their worth, he established their dignity, he served them and taught them to serve one another. He healed their physical infirmities, he opened their eyes to see spiritual realities. He fed the hungry and released those in bondage. The central purpose of his ministry is found in Luke 4:18-19, often called as *the Nazareth Manifesto* of his ministry. The prophet Isaiah has made this the manifesto of the Old Israel in their ministry (Isaiah 63:1-3). Jesus quoted this to declare the task of his ministry (so is the ministry of the church) saying, "to bind the broken, liberate the captives, release the imprisoned, and comfort those who mourn." To do this work was a noble task for which he gave his life. But God vindicated his life and work as the ideal one by raising him from the death.

Jesus' approach to greatness was through humility and service. He revolutionised the basis of human relations by his service to the lower ranks. It was in a time when the smaller should serve the greater and moreover, to serve the other was a mark of servitude and shame that he reversed the order — the greater serving the smaller until all begin to serve one another (Lk. 22:24-27). To Jesus, greatness comes not by the person's verbal claim but from the testimony of the persons served. Saint Paul put Jesus' mission in picturesque words thus:

> though he was in the form of God, did not count equality with God a thing to be grasped, but emptied himself, taking the form of a servant, being born in the likeness of man. And being found in human form he humbled himself and became obedient unto death, even death on a cross. (Phil. 2:6-8)

Jesus' ministry is traditionally analysed under three functions – as a King, as a Priest, and as a Prophet. However, this should not lead us to forget his servant role as predominant, for, the servant perspective is in all these three offices. These three offices seem to relate with the title CHRIST, meaning 'the anointed', as Healey writes:

> Christ, or the Messiah, means 'the anointed'. Eusebius (c.260-340) pointed out that, in the Bible three kinds of persons are anointed to their office: prophets, priests and kings. To avoid the dangers of discussing the prophetic, priestly and royal offices of Christ separately, it is important to emphasis the unity of Christ's work: it is all for man's (sic) salvation.[1]

This observation has also affirmed that, whatever offices Christ held, it was for the sole purpose of humanity's salvation. Christ ministered to humanity that humanity may be raised to a status, presentable to God (Jude 24). Keeping in mind the dangers of compartmentalising Christ's ministry of the above three offices we may also define each of them briefly, as each office is complementary in facilitating the main goal of his ministry – to save humankind and the whole creation.

As a **KING**, Christ is the Lord, the owner of the whole universe. He came to the world to establish God's kingdom in which every soul will know the Lord and bring honour and glory to his name. Christ's kingship is over the hearts of humans, over the whole creation. In the ministerial term of the Old Testament the king was included and all the leaders of Israel were called 'shepherds of Israel' which included the king who was also appointed by anointing. It is a spontaneous expression for the people to address God as a 'King' (Ps. 10:16; 24:7-10; 84:3; Zech 9:9). The New

Testament also has reference for God or Jesus as a King (Mt. 2:2; 22:2; 18:23; 25-34; Lk. 19:38; 23:2; Jn. 19:12). Jesus was born as a king, accused as a king, and crucified as a king, who is raised from death to be the King of kings and the Lord of lords (Mt. 27:11; Mk. 15:2; Lk. 23:13; Jn. 18:23; Rev. 19:16). However, it is important to remember that the only throne he could occupy was a throne in human hearts. William Barclay's observation is to the point:

> Jesus was the swordless king. He knew the temptation to found his kingdom on power; but his kingdom is immortal for the very reason that he founded it on love... it was the one aim of Jesus to persuade men (sic) to respond to the love of God, incarnate in himself, and to enthrone God as King within their hearts and over all the earth.[2]

As a **PRIEST**, Christ is the mediator between God and humans. The latin word for priest is PONTIFEX (bridge-builder). A priest is to build a bridge between God and humans. In the Old Testament we see the priests offering sacrifices on behalf of the people, and in turn conveyed God's blessings to the people. The Israelites as a whole were considered a priestly nation among the nations, 'to bind the broken, liberate the captives, release the imprisoned, and comfort those who mourn' (Is. 63:1-3). As a priest, Christ worked out God's forgiveness to humans by his sacrificial act in his life, death and the resurrection. He taught humanity the right way to approach God, the right way of holy living so that they can say, "Let us then, with confidence draw near to the throne of grace (Heb. 4:16). Christ's ministry as a priest dispelled the people's fear of seeing or approaching God (Ex. 33 & 20). Humanity can now meet God face to face through Christ's priestly mediation. When humanity had broken the trust relationship between them and God and when the human priests with their own imperfections could not offer perfect sacrifice to regain that relationship – Christ bridged the gap as a perfect sacrifice and a perfect priest. Unlike the levitical priests of the Jews, Christ is the priest of a Melchidzedek order. His sacrifice cleared the way between God and humans once and for all time (Heb. 10:12).

As a **PROPHET**, Christ spoke out the corrective word to the people on behalf of God. Christ, as a prophet did not do this only by words but through his words, actions and the whole life-style he lived, culminating in dying for the word he testified. By his preaching and living the word he showed how loving, compassionate and forgiving God is so that it evoked faith in God in the people. His voice called for justice and righteousness, holy living and awareness of life's purpose. The Old

Testament prophesied Jesus Christ to be born a prophet (Dt. 8:15-22; 34:10). When he was born the people recognised him as a prophet (Mt. 16:14; 21:11, Lk. 7:16; 24:19). All the four gospels recorded his self identification as a prophet (Mt. 13:57; Mk. 6:4; Lk. 4:24; Jn. 4:44). William Barclay[3] underlines the distinctive characteristics of the Old Testament prophets as follows:

(i)   The prophet is one sent by God (Judges 6:8; 2 Kings 24:19). The prophet does not choose his task but is chosen for a task. Even when the prophet realises his/her utter inadequacy one has no escape from it.

(ii) A prophet is spoken to by God (Is. 38:4; Jer. 18:1; Ezk. 20:2; Hos. 1:1; Joel 1:1; Mic. 1:1; Zeph. 1:1; Hag. 1:1). The prophet's phrase is – "Thus says the Lord". S/he has no message of his own. S/he is a mouth-piece of God.

(iii) The prophets belong to God, so God warns, "touch not my anointed ones, do my prophets no harm" (1 Chr. 16:22; Ps. 105:15). The prophet's life belongs to God.

(iv) The prophet testifies against sin (Neh. 9:26) but his aim is not for their destruction. It is to turn them back to God (Neh. 9:26; 2 Chr. 24:19). The prophet is not necessarily a messenger of doom but a recaller and a reclaimer of the people. (Barclay, *op.cit.*, p.243).

As a **SERVANT**, Jesus Christ is often portrayed with a girdle, the shepherd's crook and even with a basin at the feet of his disciples. In S.F. Winward's phrase he is 'Jesus Christ the servant King'. He was a king but a servant of God. He was a king who serves unlike the kings of the world who are served by the subjects (Lk. 22:24f). Paul puts it in plain words that Jesus came to the world in the form of a servant, emptying himself (Phil. 2:1-7). Jesus' work is described as a 'diakonia' meaning a menial service, like that of waiters at the table (Mk. 10:42-45; Lk. 22:27; Jn. 13:1-17). To John Macquire, DIAKONIA is the heart of Christian ministry and says: "perhaps there can be no healthy Christian ministry until the diaconate has been restored and its true serving function rediscovered." (Church, Ministry & Sacrament)

Diakonia refers to a service that is obscure, unspectacular. Christ as a *diakonos* directed his ministry to the sick, the handicapped, the outcasts and the rejects of the society. His work was to bring wholeness (or Salvation) to those whose lives had been ruined. This work bringing people to wholeness was described by Paul as the ministry of reconciliation (2 Cor.

5:19). The ministry of Christ was to reconcile those estranged within themselves, from each other and from God.

Christ's diakonia implied suffering. Someone rightly said, "to live is to love, to love is to serve, and to serve is to die". Suffering and death was the method in Christ's mission. For, the Christ must suffer and be crucified (Mk. 8:31). Edward Judson, speaking of the life of his father (Adoniram Judson) at the dedication of the Judson Memorial Church in New York city, said:

> Suffering and success go together, if you are succeeding without suffering, it is because others before you have suffered; if you are suffering without succeeding, it is that others after you may succeed.[4]

This exactly is what Christ did for humanity by his suffering. He loved his friends so he served them and finally died for them. He did this happily for it was his joy to serve his servants (Lk. 12:37). There should be a reciprocity of service between Christ and his people (Heb. 1:14; Lk. 22:26-27; Jn. 12:26). For, where Christ is, there his servants should also be (Jn. 12:26). Discovering life through the cross is the heart of Christian ministry.

1:2 The Church in Ministry

With the above description of the ministry of Christ we now turn to the ministry of his Body, the church which continues Christ's work. The form and pattern of the church in ministry is drawn from Jesus Christ her Lord. The adjectives of the Church like, *One, Holy, Catholic* and *Apostolic* Church of the Nicene creed are the attributes of Christ... In tracing the correlation of Christ and life of the Church, S.F. Winward underlines four meaningful propositions as follows:

> Jesus Christ the Servant-King and the Church as Diakonia;
> Jesus Christ the Shepherd-King and the Church as Pastoral;
> Jesus Christ the Prophet-Apostle and the Church as Mission;
> Jesus Christ the Priest and the Church as Priesthood.[5]

i.   *Jesus Christ the Servant-King and the Church as* **Diakonia:**

Having loved and served his followers the Lord Jesus commanded to love one another and become servants of one another even as He had done so to them. He added that even the son of man came to serve and to die for many. Therefore the pattern of the church is diakonia. This service is to be extended in the name of the Christ to God and His people.

ii. *Jesus Christ the Shepherd-King and Church as Pastoral:*

In the Old Testament, God is portrayed as the shepherd of the individual
and the whole Israel. The leaders of Israel were called shepherds (Ezk. 34,
Jer. 23:1-4, Is. 40:11) Jesus Christ used this title for himself (Lk. 15:3-7; Mt.
18:12-14; Jn. 10:1-18). The church should extend a caring ministry to the
people, with a concern also for the 'other sheep'. Every member of the
church should have a shepherd heart. The church workers should have
the attitude to turn the whole congregation to shepherds to do this common
ministry of the whole people of God (Eph. 4:13). The shepherd's crook is
a constant symbol of pastoral concern and indispensable mark of the
church.

iii. *Jesus Christ the Prophet-Apostle and the Church as Mission:*

Jesus himself was 'sent' by the Father on a mission to save the world. The
writer to the Hebrews, even used 'apostle' referring to Christ (Heb. 3:1).
As the Father sent him, he now sends the church (Jn. 17:18; 20-21). The
church is commissioned to make disciples of all nations, to baptize and to
teach (Mt. 28:19-20). It is not only the verbal proclamation but by her whole
life and action the church bears witness to her Lord. The church is therefore,
not necessarily a 'fellowship of believers' in static terms but an activity –
mission in a dynamic sense. The oft quoted proposition that the church
exists by mission as the fire exists by burning is an apt description of the
church. (See also *Mission*, below)

iv. *Jesus Christ the Priest and the Church as Priesthood:*

Although Jesus did not call himself as a priest his priestly function is vital.
Even as the old Israel was referred to as a kingdom of priests (Ezk. 19:5-
6), the church which is the new Israel, is also referred to as a royal
priesthood (1 Pet. 2:9). The function of the church's priesthood is witness.
The church as priesthood can be misinterpreted to mean every Christian
is a priest to himself or herself or that s/he is as good as the minister. The
right interpretation is that everyone is a priest to everyone else in the
Christian community. The church as a whole is a priesthood representing
the world to God and God to the world. The church exists for the world,
interceding, mediating, witnessing to and for the world.

The church is used by God in His ministry to the world. The church
does not have a ministry of its own except as a partner in the *Missio Dei*.
God's first concern is the world, not the church. The church resulted from
God's ministry to the world. God's salvific work began even before the
church came into being. Thus, the proper relationship is God-world-church

which order also does away with the idea that God cannot save the world except through the church. Similarly, God's contact with the world is first, through the individual souls. The individual is in direct contact with God through Christ. The church or its ministers, though engaged by God in His work, are not inevitable media in God's salvific economy. In other words, the individual souls who are right with God can be saved even without a system of institution. This is not to belittle the part the church can play in enhancing God's work.

The whole church is invited to join God's ministry. The oft quoted line from 1 Peter 2:9: "you are a chosen race, a royal priesthood, a holy nation, God's own people" implies the church as a whole as the people of God has a ministry and priesthood. Every Christian is a called minister, not only the ordained ministers. The only difference between the lay Christians and the full time workers is that the latter are given an extra responsibility by the church. Their duty also is to train the whole people of God for the work of ministry, for building up the body of Christ (Eph. 4:12).

The priesthood of all believers should not be misinterpreted as individualism either. Robert J. Hater, warns us, "it is a mistaken individualism and egalitarianism that talks about the priesthood of all believers as if this priesthood of the people could be divided up into equal shares among all the members of the people."

If the political theorists warn us of democracy degenerating to mobocracy (mob-rule) we should also be warned of the possibility of the priesthood of all believers turning to a church in which members are autonomous priests. Save for this danger we should not overlook the significance of the church in God's work thus: "The Spirit keeps the church in the truth and guides it despite the frailty of its members. The church is called to proclaim and prefigure the Kingdom of God. It accomplishes this by announcing the gospel to the world and by its very existence as the body of Christ."[6]

1:3 Civil Servants are God's Ministers

One important aspect of the Church's ministry which we should never forget is that the church members in civil services are in God's ministry. Jesus Christ came to claim the whole world, not only those listed in the church register. He therefore, calls all leaders, administrators, rulers and helpers to be His servants (cf. Romans 13:1, 1 Pet. 2:13-16, 1 Cor. 12:28). In the Old Testament we read about God being the head of both the State and the Religion. When human kings emerged to rule Israel they were anointed and called the shepherds of Israel. In today's language it would mean 'the pastors of Israel'. Humans have divided the World of God in to 'sacred' and 'secular', but both remain under the same divine milieu.

God called Israel out from among the nations to be the instrument to reclaim the rest of the nations for God. It was not a special privilege to escape from the world to condemn the world. It is true, Israel as the co-worker with God was told not to imitate the ungodliness poised by the world. However, God's primary concern is the world for which reconciliation Israel was called to be the instrument. So is the calling of the church, to be God's co-worker in reconciling the world to God. God's plan is not to slice out the church from the world before He destroys the latter as often mistaken by the Christians.

If God has such an inclusive shalom for the whole *oecumene*, it makes clear both the servants of the church and the servants in civil services are *diakonoi* of God (God's servants, Rom. 13:4). This bifurcation of the same world of God into 'sacred' and 'secular' has made some church ministers think they alone are doing God's work and not the civil servants. Similarly, some civil servants often legitimise their ungodly acts as due to their work being secular, leaving the whole Christian witness to the church ministers alone. In as much as there are some people of other faiths who do better work than the Christians, there are some civil servants who do better work of Christ than some church ministers. Thank God for recognising His followers not by their claims but by their doings (cf. Mt. 21:28-31; 7:21, 24, James 1:22-25; Rev. 20-12) If God cares for His people he would not leave His people one day a week in the hands of the church ministers and the rest of the six weekdays in the hands of ungodly ministers.

1:4 Call to Ministry

The priesthood of all believers does not mean confusion and lawlessness. God as a God of peace and order works through human society and hence, the need of organising the ministry. Organising the church for ministry is for the purpose of maximising the efficiency of ministry by co-ordinating its members. Proper planning, organising, co-ordinating and leading is necessary for the church to be an effective agent of ministry. It is true that there is a danger of this structure becoming a hierarchical machine that can hinder dynamism, collegiality and spontaneity. In India, the very idea of organised church is questioned sometimes, as done by the Rethinking group of Madras long ago. This resentment will continue if the church becomes a complex hierarchical structure that ignores the varied gifts of the members for the ministry. However, the organised church by itself is not detrimental to an effective ministry. Rather, it recognises the varied gifts of the whole people of God to function as a body in which the parts are complementary to each other. There is a need of teachers, healers, administrators, prophets, leaders and servers. All these works are concerted to fulfil the one purpose – to continue the ministry of Jesus Christ. None of such differentiated ministry is inherently the highest rank. For, even the seemingly humblest part can claim the highest appreciation of the Creator if one performs the task sincerely. That is the norm by which the impartial Creator judges humans.

In the context of the general call to all God's people, God also calls certain individuals, men and women rich and poor to be instrumental in accomplishing certain tasks. God's working through human personalities is proved by the Bible itself. God called Israel as a people to be His instrument but He also called certain individuals to be especially responsible in leading the people of Israel in their common task of witnessing.

Noah and family were called to exemplify obedience to God in a world of indifference and wickedness (Gen.6), Abraham was called to leave riches and family to follow God in great faith (Gen.12), Moses was called to leave his royal heritage and to become the most humble leader and liberator, a shepherd who would not enjoy heaven unless his people should also be forgiven to be there with him (Ex. 32:32). Deborah the judge was called to judge Israel and prophesy the word of God who also composed a song of victory (Jdg. 4&5). Jochebed was called to mother Moses, the liberator and the law giver (Ex. 6:20), Miriam, Pharaoh's daughter, the Egyptian maiden, were all called to save and nurture Moses the servant of God (Ex. 2:7-10).

In this group of women ministers we may also add the New Testament list like the daughters of Philip, Mary and Martha, Phoebe, Peter's mother-in-law and others listed in places like, Mt. 8:15; 27:55; Mk. 15:41; Lk. 8.3; 10:45; Rom. 16:1-6; Phil. 4:3, to mention a few.

King Cyrus, the shepherd of God, was called to liberate Israel and fulfil God's purpose (Ezra 1-5; Is. 44:28). Other examples used as common models of call are Samuel (1 Sam. 1-3), Isaiah (Is. 6), Jeremiah (Jer.1), Amos (Amos 1), Paul (Acts 9). Augustine, Sadhu Sunder Singh, Pandita Ramabai and many others from the history of Christendom to date can be listed. To some, God's call come in a slow, maturational process. For some others, it comes through sudden and dramatic experiences. Still others are called through life's crises.

The individual experience of such a call should be authenticated by the people's endorsement. One cannot simply announce God's call and claim a status or a task in the community. The believers' testimony about the called person should confirm the call. The Spirit of God which works for good always brings about the consensus of opinion among the believers to endorse such a call. Having recognised the call, a training in the field of one's designated work becomes a necessity. For, an uninformed or unskilled person cannot minister meaningfully. Therefore, besides the inner experience of God's call one should seek to get trained and go through the process of people's approval before taking up a ministry. The apostolic church had this process of authentication (Acts 13:1-3). Greenlade, has a point in this regard: "the local ministers were chosen by the people, at least in part. Clement of Rome, in A.D. 95, speaks of ministers appointed *with the consent of the whole church*, the whole local church. Cyprian of Carthage, in 250s, says expressly that the bishop should be chosen in the presence of the people and approved as worthy by their judgement and testimony, and that bishops should be ordained in their presence, so that the ordination, examined by the suffrage and judgement of all, may be just and legitimate. (S.L. Greenlade, *Shepherding the Flock*, SCM. London, 1967, p.43). Such a process of authenticating workers will also avoid unnecessary elements of confusion and heresy in the church. Churches in rural areas receive preachers to their pulpit indiscriminately, resulting in doctrinal confusion and heresy in the church. While respecting the freedom of the Spirit of God the churches should not neglect the systems by which the sanctity and harmony of the people is maintained. A humble servant of God who has accepted the call should not find it difficult to wait for the endorsement of the people with whom s/he lives. Even while visiting churches unfamiliar to them they will need commendation from a significant authority of the church concerned.

Call to ministry is not limited to the ministry of Word and Sacrament. In so far as God's ministry to the world is wholistic God appoints people also to ministry as civil administrators, scientists, technologists, healers and servants. We should consider all vocations as *diakonia* to God (Rom. 13:4), leaving nothing outside the divine mileau. The tendency to consider church ministry as divine and the secular services as mundane, creates a dichotomy in the household of God. All vocation in this *oecumnme* of God are accountable to God (see p.10, 1:3).

1:5 Ordained Ministry

The ordained ministry being a specialised function is authorised by the whole church – the body of the priesthood. For, even the human body is not a random collection of identical parts of organs. The church as the body of Christ has many differentiated, functional parts. In such an arrangement no part claims superiority to the other parts in status. Variety, while adding spice to life also does away monotony. If God is a God of beauty and orderliness He works them out through differentiation in the creation and in the assignments to His people. This is because He has the power to maintain unity in diversity. So is the gift of ministry varied but by the same spirit for the edification of the same body. If much is given to one person the giver would expect much from that recipient, too. What God expects from each of the recipients is not more than the person's ability but his/her best though humble it be. The parable of the talents portrays this truth: each according to the measure of the gift.

With regard to the ordained ministry, the Lima document (1982) on Baptism, Eucharist and Ministry (BEM) affirmed that, "the church has never been without persons holding specific authority and responsibility... the very existence of the Twelve and other apostles shows that, from the beginning, there were differentiated roles in the community."

The same document held that, the Twelve, chosen by Jesus, were promised that they would, "sit on thrones judging the tribes of Israel" (Lk. 22:30), and that they were called to be representatives of the new Israel. This is not to equate the ordained ministry with the apostolic ministry, for the office of the apostles cannot be repeated.

This is to understand the ordained ministry today as the church's attempt to engage certain people "who are publicly and continually responsible for pointing to its fundamental dependence on Jesus Christ and thereby provide within a multiplicity of gifts, a focus of its unity" (BEM).

As H.K. Moulton observed, "we are not ordained to an office; we are ordained to task, the task of service."[7] As long as the ordained ministry avoids creating a special class of ministers (hierarchical sacerdotalism) it continues to be a vital mode of ministry. For, the act of ordination indicates the minister's deeper step in obedience to Christ, a second step in commitment. The BEM document quoted above also warns us,

> "the basic reality of an ordained ministry was present from the beginning. The actual forms of ordination and of the ordained

ministry, however, have evolved in complex historical developments. The churches, therefore, need to avoid attributing their particular forms of ordained ministry directly to the will and institution of Jesus Christ."[8]

1:6 Ordination of Women for Ministry

In 1981, November, an English daily of Bangalore, reported that the Anglican Church of England took a historic step and proposed a draft legislation ordering that "within the historic three-fold ministry, the order of Deacons is an order open to women." The reporter commented, "if eventually passed, the legislation would set up a single Diaconal order giving women and men equal status."[9]

Thirteen years later, that church ordained 32 women priests at a time (1994). Here again, the reporter from Calcutta, referred to the Vatican as saying, "a major setback" about the event, but added that, "outside, the Catholic women demonstrated in support with banners saying, 'equal rights' and 'Catholic women next'."[10] This would mean there is a longing among the Catholic women also for partnership in the ordained ministry. The official Catholic Church's reaction to women's ordination may be seen from the News section of the NCCIR, January 1997 thus,

> "The Pope and the British Archbishop of Canterbury announced on Thursday that their two churches were to rethink their talks on reunification because of the obstacles to reconciliation caused by the ordination of Women."

In a rare joint declaration, they said, "in view of women's ordination, it may be opportune at this stage in our journey to consult further about how the relationship between the Anglican Communion and the Catholic church is to progress." (NCCIR, Jan. 1997, p.67). The appointment of the first Lutheran women bishop was reported in 1997. Ms. Odenberg was ordained in 1997 and became the first female bishop in Sweden. (Clar. 7-6-97). The same year another woman, Ms. Katakshamma of Andhra Pradesh became the first woman Bishop of Asia succeeding her husband, Paul Raj, as Bishop (Baptist News, Jan-June 1997, p.18).

An even more conservative group, the Seven Day Adventists of the US, is reported to have ordained three women, the first such act since prophetess Ellen D. White founded the group in 1863[11] To this may be added that a Baptist Church in North-East India has ordained eleven women, five in Nagaland, and two in Manipur, and four in Meghalaya. The church in India as a whole has some half a dozen women ordained in recent years. Such an egalitarian attitude to the ministry will bring more wholeness and effectiveness to the church. For, the church cannot leave out the greater part of its membership from the ministry. The ministry is a divine mandate to the whole people of God (See also section 2:3 and 7:3.8, *infra*).

1:7 Office and Charism in Ministry

Some ministers serve under 'Office' and the others under 'Charism'. The former is appointed by the people to work on a more permanent basis like, the bishops, pastors, the deacons, and the other church workers. The latter group of ministers are the specially gifted individuals who may not hold any office in the organised church but exercise their gifts in edifying the church. In the secular world, the extraordinarily gifted public leader, the star player in a soccer team, the famous composer, the scientific or mathematical genius may be categorised as under charism. They may not hold any office in institutions but they are an asset to the society. In church ministry, prominent evangelists like Billy Graham and others who do not hold any office in the church but edify the church by their special gifts are ministers under charism.

There is also a dialectic relatedness between the office and charism. A minister in office can become charismatic at times and the charismatic minister can also hold an office, especially when the new movement initiated by them becomes institutionalised. By virtue of popularity and insight the charismatic player in a soccer team (star player) may be made the captain of the team. This is a change from charism to office. Charism simply means a 'gift', so the ministers under office and charism in ministry can be further illustrated, thus: The Brahmins (office) and the Sanyasis (charism) in Hinduism, the kings and the priests (office) in Judaism, the priest (office) and the seer (charism) in animism, the bishops and the pastors (office) and Mother Teresa or Billy Graham (charism) in Christianity.

Official ministers can be referred to those solemnly appointed by the church authorities like the apostles or others (Acts 14:23; Titus 1:5) to special responsibilities in the church, whereas, 'charism' refers to ministry under the direct influence of the Holy Spirit. Ministry under office refers to the 'static' factor and charisma refers to the 'dynamic' factor of the church ministry. There should be no conflict between these two wings of ministry. Both are from the same Spirit for the same purpose, to serve the growth and unity of the body of Christ.

1:8 Patterns of Ministry

As the Bible does not give any particular pattern of ministry for all ministry for all time to come, churches today pattern their ministry that suits their church tradition and the cultural context. The three-fold pattern of ministry (bishop, elders, deacon) was developed in the second and the third centuries. The BEM statement on the three-fold ministry recalls:

> In the earliest instances, where three-fold ministry is mentioned, the reference is to the local eucharistic community. The Bishop was the leader of the community. He was ordained and installed to proclaim the word and preside over the celebration of the Eucharist. He was surrounded by a college of presbyters and by deacons who assisted in his task. In this context the bishop was a focus of unity within the whole community.[13]

In course of time the bishops began to take wider responsibilities, more like the itinerant task of the apostles, an oversight over several local congregations. By this time the local presbyters also widened their responsibility by taking charge of the local eucharistic communities besides assisting the bishops. The deacons as well enlarged their responsibilities. If such a classification of the ministry breeds clericalism and compartmentalisation of functions it will hinder the effective ministry of the church today. For, some have the tendency of assigning the task of oversight, preaching, and administration of the sacrament to the bishops only, the presbyters then, are the in-charge of the church discipline, assisting the bishops, exercising pastoral care. The serving part is left to the deacons exclusively. This pattern creates hierarchy in the ministry automatically. Therefore, even when the ministry is patterned three-fold there should exist collegiality, interchange of functions when necessary. 'For, Christ himself fulfilled all modes of ministry-priest, prophet, deacon, but he was always a *deacanos* more than any other form. This pattern of ministry should be a distinction for function, not for division.

The ministry, whether of the bishop, elders or deacons is exercised within the church and is not an isolated activity. It is exercised within the context of collegiality. Both the ordained ministry and the lay ministry are ministry of the people of God.

According to John Macquirrie, collegiality in ministry is recognised in recent years – the pope with the bishops, the bishops with the clergy and of the ordained with the whole congregation (*Church and Ministry*, p. 159). The Indian Church, the churches of North India and South India, are also under this three-fold ministry. An enlightened churchman of the CNI,

Late Dr. Henry Devadas, made a strong observation on the present pattern of ministry in the Union churches of India, that the pattern has "proved to be unsuitable for conditions in India. The role of the episcopacy has been largely misunderstood in India. The bishops have assumed more power than what was intended by the negotiating committee for the Church of North India."[14] Devadas continues,

> "After a good deal of thinking I am driven to the conclusion that the episcopal system is not suitable either for the CNI or the CSI, and we may have to abolish the episcopacy altogether and rethink the whole question of the three-fold ministry."[15]

Devadas fears that taking the ordained ministry as a bureaucratic hierarchy will make 98% of the church passive onlookers, thus depriving the greater mass of the church from performing their functions according to the gift given to them.

The church in India is now awakened to new forms of ministry to contextualise the ministry to the needs of today. Team ministry, lay ministry, collegiality, lay leadership training, house church, group fellowships, that strengthen each other and re-thinking the church structure are among the directions of new forms of ministry.

The other forms of ministry in India is the two-fold ministry – pastor (or elders) and deacons. This pattern is found among the free church tradition among whom the polity of the church, include Presbyterianism and congregationalism. There is a strong emphasis on the priesthood of all believers and the autonomy of the local church as in Baptist churches. In this set up, the pastor is an employee of the congregation whose voice is often as weighty as one of the congregation members. This extreme congregationalism can sometimes land the church in the hands of the untrained lay members.

The pastor in two-fold ministry is more of an initiator or co-ordinator of the people's activities. The deacons, similarly are stewards and assistants to the pastor as the latter organises and administers. The pastor is, however, responsible in giving the proper directions in the areas of the doctrine, the tradition of the church and Christian nurture.

In this two-fold ministry there are no feelings of any superiority or inferiority among the ministers. For, in all plannings and decision makings the voice of the congregation is final. The ministry is given equally to the whole people of God. The power structure here is the inverted form of the episcopacy (three-fold ministry). An important point to remember in this structure is that, though the congregation makes the final decision the final head of the church is Christ and he is the final authority. The autonomy of the local congregation should not lead to non-cooperation with the organisations outside it either. For, the leaders of the associations and conventions are also appointed by the churches by seeking the will of Christ. Christ is the head of the Church Universal. Every autonomous local congregation should keep this in mind. The saying, "No man is an island… applies to the local church and its relatedness to the church universal.

1:9 The Diaconate Ministry

Saint Paul, in 1 Tim. 3:8-13, mentions the moral qualification of the deacons rather than their functions. "Deacons must be grave…not double tongued". In Philippians 1:1 (Pet. 5:2, and Acts 20:17) the bishops and the deacons are grouped together but as two groups of ministers. The terms, bishop and presbyter seem to be synonymous, but the deacons as another category of ministers. However, Paul's use of *Diaconos*, as a general term for all ministers included the ministry of Jesus (as in 1 Cor. 3:5, Eph. 3:7; Col. 1:23; Rom 13:4). These references show *diaconos* does not refer to an order (or status) but to all who minister for Christ's sake. Even the oft quoted reference in Acts. 6, as the proof-text for the origin of the diaconate does not indicate that diaconate is an order of ministers. It rather terms both the ministry of the table (6:2) and the ministry of the word (6:4) as *diaconai*. The fact also that Philip, one of the seven was later called evangelist' (minister of the word) shows that the diaconate was not an order or official status. By the time the New Testament was written, there was no such order of deacons as a special office. However, it has been evident that by the second century A.D., the diaconate became a recognised office which ministry became very significant. By the early second century, Ignatius often referred to the order of deacons - the bishops, the presbytery and the deacons. The deacons became personal assistants to the bishops in both liturgy and the administrative works of the church.

Besides the bishop (elder) and deacons are also the ministers listed in 1 Cor. 12, Ephesians 4, including teachers evangelists, superintendents, administrators and helpers, who may also be permanent church workers.

The pastors and the deacons are engaged more in the eucharistic community, more local in jurisdiction than itinerant. The others like the evangelists, are intinerant ministers. The pastors and the deacons are the permanent ministers of the Word and the Sacrament, the ministers of nurture and caring in the local church appoints them. Among the Protestant church that appoints them. Among the Protestant churches there is an increasing awareness of the need of engaging both women and men in the ministry. The church for centuries has been under the influence of Judeo-hellinistic culture in which women were not made prominent in society. The New Testament writers were under this influence, too. However, the New Testament does mention both *presbuteros* (male ministers) and *presbutis* (women ministers) as in Titus 2:3. D.F. Hudson argues that, if the term presbyter is same as bishop or pastor, *presbutis* can be considered women pastor as well.[16] Presently, the Catholic Church is more tenacious in limiting the ministry (priesthood) to men only. The next in degree of tenacity may be the Anglican Church. However, we have also mentioned above how the breaking of the iceberg began in the Anglican church a couple of years ago, when it ordained many women for ministry in 1994.

The New Testament does not give any fixed pattern for ministry. The terms like 'elder' and 'deacon' meant at times no more than senior men and servants but which at times refers to ministerial offices. The word 'episcopos' (bishop), possibly a function-word in some instances, is also the name of an office at least in the Pastoral Epistles. While James of Jerusalem would resemble later bishop, Paul also used temporary delegates like Timothy and Titus with authority over presbyters and large areas. There were also prophets and teachers who guided and governed the church at Antioch. The apostles certainly were authoritative in the early church but their role cannot be perpetuated today. So we see a wide range of flexibility as to the pattern of ministry in the New Testament. Greenslade, observes that later, local ministry consisting of one bishop with a number of presbyters and deacons under him began to be established in the city churches. When churches began to be established in the rural areas there arose a question whether the rural churches would need bishops.[18] Such was evident through the document like, a canon passed at the Council of Sardica (Sofia) in AD 343 which says, "permission must not be granted to ordain a bishop in any village or small city for which a presbyter is sufficient... so that the name and authority of bishop shall not be cheapened."[19]

Greenslade shows a Roman clergy list of AD 251 as follows: 1 bishop, 46 presbyters, 7 deacons, 7 sub-deacons, 42 acolytes, with 52 exorcists, readers and door keepers. Later, large cities like Edessa in AD 451 had over 200 clergies of whom 14 presbyters, 37 deacons, 23 sub-deacons and 1 reader were attached to the Cathedral church (*Shepherding the Flock*, 1967).

There were other terms related to ministry in those days, like, the *archdeacon,* first mentioned by the name in Carthage in 303, who was of high importance and often succeeded his bishop. There were also the chorespicopoi (country bishops) who were men with episcopal order charged with pastoral care of part of the diocese. However, both the country bishop and the archdeacon were offices rather than status.

The Didache, dating about AD 100, bears a yardstick to test the authenticity of Christian workers which may be applicable even today.

> "Any prophet speaking in the Spirit you shall not try or test... This sin shall not be forgiven. Yet not everyone that speaks in the Spirit is a prophet, but only if he has the ways of the Lord. From his ways, therefore, the false prophet and the prophet shall be recognised.[20]

It is interesting also to note that the early ministers were not full time, and not always entirely dependent upon their ecclesiastical stipends. The presbyters in those days could also be schoolmasters, cobblers, silversmith or goldsmiths, potters and physicians. Greenslade, reports thus:

> "the labourer is worthy of his hire, and it was not disputed that the clergy might properly live from the offering of the faithful. A common practice was to divide church revenues into four equal parts, one for the bishop's expenses, one for the rest of the clergy, one for the poor, the last for the maintenance of church buildings... And some, including Cyprian, strongly held that, the higher clergy, bishop, priest and deacon, should be whole time and fully maintained, set free from the moral dangers and the time consuming demands of worldly business."[21]

It is important to note also that the early ministry became indigenous before long. The apostles and other missionaries left the ministry to the local ministers. The independent local churches decided their own pattern of ministry. Hence the need of a new form of ministry in different times and places.

END NOTES

1. F.G. Healey, *Theology: Fifty Key Words*, Lutterworth Press, London, 1976, p.8.

2. William Barclay, *Jesus As They Saw Him*, SCM Press, London, 1962.

3. Charles Wallis, *A Treasury of Sermon Illustrations*, Abingdon, Nashville, 1950, p.269.

4. Gilmore, *The Pattern of the Church: A Baptist View*, Lutterworth, 1963, p.55.

5. *Baptism, Eucharist, Ministry*, (BEM) WCC, Lima, 1982, p.20.

6. *Ibid.,* p.21.

7. H.J. Moulton, "Ministry" in *The Challenge of the Concordance*, CLS Madras, 1967, p.123.

8. *Baptism, Eucharist, Ministry, op.cit.,* p.23.

9. D.H. Hudson, "Diakonos and its Cognates in the New Testament", *Indian Journal of Theology*, April-June 1965, p.138f.

10. *The Telegraph*, April 14, 1994.

11. *Forerunner*, (Bangalore), No. 165, November, 1995.

12. *Ministry in the Church in India,* CBCI, 1976, p.21, 43.

13. BEM, *op.cit.,* pp. 24, 159.

14. John Macquarrie, *Theology, Church and Ministry*, SCM, London, 1986.

15. Henry Devadas, *Christ inspires Human Freedom and Justice*, ISPCK, Delhi, 1993, p.13.

16. D.F. Hudson, *op.cit.*

17. *Ibid.,* p. 138.

18. S.L. Greenslade, *Shepherding the Flock*, SCM London, 1967, pp. 34, 36.

19. *Ibid.,* p.37.

20. *Ibid.,* p.41.

21. *Ibid.,* p.44.

CHAPTER 2

Biblical Foundation of Ministry

2:1 Introduction

Jesus is the head of the Church, his body. He called the Church, saying "Come unto me", so that he may send her out, saying, "Go therefore" (Mt.11:28; 28:18-20). The Church derives her authority to minister from this "Go" of her Lord. As a sign of the presence of the Kingdom of God, Jesus healed a man of demon possession and told him to testify it, saying, "Go home to your friends and tell them how much the Lord has done for you... (Mk. 5:19). The Church ministers to express this goodness she has received from her Lord. The sending by the Lord is the foundation of the ministry of the Church.

A pioneer pastoral theologian and counselor, Steward Hiltner (1958, p.147).[1] underlines three types of pastoral care, namely *Healing, Guiding* and *Sustaining* and says, all these three modes of pastoral care are present in the helping act of the Good Samaritan. Binding the wound of the victim is healing; giving a drink from his bottle is a sustaining ministry; and taking the wounded to the inn is a guiding ministry. Jesus told a seeker of eternal life to "go and do likewise" (Lk.10:37), that is, to do like the Good Samaritan, attending to the needs of the people in the society. The pastoral carer derives his/her mandate from this "go and do likewise" of the Lord, and ministers along the modern Jericho road. The compassionate Lord sends his servant church to the wounded and fractured world to heal, to comfort and to guide to make humanity whole. Jesus Christ is a Shepherd King and his Church is therefore, pastoral.

Underlining the biblical foundation of ministry this section attempts to clarify concepts, like the church, ministry, them Minister, the individual, pastoral care, pastoral counseling and pastoral psychotherapy and mission.

The general term 'Man' is used sometimes in this section without implying discrimination of sex, to refer to humanity in general.

2:2 The Church

The community gathered by God through Christ has been called by different names in the New Testament. In the Old Testament, the word used to refer to such gathering was 'Qahal' which is translated 'ecclessia' in Greek. The LXX equivalent of 'Synagogue' also means a gathering of any kind like 'ecclessia'. When these terms are used to refer to the community gathered by God, the 'purpose of such gathering and the people there are different from other gatherings. *Such an ecclessia belongs to God because He called it into being, dwells within it, rules over it and realises his purpose through it.*[2] In the New Testament, that community gathered by God through Christ is identified by various names (or images). Paul S. Minear (1961),[3] identified almost one hundred different images given to that community in the New Testament, like, Salt, Vine, Flock, People of God, New Creation, to cite a few. Minear grouped all these under four major images, namely, *People of God, New Creation, Fellowship in faith* and the *Body of Christ.* Today this community of God is universally called 'the Church'. Jesus used this term only twice (Mt. 16:18; 18:17), and this becomes the important name for the followers of Christ today.

The New Testament has varieties of names for the church because of the nature and the varied functions of the Church. There are those who call the Church as 'Fellowship of Believers' as Baptists do, while there are others who argue that the church should include the new converts, the children and the unbaptised (Winward, 1963, p.60).[4]

It is generally accepted that though the church can be the sign of the Kingdom of God it is not necessarily the Kingdom of God. However, it is the community which has recognised the working of God in the world and has responded to God's call for obedience. It is the community of the first fruit of the new humanity through which God's mission is to be accomplished. The church is founded on Christ (1 Cor. 3:11), and on the witness of the apostles (Eph. 2:20). Christ, on whom the church is founded has been called 'the man for others'[5] and his church has been called 'the church for others.'[6]

The church, in brief, is not the safety boat outside which all are considered lost, nor is the community of the few especially favoured people. The relationship among its members is not pyramidal but circular. Dr. Amalados (1976, p.379),[7] speaks of a new model of the church as that of 'encounter group' of therapeutic situation where the members are equals, each responsible for his/her own liberation and growth. In such a group, everyone facilitates the growth of the others as well. The leader of such a group (Church) is a facilitator. The goal of the church is growth in the spirit of each person. This group *"provides an atmosphere of acceptance and assurance through its faith in the risen Lord. It provides healing and reconciliation."*[8] The only master and Lord of this community is Jesus Christ who continues his mission through this community, preaching good news to the poor, proclaiming release to the captives, restoring sight to the blind, setting at liberty those who are oppressed, proclaiming the acceptable year of the Lord (Lk. 4:18-19). The purpose of the church, as Niehbur (1956)[9] and friends affirmed, is, 'to increase among men love of God and love of neighbours'. The attributes of the church like, *Holy, One, Catholic* and *Apostolic* are derived from Jesus the Lord, thus, the Church is Diakonia, because Jesus was a Servant-King; the Church is Pastoral, because Jesus Christ was the Shepherd-King; the Church is Priesthood, because Jesus Christ was a Priest; and the Church is Mission, because Jesus Christ was a Prophet-Apostle (Winward, 1963).[10]

While thinking about the Church in relation to God's mission in the world we are reminded that God's primary concern is not the Church, but the world. God's love for the world caused Him to send His Son, Jesus. Jesus continues this 'Missio Dei' through the body, the Church. The Church is only a partner of God in history to promote God's *Shalom* to the world. The church, therefore does not have any ready-made agenda of her own. The world, which is God's field provides the agenda of her own. The world, which is God's field provides the agenda for her ministry (*The Church for Others*, 1968, p.20).[11] She goes to serve where the hungry, the thirsty, the naked and the imprisoned, the sick and the broken hearted are found. A study group of the WCC on 'A Structure for a Missionary Congregation' reported once, thus, "Since God is constantly active in the world and since it is the purpose to establish shalom, it is the church's task to recognize and point to the signs of this taking place... Each time a man is imprisoned, tortured or destroyed, the death is at work. But each time a man is a true neighbour, each time man lives for others, the life giving action is to be discerned. These are signs of the kingdom of God and of the setting up of *Shalom*."[12] The ministry of the church, therefore, is for the setting up of God's shalom in the world.

The ministry of the church began when Jesus said, 'I came not to be served, but to serve' (Mk.10:45). The incarnation of Jesus is an embodied message of God's love for mankind or the word becoming flesh (Jn. 1:14).

The good intent of God in reconciling the world to himself was to be accomplished through Jesus Christ and thus Jesus' mission was to do the will of the Father (Jn. 434). The church in mission should also seek to do the will of the Father.

2:3   The Ministers

The Hebrew word 'Shereth' (meshareth) meaning a 'minister' or a 'priest' is translated 'Latourgein' in the LXX meaning 'minister' in the latinised form. Shreth in O.T. meant a ministration toward a higher being, as the priests to God for the common good (Ex. 29:30; 28:35), or one human being to another for common good, as Joshua to Moses (Jos. 1:1). The LXX use of 'Leitugein' meant (Ergon+leitos, or work+people), public duty discharged for the State by richer citizens at their own expense.

The other word for minister in the Old Testament is 'ebed' meaning a slave, or a servant. The word 'ebed' covers varieties of services. According to E.C. John, "Ebed, literally a slave or servant, can be the title for a king in relation to his God, for an official of a king and also the domestic slave. In addition to the notion of work, the relationship category of obedience and loyalty is an important aspect of 'ebed'... Commitment to God's call to do a particular task as a life-long vocation is the essential characteristic of being the servant of God."[12b]-E.C. John sees the main functions of the O.T. mediators as *liberation* and *maintaining justice* in the society, as did by Moses and the judges. He points out the teaching function of the *priests* as one important ministry, the priest as one who instructed the people in the way of God (Torah). For, the priests know the divinely appointed order of life for mankind. The prophets had access to the council of God and they perceived the divine demands and vision of a just society, of God's rule on earth. The *wisemen* were the counselors, who out of their own experiential knowledge were able to counsel others so that people may not be misled by false ideas and hopes which ultimately led to ruin. Lack of wisdom leads to immoral actions, and to the wisemen, the fear of the Lord was the beginning of wisdom.

D.F. Hudson (1965),[13] examined the New Testament words for minister, like, *hierus, episcopes, therapon, presbuteros; leitourgous, huberetes, doulos* and *diakonos,* and found the last, *'diakonos'* nearest to the work of Christian ministry. The New Testament presbuteros, 'Leitourgein' as 'diakonein', meaning both the service of the priest and the people. Diakonia means ministration which is the primary aim of all Christian actions (Eph.4:12). Diakonia is the meaning of ministry whether rendered to God (2 Cor. 6:4) or to Christ (Col. 1:7), to the Gospel (Eph. 3:7) to the Church (Rom. 12:17), or to the saints (Acts 6:1-2), or to Paul (Acts 19:22).

Having listed the New Testament terms for minister which are all masculine, a word about women ministers may be added here. From the earliest history of God's liberation, say the Exodus event, it was not Moses alone who was the agent of God's purpose. The mother and the sister of Moses, the daughter of Pharaoh, and the midwives who disobeyed Pharaoh, were all instruments of God's liberation. So also were the women judges and the prophetesses in the ministry of God's people. In the words of Hudson, "I have heard people argue that 'presbuteros' in the pastoral letters could be translated 'priest' in modern terms, but they do not seem to want to translate 'presbutis' in Titus 2:3 as 'women priests' which would seem to me to be only logical" (Hudson, *op.cit.*). An agreement on Ministry at world level (the so-called, Lima Document) 1983,[14] has a phrase in favour of women's ministry, which says, "the ordained ministry of the church lacks fullness when it is limited to one sex... women's gifts are as varied as men's and that their ministry is as fully blessed by the Holy Spirit as the ministry on men." Hudson asserts that *diakonia basically concerns with doing things for other people.*[15] Bayer calls diakonia as a "discharge of service in genuine love."[16] (See also section 1:6 *Supra).*

The model of diakonia was laid by Jesus when he said to the disciples, "Let him who wants to be your leader be as your servant" (Lk.22:26). The diakonia had two aspects: the diakonia of the word as the apostles did, and the diakonia of the table as the Seven did (Act.6:2).[17] There is no 'orders' of ministers in doing diakonia, for every person has his/her part in the ministry.[18] Naturally, the greater one is served by the smaller ones, but Jesus instituted a new pattern of human relation. He as the Lord of the kingdom of God (Lk.22:29) who can summon the disciples to judge Israel with him is among them as a servant (Lk. 22:30; Mk. 10:45). To Jesus, the one way to greatness is humility and service.

The ministry is given to the whole people of God and the Holy Spirit gives diverse gifts to the people. The Lima Text on ministry declares: "These are for the common good of the whole people and are manifest in acts of service within the community and to the world. They may be gifts of communicating the gospel, in word and deed, gifts of healing, gifts of praying, gifts of teaching and learning, gifts of serving, gifts of guiding and following, gifts of inspiration and vision. All members are called to discover with the help of the community, the gifts they have received and to use them for the building up of the church and for the service of the world to which the church is sent."[19]

Within this general call is again a special call, an ordained ministry. The ordained ministry is not a specially privileged status as often misunderstood. It is a ministry to facilitate, equip the whole serving community (Eph. 4:11-12). The ordained ministry is a three-fold ministry in the episcopal churches, and a two-fold ministry in the non-episcopal churches – bishops, presbyters and deacons, or the last two respectively. The difference between the three-fold ministry and the two-fold ministry are functional rather than hierarchical. The priesthood referred to in the New Testament is to the community of saints, as Lightfoot puts it thus: "The only priest under the gospel designated such in the New Testament are the saints, the members of the Christian brotherhood."[20]

The interchangeability of function among the ordained ministers is evident from Acts 20:28, where Paul called together the 'elders' of Ephesus and told them to exercise their oversight (bishop) and care (pastoral) of the church of God. In Philippians 1:1, Paul seems to address the bishops and the deacons and the people. However, whether it is a bishop, a pastor or elder, the nature of service is always a diakonia, to be Christian service. Their task is the ministry of reconciliation.

John Knox has rightly observed that, "A minister of Christ is useful to Christ, assisting in the fulfilment of Christ's purpose in the world. A minister of the Church is useful to the Church, serving its members in all possible ways and contributing to the growth and effective functioning itself. A minister of the gospel is useful to the gospel, making known the good news of what God has done in Christ, so that the gospel may reach those for whom it is intended and may have its true fruit."[21]

The types of ministers are, the apostles, prophets, teachers, miracle workers, healers, helpers, administrators, speakers in various tongues (1 Cor. 12:28); bishops and deacons (Phil.1:1), Exhorts, Service, contributors, presidents, mercy acts, cheerfulness (Rom. 12:6-8); pastors (Eph. 4:11). Though the elders are not in Paul's list, they were the shepherds of the flock of God (1 Pet. 5:1-3). The elders prayed and anointed with oil in the name of the Lord (James 5:14), they are of the same ministers. It is quite possible that the elders were called bishops to make it intelligible to the Greeks."[22]

2:4 Ministry of Care and Counseling*

The functions of the church is sometimes compared with the four walls of the church building, namely worship, fellowship, education and evangelism. Through these functions the church prepares people to live in harmony with the will of God. Howard Clinebell (1984) has shown the traditional functions of the church as fourfold: *Kerygma*, (Proclaiming the good news of God's love), Didache (teaching), Koinonia, the establishment of caring community with a vertical dimension, and *Diakonia*, the expression of the good news in loving service.[23] Clinebell considers Pastoral Care as basically an expression of Diakonia, but also covering all other dimensions.

The three traditional functions of pastoral care, as Hiltner specified, are:[24] Healing; Sustaining and Guiding, as mentioned earlier. They are described briefly as follows:

1. *Healing:* The type of pastoral work in helping persons becoming whole or re-becoming. It is the process of restoring functional wholeness that has been impaired as to direction and/or schedule.

2. *Sustaining:* The aspect of the therapeutic perspective that emphasises "standing by" when the situation is such that, at least for the time being, change is not possible, one stands by and makes sustenance available. "This is the ministry of comforting.' To this may be added Wayne E. Oates' maxim that the task of the Pastoral Counselor is **"to heal sometimes, to remedy often, but to comfort always."**[25]

3. *Guiding* : This is not an authoritarian directive when the client remains passive. Hiltner calls, this an 'eductive guiding', (eductive, from educare) that is, to make available something which is already within or around the person. Such guiding cannot be coercive. The Pastoral guide makes the choices available and the person makes the decision.

    To these three traditional types of caring, two Church historians, Clebsch and Jaekle (1964),[26] added one 'Reconciling'

4. *Reconciling* : Reconciling is the task of re-establishing broken relationship between men and fellow-women, and between human and God. This can be done through discipline and forgiveness.

    To these four types, Clinebell (1984)[27] has added one-Nurturing.

---

5. *Nurturing:* Nurturing is known in the historical expression as "training new members in the Christian life, or religious education. In modern concept it is an 'educational counseling' and 'care through developmental crises.'[27]

The ministry of care is understood in terms of *Pastoral Care in general, Pastoral Counseling and Pastoral Psychotherapy* in particular situations.

Clinebell defines pastoral care as "the broad inclusive ministry of mutual healing and growth with a congregation and its community, through the life-cycle."[29] To Don Browning (1985), pastoral care is the most inclusive activity, an "unstructured general work with youth, couples, adults and other such groups in various types of informal conversations' dialogue and other communicative interactions."[30]

Browning sees pastoral care as of two dimensions: the activity in incorporating members and their discipline in the group goals and practices, and the assistance of persons in handling certain crises and conflicts.[31] According to Clebsh and Jackle, pastoral care consists in "helping acts, done by representative Christian persons, directed toward the Healing, Sustaining, Guiding and Reconciling of troubled persons whose troubles arise in the context of ultimate meanings and concerns"[32] To John Patton, pastoral care is the broad response of the Christian community through her ministers to persons who are in some way alienated from their faith or from other persons."[33] One important point to note is that, unlike pastoral counseling which is mostly a crisis intervention, pastoral care is an ongoing programme of the church attending to the person from birth to death.

Clinebell describes pastoral counseling as one dimension of Pastoral care which is "the utilisation of a variety of healing (therapeutic) methods to help people in their problems and crises more growthfully, and thus experience the healing of their brokenness. Pastoral counseling is a reparative function needed when the growth of persons is seriously jeopardised or blocked by crises. People need pastoral care throughout their lives. They may need pastoral counseling in times of severe crises, usually on a short term basis."[34] Pastoral counseling, according to Oglosby, is needed "when under circumstances the persons are so wounded, so cut off from the life-giving relationships; so deeply entrenched behind the deadly facade of destructive behaviour that concentrated attention is required for restoration."[35] One new emphasis in Pastoral relationship comes from John Patton (1983) when he sees it as an "offering of humanness in relationship which is in some way patterned after the humanness of

Christ for us."[36] R.J. Hunter, in his most recent work (1990) sums up the difference/similarity of the ministry of Care and Counseling thus, "In earlier literature Care and Counseling were often used synonymously; their gradual distinction no doubt reflects the emergence of counseling as a specialised ministry. Today there is a question as to what extent and in what respects the general ministry of care should be guided by the methods and the principles of specialised counseling, which has heavily influenced its modern development."[37] Pastoral Counseling therefore, is a specialised ministry within the broad range of pastoral care. It is an offering of genuine human fellowship to a person or persons in crisis with a supportive nature. When necessary, moral questions are bracketed, at least for a while, in pastoral counseling. The question of whether pastoral counseling should be proclamatory in nature or therapentic is often debated. However, in all situations, the modifier 'pastoral' should not be out of sight. That makes the counseling situation not only therapeutic but also redemptive. This makes also the pastoral counseling different from other secular therapies.

Some people consider pastoral psychotherapy as a synonym to pastoral counseling. However, Clinebell (1984) defines pastoral psychotheraphy as "the utilisation of long-term re-constructive therapeutic methods when growth is deeply and/or chronically diminished by need-depriving early life experiences or by multiple crises in adult life."[38] Pastoral psychotheraphy, like pastoral counseling is more specified activity but "with time limited constant covering length and frequency of pastoral conversation."[39] This will require insight from the science of human behaviour, social science and spiritual values for effective helping. The question of competency in such professional enterprise for all ministers is to be considered also. Christian ministers are not easily trained in effective psychotheraphy. There may also be a professional encroachment on the part of the ministers, unless the minister is so-trained.

A word about the modifier 'Pastoral' may be said here. Clebsch and Jackle would have used the term 'representative Christian person' as seen above.[40] John Patton observes that 'pastoral' in general refers to the church's care for persons through one of her representatives rather than a reference to the service by the administrator of the parish."[41] Patton (1983) believes that what is pastoral is a 'relational humaness' in our approach to humans in need. Relational humaness takes life as neighbourhood, or an I-Thou relationship that reveals God's relationship to us and it results in healing.[42]

The history of Pastoral Care reveals how there has been a constant fear by certain sections of the ministers for losing this 'pastoral' from the ministry that is the fear of sacrificing the pastoral in favour of 'clinical' or 'therapeutic' among the pastoral counselors.

2:5 Conclusion

Our ministry begins from God's initiative to reconcile the world unto Himself. Jesus Christ is the chief instrument of God in this reconciling Mission of God. Therefore Jesus came to the world as a servant to minister, not to be ministered to. Jesus set the model, content and the authority for ministry to the church, his body. Jesus gave gifts to all the parts of this body, so that the ministry belongs to the whole people of God. Within this general ministry of the whole body, there are also specialised ministries to meet some specific situations. In general, whatever the Church does in the name of Jesus is pastoral, but we can also speak of ministry in specific situations like Pastoral Care and Counseling. This aspect of the ministry takes its mandate from Jesus Christ the Shepherd-King. Pastoral Care and Counseling draws insights from both human sciences and faith tradition. God is understood as a listening God, an accepting and an understanding God who respects human freedom which He gave them. The modifier 'pastoral' indicates a theo-centric nature of the ministry.

Counseling has a lot to do with psychology, the science of human behaviors. For those who consider the Bible as the absolute description of human nature and its message as the panacea of all human problems they will not find psychology as a helpful source for understanding and healing human problems. W.T. Kirwan, + an evangelical Christian psychologist maintains that there is nothing in the Bible that contradicts psychological statement on human nature and for that matter the insight from psychology in healing human problems. He presents the following three statements to this effect:

1. Psychological laws are integral part of the creation order itself and everywhere assumed in the Bible.

2. Throughout scriptures there is a stress on the human need for relationships.

3. The Bible is replete with data on the chief dimensions of the human personality – knowing, being, and doing.

The Bible has also several references on human destructive emotions like, anger, anxiety, guilt, aggression, and depression. These emotions cannot be resolved easily by pronouncing scriptural sentences on them. The *neuthetic* counselors hold that the scriptures are the sole healing means and nothing else, including the science of human behavior. While we all trust the scriptures as an important source of healing we cannot simply tell an angry man, *"Do not be angry, for it is sinful to be angry."* Psychological counselor can help in dissolving the anger healthily. Anger and any other strong emotion cannot be hushed up without dealing with it carefully. Again, when we tell the bereaved mother not to cry, as she will meet her deceased daughter in heaven we are just jumping the boundary of humanity and escaping to idealism. This is not to deny the place of faith in counseling but to recognise the fact that Jesus the human cried when his friend Lazarus died and thus touched by the agony of the sisters. The Bible will also approve any such healthy way of dealing with the flesh as Jesus did when he wept (John 11:35). For, the message of the Bible seeks to nurture a person to health, sincerity, maturity, and reliability, which psychology attempts also to lead humans to these ends. Similarly, the Bible teaches the person the right way of relating to self, others, and God. Eric Berne, in his Games People play ++ how people at time relate with one another in a harmful ways- through games that have hidden agendas and superficiality than in ways of love and intimacy. Both the Bible and psychology try to remove superficiality in human relations, ulterior motifs, insincerity and immaturity in dealing with one another. We can safely say that psychological counseling attempts to elaborate the teaching of the Bible, which we find in concise presentation, often in pronouncement sentence. Psychological counseling helps the person to understand the situation from human perspective and in sympathy with our humanity. Therefore, Christian ministers who know the scriptures as well as the science of human behavior are better equipped than those who depend only on one of the two sources of our knowledge in dealing with human problems, wellness, joys and sorrows.

ENDNOTES

1. Seward Hiltner, *Preface to Pastoral Theology,* Abington, Nah, 1958, p.147.

2. Paul S. Minear, 'Idea of Church' in *IDB*, Vol. 1 (AD) Abingdon, 1985, p.608.

3. Paul S. Minear, *Images of the Church in the New Testament,* London, 1961.

4. S.F. Winward, 'The Church in the New Testament' in *The Pattern of the Church: A Baptist View,* Gilmore (Ed.), London 1963, p.60.

5. Erik Routley, *The Man for Others,* 1964.

6. Charles Royal, *The Man For Others,* 1973.

7. Fr. Amalados, 'Models of the Church and the Concept of Ministry in *Ministries in the Church in India,* CBCI Centre N. Delhi 1976, p. 379.

8. *Ibid.*

9. Richard Niehbur, et.al. *The Purpose of the Church and Its Ministry*, Harper and Row Publishing, N. York, 1956.

10. Gilmore (ed.), *op.cit.*

11. The Church for Others, *op.cit.,* p.20.

12. *Op.cit.,* 12b. E.C. John, 'Christian Ministry: A Biblical Perspective' in *Masihi Sevak,* UTC, March 1988, p.38.

13. D.F. Hudson, 'Diakonia and its Cognates in the New Testament' in the *India Journal of Theology,* April, 1965, p.138.

14. Report of Faith and Order Commission, WCC, Lima, Peru, *Growth in Agreement,* Editors: Meyer and Vischer, Paulist Press, N.York, 1984.

15. D.F. Hudson, IJT, *op.cit.,* p.142.

16. Beyer, 'Diakonio' in *Theological Dictionary of the New Testament,* Vol. 2, Ed. G. Kittel, WB Eerdsmans Publ. Co. GR Michigan, 1964, p.81.

17. Lancaster, 'The Theology of the Diakonate' in *IJT,* Dec. 1959, p.151.

18. *Ibid.,* p.151.

19. *Growth in Agreement, op.cit.,* pp.438-484.

20. Lightfoot, 'Christian Ministry' in his Epistle of *St. Paul to the Philippians* (2nd Edn.) London, Cambrige, McMillion, 1869, p.182.

21. John Knox, 'The Ministry in the Primitive Church' in the *Ministry in Historical Perspectives* (eds.) R. Niehbur and D.D. William Harper & Row, NY, 1956.

22. *Ibid.*

23. Howard, J. Clinebell, *Basic Types of Pastoral Care and Counseling,* Nashville, 1984, p.66.

24. Seward Hiltner, *Preface to Pastoral Theology, op.cit.,* p.89f.

25. Wayne E.Oates, *Pastoral Counseling,* Westminister Press, Phila. 1974, p.9.

26. Clebsch and Jackle, *Pastoral Care in Historical Perspectives,* Prentice Hall Inc. Eaglowood Cliff, N. Jersy, 1964, p.9.

27. Clinebell, *Basic Types of... op.cit.,* p.26.

28. *British Association for Pastoral Care and Counseling,* (n.d.) Constitutional Papers, p.9.

29. Clinebell, *Basic Types... op.cit.,* p.26.

30. D.S. Browning, 'Introduction to Pastoral Counseling' in *Clinical Handbook of Pastoral Counseling,* eds, Wicks Person & Capps. Paulist Press, Integration books, N.Y. 1985, p.5.

31. D.S. Browning, *The Moral Context of Pastoral Care,* The Westminister Press, Philadelphia, 1976, p.29.

32. Clebsch and Jackle *Pastoral Care in Historical Perspective, op.cit.,* p.4.

33. John Patton, *Pastoral Counseling: A Ministry of the Church,* Abington Press, Nashville, 1983, p.16.

34. Clinebell, *Basic Types... op.cit.,* p.26.

35. William Ogleby, *Biblical Themes for Pastoral Care, Abingdon,* 1980, p.42.

36. John Patton *Pastoral Counseling, op.cit.,* p.14.

37. R.J. Hunter (ed), *Dictionary of Pastoral Care and Counseling,* Abington, 1990, p.845.

38. Clinebell, *Basic Types of... op.cit.,* p.26.

39. *Ibid.*

40. Clebsch/Jackle *Pastoral Care...op.cit.,* p.4.

41. Platton, *Pastoral Counseling, op.cit.,* p.16.

42. *Ibid.*

CHAPTER 3

Preaching and Worship

WORSHIP

We are familiar with the word 'liturgy', which means, 'an act of worship'. Singing, prayers, readings and other worship elements arranged to be used in a worship are also called a 'liturgy'. The word 'liturgy' comes from a Greek word *'leitourgos'*, meaning, *'one who performs service to public at one's own expense'*. Such act of free service to the public was called 'leitourgis', from which the present English usage 'liturgy' comes. In the New Testament, a minister or a servant was described by that term (Rom. 13:6; Phili. 2:25). The word 'Latria' means both *service* and *adoration.*

The English word 'worship' as we use today, comes from an Anglo-Saxon word, WEORTHCIPE, meaning 'honour' or 'worthship'. Worship declares God's worthiness to be praised. Worship is the creature's act of ascribing what is due to the Creator. Worship is primarily the creature's duty or service to the Creator (the objective) and not necessarily a means of emotional satisfaction (the subjective) of the worshipper. However, it is true that worship contains the **subjective factor** (adoration, praise, singing and prayers etc.), and the **objective factor** (reading of the Word, preaching to which the worshippers listen and sacraments etc.)

MacNutt shows us some of the *definitions* of worship,[1] as, "certain type of activity of the soul of man" or, "certain type of response of the creature to the Eternal" (Underhill). "Worship is the adoration of God, the ascription of supreme worth to God, and manifestation of reverence in his presence" (Sperry). "It is an inner posture of the individual, his/her attitude toward God" (Brightman) For, no true worship is transacted without a conscious attitude to God.

The principles underlying worship are:

(a) that worship and mission cannot be separated (liturgy and life)

(b) It is a celebration of what God has done (by a congregation), so the structure of the worship should be arranged like a story.

(c) Worship consists of an objective factor and a subjective factor: that is the divine message and the human response.

(d) Worship must be done decently and in order. Indisciplined worship is a confusion.

(e) It should contain congregational participation. The pulpit should not obstruct the view of the congregation, and the leader should face the congregation.

Worship is a state of mind. It can be a *private* activity as in our personal devotions. It can also be *public* as in our group worships, like the one in the Church, in institutions, homes and other places.

3:1 Liturgy and Life

Christian worship always begins with God. It is a creature-Creator encounter. God is the object of worship and the worshippers are the subjects. Worship takes place where there is a divine revelation and a human response to that disclosure of God. Niguidula rightly puts it thus:

> "Worship is man's response to an awareness of the presence of God. The response may be in praise and thanksgiving, in utter contrition, or in selfless commitment to the cause of the one worshipped. Worship always has this two-fold action: an awareness or consciousness of a revelation of God and of God's presence, and a corresponding response or reaction of the worshipper to such an awareness. Where one of these aspects is absent, worship has not taken place."[2]

In the worship experience of the prophet Isaiah (Is. 6:1-8), he saw the Lord and heard the angelic voice (revelation), he realised that he was a man of unclean lips (confession), then he experienced the cleansing touch of God (sanctification); and he responded to the call to go out of the place of worship, to the world as a witness (mission). Worship always leads to action, as Isaiah experienced. The meaningfulness of a worship inside can be determined by what follows outside in the daily lives of the worshippers. Niguidula puts it thus:

> "What happens during the worship is as important as what happens after it. For the essence of worship is not how man encounters God,

or that man has met God, but what he does about it... for a man's worship determines the quality and the pattern of his life."[3]

Passages like Isaiah 58:1-7; Amos 5:21-25; Micah 6:6-8; are few examples from the prophets showing how God wants his worshippers to live their daily lives worthy of their worship. God associates inner purity and spirituality with our function in the society as the salt, and the light. In the Isaiah passage (58:1-7), God told the Israelites that true austerity (worship e.g.), before God is to do good to His people in the society. This is illustrated in, the Amos passage too (5:21-25). God, similarly, resented the lip service in the temple and demanded that justice and equity be promoted in the society. In the Micah passage (6:6-8), the same demand is made from the worshippers. In the New Testament, Mt. 25:31-46, shows how Jesus taught that people who live close to God order their daily lives in acts of kindness to their fellow beings, especially those in need. Jesus also taught to the effect that peace and harmony with our fellow beings should precede worship (Mt. 5:23). John wrote to the effect that our love of God is seen in our love of fellowhumans (1 Jn. 4:20). These few references are cited to show how worship is related to mission in the world. Our solemn worship and fellowship with God should be a time of preparation for our mission in the world. J. Morikawa, speaks of the Sunday morning worship as a reminder of what our lives at any given moment should be, rather than considering it as the only true worship. He says,

> "It recalls us to the central end of life, that it be lived in worship and adoration. Man should live always in worship, glorifying God in all that they do. But being frail humans prone to forget Him, men need at regular intervals vivid reminders of the central end for which they live."[4]

3:2 Elements of Worship

There are some essential *elements of worship*. The pastor as the leader of the congregational worship should plan to incorporate the traditional heritage as well as the needs of the worshippers today as s/he plans the worship. The language of the worship should be intelligible to the people. Where possible, indigenous expressions should be encouraged in worship. The worship leader should know the needs, hopes and aspirations of the people. Sometimes the people themselves may be involved in planning the worship, like in selecting the hymns, suggesting prayer items or ideas for the sermon.

The following are two samples of worship order showing the important elements of worship, one from the *Worship Manual* (F.S. Downs) Commonly used in our churches, and the other from the *CELEBRATION: A Source Book For Christian Worship* (Niguidula: Philippines).

F.S. Downs' Model	**L.N. Niguidula' Model**
* Prelude	
1. Call to Worship	**1. Praise and Adoration of God**
2. Invocation	a) Introit
3. Adoration and Praise	b) Call to Worship
4. Prayer	c) Invocation
5. Confession of Sin	d) Hymn of Praise
6. Assurance of Pardon	e) Psalter or Creed
7. Thanksgiving	f) A Canticle or Doxology
8. Supplication	**2. Confession of Sin and**
9. Intercession	**Assurance of Pardon**
10. Hymns & Special Numbers	a) Call to Confession
11. Responsive Readings	b) Prayer of Confession
12. Scripture Lessons	c) Kyrie Eleison
13. Sermon	d) Assurance of God's Pardon
	e) A Canticle
14. Affirmation of Faith	**3. Intercession for God's**
15. Consecration	**People**
16. Offertory	a) Sharing of the Church's Concerns
17. Benediction	b) Pastoral Prayer or Morning Prayer
*Postlude	c) The Lord's Prayer
	d) Gloria

4. Proclamation of the Word of God

    a) Hymn of Proclamation

    b) Reading of Scriptures

    c) Anthem or Gloria Patri (if not used above)

    d) Sermon

5.   Dedication of Lives and Offerings

    a)   Call to Offering

    b)   Presentation of Offerings of life and labour

    c)   Offertory Anthem or Hymn

    d)   Doxology (if not used above)

    e)   Prayer of Dedication and Thanksgiving

    f)   Hymn of Dedication or Consecration

    g)   Benediction

    h)   Ascription of Glory

    i)   Choral or Congregational Amen.

These two samples contain the essential elements of worship. We can see how many of them can be found in our worship items, even from that of F.S. Downs' list. We are familiar with most of them though how we make them meaningful to the worshippers is not sure. This is true even of the more common features like, *Thanksgiving, Confession and Intercession.* For instance, Confession is an important element of worship done in many churches through congregational responses. At the end of this congregational confession comes the assurance of Pardon (absolution) where the leader pronounces:

> "May the Almighty and merciful Lord grant unto us Pardon and remission of all our sins, time for amendment of life, and the grace and comfort of the Holy Spirit. Amen."

I find this pronouncement very comforting when I attend churches using the absolution. I am sure many wearied souls in the worship (including the guiltridden worshipper) will find great release of tension and experience of forgiveness. Other simpler items like, *'Gloria Patri'*, *Doxology, Kyrie Eleison* can help moulding the worship spirit. Use of Prelude and *Postlude,* can also make the worship experience very inspiring. The prelude can be done by a prayerful singing of verses like, "The Lord is in His holy Temple, let all the earth keep silence before Him" by the choir or an appointed group. This helps the congregation to shut out the outside thoughts and concentrate in worship and meditation. The postlude can be done by the same group singing the AMENs as soon as the benediction is pronounced. Churches having instruments like Piano or Organ (or any other musical instruments) may do the prelude and the postlude through musical items.

3:3 Indigenisation of Worship

If the church should be rooted in the soil of the land, its worship should also be rooted in the culture of the given people. Devotees of a certain culture have their own special appeal to the mind. When the Jews and the Western world have used such objects, postures, arts and symbols of their culture, we in India should also use vehicles common to our Eastern mind in worship. In India, the worship place, its structure, the postures and the sitting arrangements of the worshippers are made Indian as far as possible. The use of dance, *bhajans*, lyrics and musical instruments commonly used in India are extensively used in worship. Religious festivals, feasts with Indian food items and utensils, leaves, flowers and colours add to the Indianess of the worship and fellowship. Physical cleanliness of the devotee, the attitude and approach to the sacred, the place of silence and meditation in Indian culture are all sources of deepening solemnity and communion with the deity.

A good example of indigenising worship in India is given by Eric Lott, who re-wrote the Eucharistic liturgy into five moves using Indian terminologies, thus:

1. *Pravesa* (Entry into presence of God): The worship leaders enter the church in procession while the rest of the worshippers remain standing. The Bible is brought in with the procession and kept behind the lamp. Then the first part of the worship begins.

2. *Prabodha* (Awakening to the Word of God): The reading and preaching of the Word takes place.

3. *Smarana* (Recalling and offering): Here the offering is taken, the bread and wine are brought and an intercessory prayer offered.

4. *Prasada* (The sharing) Here the elements are shared and taken by all.

5. *Preshana* (Blessing and commission). Worship in Indian Context.[5]

To the tribals like the Nagas, the common houses in each of the sectors of the village (Morung) is a distinct and a commanding structure in the village. The structure of the morung, its pedagogical role in the society's nurture, its community experience of the village can influence the Naga church structure (architecture), its moral and religious teachings and the corporate life much like the Synagogue has done to the Christian worship.

The Nagas feasting among the members of reconciling villages and communities can throw light to their understanding of the Eucharist. Their use of bamboo, especially the arching young shoots in religious ceremonies, utensils made of it, use of fresh leaves and scented herbs, eggs, rice, other food items to approach the supernatural can be retrieved with Christian meanings. The tribals, especially the Nagas, have many beautifully harmonised traditional tunes. Tribal songs, usually, are mostly group songs sung anti-phonally. These songs can be used with gospel words in worship. Once they begin to use them they will bring the same devotional effect in worship. The benevolent and therapeutic expressions of the prayers in the old faith can be used in praying to the God they worship today.

3:4 The Eucharist (or, The Lord's Supper, or The Holy Communion)

The Lord's Supper is an important element of worship which comes under the 'objective factor' in worship. It is a dramatic way of communicating the divine truth to us. It is an act by which the self-giving love of Christ for his people is enacted and proclaims his death until he comes again. Among the Free Churches, the Baptist churches of North-East India celebrates the least though some of them do it at least once a month. The New Testament references of this dominical ordinance are found in 1 Cor. 11:23-25; Mt. 26:26-29; Mk. 14:22-25; and Lk. 22:14-20.

The well-known text, 'LIMA DOCUMENT' of 1982 on Baptism, Eucharist, Ministry (BEM), underlines at least five meanings of the Eucharist emphasised by different church traditions as they celebrate it, thus:

1.   The Eucharist as a Thanksgiving to the Father

2.   The Eucharist as Anamnesis (or memorial) of Christ

3.   The Eucharist as Invocation of the Spirit

4.   The Eucharist as Communion of the Faithful

5.   The Eucharist as Meal of the Kingdom[6]

As the document declares:

Every Christian receives this gift of salvation through communion in the body and blood of Christ. In the Eucharistic meal, in the eating and drinking of the bread and wine, Christ grants communion with himself. God himself acts, giving life to the body of Christ and renewing each member. In accordance with Christ's promise, each baptised member of the body of Christ receives in the Eucharist the assurance of the forgiveness of sins (Mt. 26:28) and the pledge of eternal life (Jn. 6:51-58).[7]

When the Eucharist is included in worship, it is convenient to divide the worship hour into two parts: *The Ministry of the Word* and *the Ministry of the Table.* For the appropriate order of its celebration the readers may consult worship manuals of their church tradition. The following elements of the Eucharistic worship is the so-called, *'The historical elements of the Eucharistic liturgy'* quoted here for comparison with each denominational elements:

- hymns of praise

- act of repentance

- declaration of pardon

- proclamation of the Word of God, in various forms;

- confession of faith (creed)

- intercession for the whole church and for the world

- preparation of the bread and wine

- thanksgiving to the Father for the marvels of creation, redemption and sanctification (deriving) from the Jewish tradition of the *berakah.*

- the words of Christ's institution of the sacrament according to the New Testament tradition.

- the *anamnesis* or memorial of the great acts of redemption, passion, death, resurrection, ascension and Pentecost, which brought the church into being.

- the invocation of the Holy Spirit (epiklesis) on the community, and the elements of bread and wine (either before the words of institution or after the memorial, or both; or some other reference to the Holy Spirit which adequately expresses the epikletic character of the Eucharist).

- consecration of the faithful to God

- reference to the communion of saints

- prayer for the return of the Lord and the definitive manifestation of his kingdom

- the Amen of the whole community

- the Lord's prayer

- sign of reconciliation and peace

- the breaking of the bread

- eating and drinking in communion with Christ and members of the church.

- final act of praise

- blessing and sending.[8]

PREACHING

Preaching is the proclamatory function of the church (Kerygma). It is the proclamation of God's salvation. *Teaching* (didache) is another important function of the church. Teaching is more of an ethical instruction, whereas, preaching is, basically, the public proclamation of Christianity to the non-Christian world (C.H. Dodd).

3:5 Preaching Defined

Preaching is defined as the 'communication of divine truth through human personality" (Philips Brooks). God uses human personality as a highway to come to human and for human to come to God – a personal encounter through the preacher's personality. Preaching is not only a proclamation of the historical events of Christ's life and work – it is done through the channel of human personality. Therefore, the preacher's sincerity, dedication is required. No one can preach effectively without a genuine sense of call from God. Bernard Meaning's definition of sermon is short and to the point: A sermon is "a manifestation of the Incarnate Word from the Written Word by the spoken word." Sangster would define: "A sermon is not a lecture because its aim is not simply to inform. It is not a platform speech because it is not the delivery of one man's thought to others. It is nearer the work of a herald, yet with this important difference: a herald today is merely a mouth-piece, and a preacher when he preaches must give himself."[9] Preaching can be invalidated by the preacher's life that contradicts the message. For, the preacher's life is the greatest sermon s/he can ever preach.

3:6 Goals of Preaching[10]

To instruct: God has given the gift of preaching to the church to convey the facts and content of God's revealed truth. This is to 'preach the gospel to every creature' (Mk. 16:14). This task is essential to faith and salvation of humankind (Rom. 10:7). All preaching must contain instruction about this gospel truth. The preacher interprets this revealed truth in the light of inspiration and patient scholarship. To do this the preacher consults the language of the scriptures, grammar, and the commentaries of the sound thinkers of the church.

To persuade: The preacher persuades the people through the powerful appeal to their motives, to make the gospel truth true to them. This is more than a mere instruction. Persuasion is 'speaking the truth in love' (Eph. 4:15), appealing to the will for moral affection. The preacher should have a zeal to save souls by persuasion.

To edify: This attempts to build up the soul in holiness and righteousness, to make souls 'Christ-like'. The work of the preacher is to 'perfect the saints' for the work of the ministry, for the edifying of the body of Christ, till we all come in the unity of the faith, and of the knowledge of the son of God, unto perfect man unto the measure of the stature of the fulness of Christ." (Eph. 4:12-13). Hoppin maintains that the immediate aim of preaching is *soul-enlightenment* and *soul* conversion but the final object of all true preaching is soul-edification,, that is, the formation of a true personhood in Jesus Christ. Saint Paul spoke of the goal of proclamation as, to 'present every man mature in Christ' (Col. 1:28). It will be interesting to know if our preaching have these goals. Many a times our preaching may be a pre-dominantly expression of our needs and scoldings of those we think would not agree with us. It will be unfortunate if our preaching to 500 people are determined by what we want to tell few individuals. It may also be found that most of our messages contain threat and judgement of people rather than announcements of the glad tidings. Sometimes our preaching can be so mechanical and routine that the needs of the hearers are not met. It will be helpful if we sometimes invite feed-back to see if our preaching are so distant from the daily experience of the people.

There is also the temptation of reading certain texts from the Bible and telling our own story, rather than the content of the passage reading. Sometimes excessive use of unexplained foreign words (like English) in our preaching mar the impact of the message. Some preachers are very fond of hypothetical stories, wonder stories from far countries, mysterious and superstitious stories to amuse the hearers. Use of stories (hypothetical or factual) should directly support the point the preacher is driving home. Irrelevant use of illustrations always ruin the sermon. A sermon should be properly introduced, explained or argued and concluded with a challenge for a response in action.

Preaching should touch the cognitive (intellectual understanding), the affective (attitude and feeling) and the executive (action) parts of the listener. Though preaching should appeal the emotion (affective) it should not be a mere emotional exercise. Our churches receive a heavy dose of emotional preaching but very less detailed teaching of the Bible. Our churches should have strong Bible Study programmes to strengthen the Word preached. The Word should take root in the depth of the heart, not only on the emotional level.

Jitsuo Morikawa, states a case of an American lay group who were asked for "the frankest disclosure of their deepest feelings in relation to their Christian faith and Church"... *"First,* they saw little relationship between the sermon they heard on Sunday and the life they live during the week, especially in their places of daily work. *Second,* very little genuine conversation and dialogue took place between the pastor and the laymen. *Third,* they confessed painful ignorance of the central message of the gospel."[11] Forget about the learned Americans, and think of our pre-dominantly rural congregations how far they can be aware of the central meaning of the gospel. This can happen when the pastor assumes the role of an authoritarian speaker and announcer while the people are expected to listen passively and simply to follow. The pastor preacher should be able to receive feedback through occasional sharing with the lay people.

3:7 The Church Year (Feasts and Seasons unfolding the Story of God in Christ)

One important task of the preaching pastor is to feed the congregation with a balanced diet, a systematic feeding with the Word for an all-round healthy growth in Christian life. Perhaps our sermons are so centred around certain themes and topics we are familiar with, or certain idealogies we tend to propagate. Our congregation may have become bored of hearing the same type of sermon Sunday after Sunday. One way to avoid such an uncharted preaching is to follow the *Christian Year* (or Church Year, or, Church Calendar)[12] in our preaching. Many pastors do not seem to know what 'preaching the Christian year' means. The Christian Year is the cycle of events in the salvation history – events in the life and ministry of Jesus Christ the Saviour, plus the important events from the tradition of the Church (like Reformation Sunday, Race Relation Sunday, Mothers' Day and others). Our churches do not seem to give importance to the saving acts in our preaching. We do celebrate Christmas, Easter and Good Friday (these few of the many events) but what message we impart on these occasions is to be ascertained. These events are now so commercialised that we may be enchanted to observe them in festive mood alone, leaving out their eternal messages. Such events are the preacher's opportunities to present the Word at the right time. Many of our village churches may not know what is Lent or Passion Week. Some churches around the world would not fix times of merry making and festivities (such as weddings) on such great events of the church to show solidarity in Christ's suffering and death. It is the preacher's task to arouse an appropriate response from the congregation on such events.

Preaching the Christian Year should not make us ignore the life-situation messages. The preacher should be able to incorporate messages of current needs without neglecting the message of the given occasion. It is important for the preacher to be in touch with the current life experience of the congregation to preach a relevant sermon. Preachers of advanced countries are advised to keep the daily newspaper in the left hand as they hold the Bible by the right hand in preaching. This precisely is to make the Word of God a living word, applicable to all situations.

3:8 The Church Calendar

CHART OF THE CHURCH YEAR

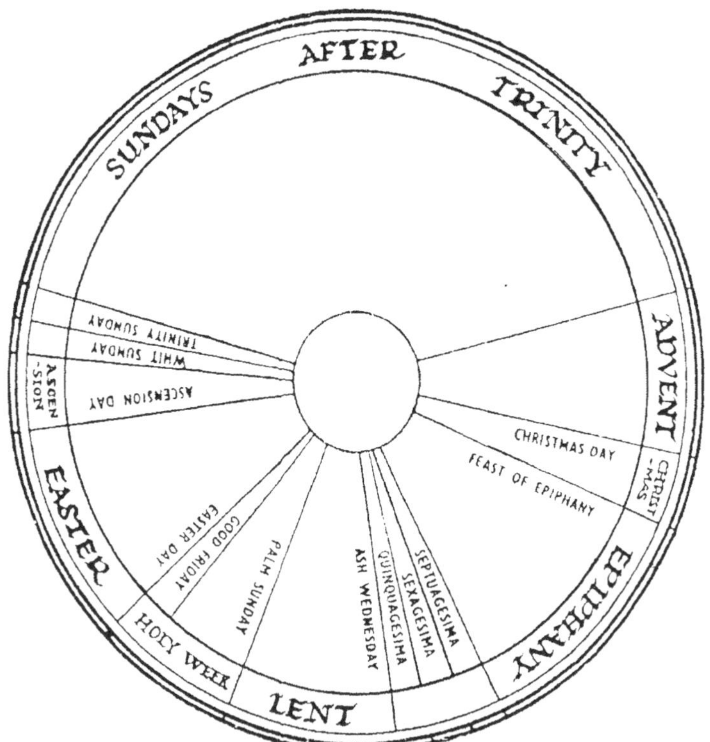

1. *Advent Season*   – Four Sundays before Christmas Day, December 25, designated as *Sundays in Advent.*

2. *Christmastide*   – Christmas day, and one or two Sundays between December 25 and January 6, designated as *Sundays after Christmas Day.*

3. *Ephiphany Season*   – Four to nine Sundays between January 6 which is Epiphany Day, and the beginning of Lent, which depends upon the date of Easter Day, designated as *Sundays after Epiphany Day.*

4. *Lenten Season*   – Six Sundays before Easter Day, designated as Sundays in Lent, of which the fifth may be called *Passion Sunday and the sixth Palm Sunday.*

5. *Eastertide*   – Easter Day and Six other Sundays designated as *Sundays after* Easter Day, of which the last may be called *Ascension Sunday.*

6. *Pentecost Season*   – From eleven to sixteen Sundays beginning with Pentecost Sunday, the seventh Sunday after Easter Day, and continuing through the next of the last Sunday in August, designated as *Sundays after Pentecost.*

7. *Kingdomtide*   – Thirteen or fourteen Sunday beginning the last Sunday in August and continuing until Advent, designated as Sundays in *Kingdomtide.*

Besides the above there are some locally relevant Special Days which may include: Bible Sunday, New Year Day (or Watch Night), Festival of Christian Home, Independence Day, Mothers' Day/Fathers' Day, Labour Day, Reformation Day, All Saints' Day, Thanksgiving Day... etc.

Easter Sunday does not fall on the same date every year because it falls on the first Sunday after the first full moon following *the 21 of March* (*Spring Equinox*) Easter Day is thus 'moveable' which affects other special days. Forty days in Lent prepares for the Easter, and from the Easter Day to the Ascension Day is another forty days.

Other occasions related to Lent/Easter are:

Ash Wednesday — The first day of Lent, so called from an ancien custom ofsprinkling ashes upon the heads of believers. Ashes in the Bible are signs of repentance and mourning (Esth. 4:1, Job 42:6, Mt.11:21) and some still follow this custom.

Maundy Thursday — This recalls the Last Supper and the beginning of the Holy Communion (Lk. 22:7-14). It also recalls how Jesus washed his disciples' feet (Jn. 13:3-5), and gave the new commandment that we love one another (Jn. 13:34).

Low Sunday — The first Sunday after Easter, continuing to celebrate the resurrection of Christ. The risen Lord met Thomas the doubter on this day. This was another first day of the week on which the Lord appeared again to his followers. This led to the idea of the Lord's Day (Sunday, the first day of the week, not seventh day of the week which was the sabbath for the Jew).

Septuageisima — The word means "Seventieth' since the day is roughly seventieth before Easter.

Sexagesima — The word means 'sixtieth'. No social theme is suggested for this Sunday.

Quinquagesima — The word means 'fiftieth', and unlike the previous two Sundays this is strictly correct, being fifty days backward from Easter. The theme here is *Love*. That is to consider God's love for us and our love for Him. We love him because he first loved us (1 Cor. 13; 1 Jn. 4:7-21).

Palm Sunday — The last Sunday in Lent recalling how Jesus entered into Jerusalem to claim the kingdom, and how the people received him as he approached the end of his earthly ministry. In those days palm leaves were used as a sign of victory. The people came with palm leaves to meet the triumphant King, Jesus;

Whit Sunday — (The Power of The Pentecost). PENTECOST was the name of the Jewish festival which was linked with the giving of the Law on Mount Sinai. It was so-called because it fell fifty days after the feast of the Passover: (Pentecost, comes from a word meaning fifty). Later, it came to be called 'Whit Sunday', probably from the term 'White Sunday' because this was the day on which they wore, after baptism, their white garments.

Trinity Sunday — Trinity Sunday is the first Sunday after Pentecost. It presents both an opportunity and a challenge to the preacher. We must show that there is one God, but three persons within the divine nature; Father, Son, and Holy Spirit. Christians do not worship many gods as often misunderstood by others. The purpose of this Sunday is to teach the Christians to understand the Holy Trinity. This event follows the Pentecost feast which completes the revelation of the persons in the Trinity, (i.e., God seen as Father, the Son, And the Holy Spirit), in the preceding events.[13]

3:9 Preaching, Sermon, and Teaching

The messages given in evangelical campaign and public worship have been termed 'preaching'. However, to C.H. Dodd, preaching (kerygma) is "the public proclamation of Christianity to the non-Christian World" as mentioned earlier, Thus 'kerygma' is done in street corner, market place, saloons, and is not the New Testament word to describe the Sermon within the sanctuary. The Sermon in the Church, as on the Lord's day are *"paraclesis or homilia"*, the specific intent of which is to 'revitalize' the faith of the believers, the reviving of those once 'vived'. The sermon is thus, addressed to a congregation already in faith (Dodd). The pastor, through his/her sermon reminds the congregation something loved long since and, may be, lost a while (J.T. Cleland). The other important aspect of preaching is the often neglected 'teaching' (didache). Teaching in sermon explains, instructs and gives lesson for the faith professed. However, the presence of teaching in preaching should not make us neglect its distinct function from preaching. C.H. Dodd points out how teaching and preaching are inseparable, as in Jesus' Sermon on the Mount which opening words says, "He opened his mouth and taught them saying..." (Mt. 4:23; 11:1; 9:35 etc). These examples show that there are some amount of preaching, some amount of proclamation, some amount of exhortation and some amount of instruction in preaching.

3:10 Exegesis, Exposition, and Application

The three interrelated branches of preaching are the exegesis, exposition and application. Exegesis critically analyses the word in its geographical, political and cultural setting. It attempts to discover what the particular word meant to the original hearer of the word. The reader makes linguistic, literary and historical approaches to discover the original content of the word.

Exposition seeks to find out the eternal validity of the word so given in a particular period of time. The relevance of the word throughout the centuries, what is the very heart of the word for all centuries?

The application: The word so discovered by exegesis and refined by exposition is applied to life situations today – the situation of the preacher and the hearer (J.T. Cleland).[14]

3:11 Preaching as Communication

Modern preaching has been much enriched by the techniques of modern communication. Every student of preaching should use both the traditional and the modern media of communication in preaching the gospel. The modern media is often criticised as consumer oriented than human dignity but that does not mean we should throw away the baby of media with its bath water. We believe God inspires inventions and technology as well as human science. The knowledge of human behaviour – the behaviour of both the communicator and the recipient of the message helps in determining the actual content of the message. A simple knowledge of analysing the audience makes the preacher present the gospel within the frame of reference of the gathering. So also, the preacher's awareness of the barriers of communication (noise in electronic media) can help him/

her present the message more effectively. Knowing the psychology of advertising will help the preacher make better presentation of the Word.

Dr. C.R.W. David, a professor in communication, gives the following as useful criteria in **analysing modern preaching**:[15]

1. What was the theme of the sermon? Did it come from the lectionary or the preacher's choice?

2. How relevant was the theme for the context?

3. Was there evidence that the preacher has done enough preparation for the sermon?

4. How communicative was the delivery of the sermon? Was it understandable to the people?

5. What was the reaction of the congregation? Did they show signs of approval or appropriation during the sermon? What was their reaction when you asked some of them after the worship?

6. Is there a particular style of preaching dominant in the area? For example, preaching with a written script, preaching extempore, preaching in a 'revival' style etc?

7. Were any of the socio-economic and political problems of the day touched upon in the sermon? If so, what is the kind of treatment these issues received, individualist or structural approach?

8. Having listened to the sermons on two or more consecutive Sundays, do you find any particular trend in the sermons such as, evangelistic, revivalist, individual-moralistic-oriented and so on?[15]

Earlier, preaching was considered one person's activity in which the preacher would prepare a talk and deliver to a passive congregation (one way traffic). In this monologue the congregation is not given to reflect and ask questions on the sermon. Perhaps the listeners themselves thought it was their religious modesty not to question anything given on the pulpit. Besides, the preachers themselves might not entertain any such feedback. According to Lasswell, communication is complete only with the feedback. Preaching will be more effective if the preachers can take in feedback constructively. In modern preaching, there is even a thing like 'collective sermon preparation' where the congregation helps the pastor-preacher in preparing the message. Dr. Surya Prakash presents a new method of improving the sermon by "W.H. Williamson's Sermon reaction Questionnaire'.[16] Which contains 24 questions to be given to the listeners following the preaching requesting them to give a frank response. The questions touch a wide range of homiletical principles. Such will surely be a threat to those who would monopolize the ministry of the Word. On the other hand, such a corporate shaping of the sermon will motivate everyone to accept what they prepared.

3:12   Conclusion

Worship, whether private worship or public worship is an act of homage to the Creator. Worship is not only an external act, but more of an attitude. The moment of worship is a dramatisation of what life at any moment ought to be. Therefore, worship has an indispensable counterpart – life and mission to the world. Worship is both a celebration of a past event and a renewal of our commitment to God. The pastor as a leader of congregational worship should lead the worship of the people using the essential elements of worship, providing the participation of the people. The worship should be arranged logically and in order. The sermon, the prayers, songs and the other items should be co-ordinated to form a connected theme.

The constancy of preaching is stated as "in season and out of season", and its urgency as like a dying person communicating to a dying person. Preaching forms an integral part of the total worship service. In the free churches (like the Baptists) the ministry of the word is the most important part of worship. To recall Sangster's quote, it is a communication of the Incarnate Word, from the Written Word by the spoken word. Preaching is not a time of scolding but of announcing the glad tidings. Whether the sermon is textual or life-situational, it is always the application of the word of God to a human situation.

ENDNOTES

1. W.R. Macnutt, *Worship in the Churches*, Judson Press, 1941, p.21.

2. L.N.Niguidula, *A Source Book for Christian Worship: Celebration*, Philippines, 1975, p.1.

3. *Ibid.*

4. Jitsuo Morikawa, *Pastors for a Servant People;* Baptist Jubilee advance, American Home Mission Society, N York, 1961, p.28.

5. Eric Lott, *Worship in Indian Context*, UTC, Bangalore, 1986, p.65.

6. *Baptism, Eucharist, Ministry*, WCC, Geneva, 1982, p.10.

7. *Ibid.*

8. *Ibid.*

9. W.E. Sangster, *The Craft of the Sermon*, Epworth, London, 1961, p.22.

10. Hoppin, *Homiletics.*

11. *Morikawa, op.cit., p.24.*

12. On the Christian Year Books within our reach are like : *Worship Resources,* Charles Wallis, Harper and Row, N. York, 1964.

13. David Livingstone, *The Saving Events: An Explanation of the Christian Year,* Key Books, CLS, Madras, 1996.

    See also: R.H. Fuller, *Preaching the Lectionary: The Word of God for the Church today:* Liturgical Press, Minnesota, 1984.

14. James T. Cleland, "Preaching" in *Dictionary of Christian Education:* Philadelphia, 1963, p.512.

15. C.R.W. David (ed.), *Communication in Theological Education.*

16. *National Council of Churches in India Review,* 1993, January.

Postscript: A word may be added about the place of the Lord's Supper as a part of worship experience. The elements come under the objective factor of worship in that it is a dramatic way of communicating the divine truth to us. It is an act by which the self-giving love of Christ for his people in enacted and his death proclaimed till he comes again; Baptist churches elsewhere administer it to the worshippers at least once a month, but many churches in the CBCNEI do not administer it more than once or twice a year. When this ordinance is included in worship, the worship is divided into two parts: the ministry of the Word and the ministry of the Table.

CHAPTER 4

The Teaching Ministry

"Were there neither soul, heaven, nor hell, it would still be necessary to have schools for the sake of affairs here below." (Martin Luther)

4:1 Imparting Faith Tradition

It is questioned sometimes whether, religion, being a matter of feeling can be taught. Common sense will tell us that a complete and proper knowledge of faith and practice requires education. Religion consists of an objective factor (God) and a subjective factor (the adherent), and there is also the human freedom which can deny or reject God's proposal. Teaching alone, therefore, cannot transfer faith from the teacher to the learner. For, the learner has a God given freedom to accept the teaching or remain indifferent. This means that religion cannot be imparted automatically or coercively by external teaching alone as if it is a mathematical truth. A mathematical truth like, the sum of two plus two is four, can be taught to a person after which the person has no choice to deny or reject. Religion and morality cannot be communicated in digital figures like a scientific truth is. For, the centre of decision is in the learner concerned determined by the quality and level of commitment s/he had made with God. A young person coming to Seminaries to learn spirituality by objective input alone will go back without getting it. Teachers can guide people to spirituality but cannot impart it unless there is readiness in the learners. As T.H. Fickes observes, "It is not within the province of education to control or to supplant the operation of the divine spirit in the heart and mind of the individual. Teaching can stress this experience but cannot impart it."[1] There is also a thing like, "Readiness for Religion" as Ronald Goldman talks of. Rosseau, talks of hiding adult values from the child which includes religion. He said, "To overheat the imagination of a youngman with the idea of God would turn his head, and in the end he would make him a fanatic instead of a believer."[2] To Rosseau, moral questions like right or wrong should be taught only when questions arise from the child. This is not to mean children cannot be taught religious truth. It is important to know the right stage of teaching the right content. Readiness is required for all ages to accept abstract truth like religion and morality.

4:2 Teaching by Relating

To the younger persons teaching can be done through relationship. If, as the developmental psychologists say, the mother's relationship with the baby can create a basic trust (or mistrust), and if that seed of infantile trust can germinate to adult religious faith in God, how important is that trust relationship? Jesus was a teacher who taught of the kingdom of God more by the way he lived with the people than by words. This is to say that teaching by relationship in life together is a method suitable for both the child and the adult. Educators often forget the magnitude of human relationship and life testimony by their overemphasis on mechanical catechism.

Christian education is sometimes defined as, "the process of communicating the Christian gospel to others in such a way that all of life is surrendered to the lordship of Christ."[3] Or, "It is helping the person to accept the Christian faith not only as intellectual assent to formal theological propositions, but as the active living out of that faith in the experiences of their common life."[4]

The great educationist, R. Howe, emphasised the language of relationship besides the language of words though both should be correlated. After the trust is communicated by relationship anything about trust we teach will have meaning in the learner. Howe spoke of the back of the word, where lies the meaning and the back of the meaning lies the experience. He says, "The child learns how to trust his mother not by a gospel of trust but by a kind of relation that would awaken the child's trust." Trust cannot be taught verbally, it can only be awakened in a person. After it is awakened, they can be instructed through words, books and other resources. Howe laments that the church in its teaching function has used too much of language of words and used too little the language of relationship: He says,

> "I need the grace to be, in order to help my child, my wife, my friend, my student to become. And what do I mean when I suggest that your becoming is dependent upon my being? Simply this : my friendliness

helps you to become friendly my trust-worthiness helps you to become truthworthy; my hostility causes you to become hostile, my anxiety causes you to become anxious. If I affirm you will become affirmative. This is what I call the language of relationship, the communication that results from living together and which gives us the basic and personal meanings for the words we hear and use."[6]

As the above definition has it, Christianity is not only of reaching an intellectual assent nor a philosophical conviction but the consent to a relationship with a living person. Religious education should consist of encouraging the child to enter into a personal and living relationship with God and people with whom the learner lives.

Sherrill, who seems to be the first to present relationship theology in Christian education theory would mean by relationship, "to God, to other men (sic), and to self."[7] Similarly, Paul Tillich, taking the individual's separation from God and humans as sin, says that all our life is an effort to overcome our separation and to find each other in fulfilling relationship. He says, "the deepest significance of religion have to be with our attempts...to mend the break between ourselves (others) and our God... we want to be 'at one' with Him who is the ground of our being."[8]

Someone rightly observed that, before the fall God's concern with humans was to maintain good relationship. When the human rebelled and broke the relationship it becomes God's concern to bridge that broken relationship. It was considered God's change of method in educating the human from maintaining peace to reconciliation. In either case, the main concern is the relationship.

J.D. Murch has reminded us how the educational task in the apostolic church was to continue steadfastly in the apostles' teaching with its sublime object "to fit men to live in perfect harmony with the will of God"[9] as summarised in Acts. 2:41-42. This is also to bring the person in perfect relationship with Christ.

The Judeo-Christian religion is not a matter of an abstract philosophy. It is a matter of relationship. It can be best taught by personal relationship as much as the goal of teaching is to experience a perfect relationship with God and neighbours. This must have led the early Christians to live in a relationship of love so that the onlookers remarked, "see how much they love one another". Such teaching of the faith by a living reality is the best method of teaching religion. Coming to know Christ through reading and hearing alone cannot bring people to Christ as it was in the case of Mahatma

Gandhi who loved Christ, but could not be convinced by the Christians. It requires living out the faith to communicate it.

God was the teacher of his people Israel. He was the subject matter of the Jewish education. The patriarchs, the priests, the prophets, the wisemen and the parents were the agents of their education. The objective of their education was to live a holy life before God, fully dedicated to the service of God. Later, this teaching by use of external agents did not bring satisfactory result. Therefore, God decided to teach His personal relationship with the people through His Son Jesus Christ (Heb. 1:1-2). God communicated Himself by the incarnation showing his nature to the people by living with them. Jesus taught more by his being and doing than his speech. Paul's appeal to the Christians to be a "living sacrifice" is to show their faith by living it. Jesus is often referred to as a teacher who followed the method "do as I do" rather than "do as I say". That unique quality in him made the difference - a teacher different from the other teachers of the world. Living out what he taught himself made him live "the man for others" and dying for those he loved. The cross has become the ideal living reminder of the truth about God which is the core of Christian teaching. Dorothy Scott is right in saying that the curriculum of Christian education is being lived rather than spoken.[10]

Williamson, who reviewed several literature to pinpoint the core of curriculum for Christian education came up with more than 50% of them centering around "Experience (life itself)." Those statements quoted by Williamson centre around the experience of the learner, not verbal teaching of some stories. This is also in line with Howe's affirmation, that, back of the word is experience (supra) f.n.5.

The definitions of a curriculum show the total experience of the learner with the teacher as the core of education the church should reconsider as her educational role today. It is not an armchair dictation of the good news about Christ but the sharing and living a Christ-like life with the learner. Has the Church in India been teaching the people both Christians and people of other faiths in that manner? An emphasis on life and work has become more important in teaching the faith.

4:3 New Direction in Teaching

Dr. Poerwowidagdo[11], talking on a paradigm shift in theological education, includes the following emphases which are applicable also to the Christian education in general. That the shift be made from:

Old Paradigm	New Paradigm
• Male dominated education	Inclusive, male-female balance.
• Campus and classroom based	Local church and community based.
• Standardised, fixed curriculum.	Flexible, module system curriculum.
• Top down teaching process	Group teaching-learning process.
• Encourage submission and loyalty to the doctrines and the traditions of the church.	Encourage critical acceptance of the teaching of the church, existential reflection and creative innovation.
• Biblical-historical oriented	Biblical contextual oriented.
• Individual and heaven oriented.	Community and God's world oriented.
• Narrow confine of Christian doctrines.	Wider appreciation of liberating motifs in other faiths.
• Local and anthropocentric	Global and Ecocentric.
• Teachers monologue	Teacher-learner dialogue
• Liturgy and rituals	Life and spirituality
• Spiritual focus	Holistic focus
• Children education oriented	Whole life oriented
• Life and world negating	Life and world affirming.

4:4 The Cognitive and the Affective in Learning

In this brief introductory section on education we underline yet another vital point in imparting truth. The teacher may simply impart the factual materials without actual experience of the fact, and the learner accepts the truth without emotional involvement. This is so also in learning geography, hygiene, language or science. However, even in secular education, subjects like history and political theories needed to touch the affective part of the learner if such learnings should result in revolution and change.

Religious education, without fail should touch the affective part of the learner because its objective is to result in a healthy relationship with beings (God and humans). Without some emotional involvement there cannot be a relationship in emotional involvement. Therefore, the teaching of religion should touch the affective part of the learner. This does not mean the religious education should neglect the cognitive aspect of the person. The teaching should touch the cognitive (understanding intellectually) part of the learner. Without the gospel being rooted in the intellectual part of the person the seed is sowed only on the thin soil of emotionalism. This learning can be short lived. This often happens in evangelical sermons where the audience is taken up temporarily to fear and excitement. Some parts of the sermon may be remembered but the greater part of the subject is often forgotten. A Sunday School class or theological classrooms have the activities of reaching this cognitive part. An affective response resulting from this cognitive input is a lasting knowledge that leads to action (executive).

In the churches there are a lot of emotional activities but without proper cognitive root. Emotion is necessary to express the knowledge but emotionalism is shallow and short-lived experience.

It is here that the church should continue the task of both preaching and teaching as Jesus began and the early church continued. The teaching task of the church is to impart the truth of the gospel and of life in a systematic and critical treatment which may not always involve emotional experience. Preaching, though it has also a teaching content has the task of persuading and challenging the learner emotionally. In any proper learning, both the aspects of cognitive and the affective parts of the learner should be touched. What Gilbert[12] proposes will be a fitting model in this regard.

Gilbert observed that the relationships within which the individual matures are of various dimensions of which six dimensions are given as examples. These six topics are among the learning frontiers of the person which should be assimilated in the cognitive and the affective regions of the person and finally put that learning to action. Only three examples are presented here, namely GOD, SELF and NEIGHBOURS. For example, the learner should understand (cognitive) who God is, then s/he is moved emotionally (affective) to love God, and finally s/he lives to love and serve Him is daily life (executive). This is the learning process proposed by Gilbert:

Topic	Cognitive	Affective	Executive
GOD:	Understood as Creator and sustainer who loves all people and the world	experiences faith in God develops reverence, love and willingness to serve Him.	worships Him, obeys Him in daily life and serves Him.
SELF :	Understands self as a justified sinner, redeemed by God in order to serve Him	filled by gratitude, have humility, self-respect, honesty, forebearance, and a desire to fulfill his/her God - given potential	live a life befitting his/her redemption and vocation
NEIGH-BOURS:	Understand them as individuals who though sinful are God's creation to be loved because of God's love for all.	as individuals whom s/he to whom s/he witnesses and with whom s/he shares and co-operates	as individuals from whom s/he feels love, concern friendship, respect, forgiveness.

ENDNOTES

1. Price, Chapman, *et.al. A Survey of Religious Education,* p.16.
2. Robert Ulich, *History of Religious Education,* N. York, 1968, p.286.
3. Williams Williamson, *Language and Concepts in Christian Education.*
4. *Ibid.*
5. Reuel Howe, *Man's Need and God's Action,* p.70.
6. *Ibid.*
7. Williams Williamson, *op.cit.,* p.80.
8. *Ibid.*
9. James Deforest Murch, *Christian Education in the local Church.*
10. Williamson, *op.cit.,* p.130.
11. Judo Poerwowidagdo, *Towards the 21st Century and Opportunities for Theological Education,* WCC, Geneva, 1993, p.61.
12. W. Gilbert, *As Christians Teach,* Fortness Press, 1962.

CHAPTER 5

Ministry: Its Relation to Theology and Psychology

Having discussed the biblical foundation of pastoral ministry in the previous section, we now turn to consider how pastoral ministry is informed by/and contributes to theology and human science. It is understandable to speak of the ministry being informed by the faith reflection (theology) of the church, but for many people it may sound novel to speak of the ministry drawing insights from human science. There are some thinkers who claim that nothing in this created world is outside the milieu of God (that is, both the sacred and the secular belong to God). This is to say that it is not theology alone that heals humans. Natural science is equally God's wisdom in making humans whole. Though theology and psychology may speak different languages, both address the person. Pastoral ministry has a special concern for the individual and thus draws insights from both theology and psychology. It is the present writer's belief that God can mobilize all resources from his good creation in re-making the fractured world to wholeness.

5:1 The Individual Person in Pastoral Care

Pruyser (1976), observed that "the subject of pastoral theology is the person, the concrete man, woman, or child in his personal interactions, not a disease, a disorder, vice, deviation or defect,"[1] Pastoral care and counseling, and also pastoral psychotherapy, is a general ministry of the church, but more directed to the care of persons. Hiltner (1958) uses the term 'shepherding' for pastoral care and sets its aim as "the quest for the good of the person or persons involved – temporarily, if need be, without thought of the larger groups or institutions. It is simply the good Samaritan's principle in operation."[2] Hiltner goes on to say that the good Samaritan, though in hatred with the Jews did not think of that larger society in conflict (Jews and Samaritans) and attended to the immediate need of the person wounded and so in need of help. This is analogous to Jesus' concern for the one lost sheep (individual) leaving aside the ninety nine for that moment (Lk. 15:3-5).

Paul Tillich[3] calls psychology predominantly a 'doctrine of man' and that pastoral psychology, even while using the insights of general psychology deals with man/woman both in their essential potentialities and their existential activities. C.F. Horne[4] sees a person as a composite of the image of God and rooted in nature. That is, humans, though created in the image of God, has the 'dust' part and life goes through the cycle of births, growth, maturity and death. There is no dichotomy of body and soul in humans. Therefore, the ultimate end of life is not freeing the soul from body. Life is one and the whole life is to be saved and made whole. What Horne says is that the persons's *theological and psychological* aspects cannot be separated. Doughlas Lewis (1964)[5] similarly, holds that a person should be considered theologically and psychologically. He/she is created in the image of God but lives as a child of nature, ambivalent, having roots of both good and evil (Eros and Thanatos). We can speak of the good natured human who is also in constant influence of the unconscious that directs his/her thought and behaviour. Browning (1985)[6] speaks of humans as a synthesis of nature and spirit whose behaviour is a product of both free decisions and various forms of 'conditionedness'. That means humans are subject to biopsychological development as well as the conditioning of the environment.

Finally, Whitlock,[7] considers the person like that of the Hebrews' view, as related to healing. Whitlock examines the terms like 'basar' (flesh) differentiating it from the Greek concept of 'sarxs'. *Ruach* is the spirit or power of God at work in man. *Nephesh,* is the soul by which humans live or die. He says, *ruach* is the power or energy which moves the individual, but it is the Nephesh which exhibits the power energy.[8] When ruach was breathed into the dust, biologically the person became a living person (Nephesh). He says, "It is true that man was created from matter (dust of the earth) and from spirit (Ruach of God) but once he was created he was a unitary organism".[9] Whitlock sees the Hebrew view of man as a "Clinical Understanding" and says that the modern development of psychosomatic medicine is a recognition of the unity of man. This is theological as well, for Whitlock says, the mind cannot blame the body for deceiving it. In dualism, evil resides in the flesh or the mind. But to the Hebrews, it resides in the total person and it is the total person that sins.

One important remark of Whitlock that makes the person respond to theology and therapy is the 'ruach' which is a gift of God to humans.

The Ruach's function in the person is known through the person's emotions, actions, the will and the intellect of the person. Hence, "it is the ruach of God which enables man to make an about face in a religious conversion or to gain insight by therapeutic relationship. Hence, man has responsibility to act, but it is the *ruach* of God which enables him to act."[10]

The understanding of the self by the carer becomes the central focus in pastoral care. In fact, Holifield (1983)[11] has written the whole history of pastoral care in America pivoting around the varied understanding of the self throughout the centuries, e.g., from *self-denial to self-love, self-love to self-culture,* and *self-culture to self-actualisation,* etc.

In pastoral approach, what the pastor considers the person to be is very important. One may have a Rogerian understanding of the capable person, or the opposite as Rienhold Niebuhr's understanding of the person (Neo-orthodoxy). However, as Wayne Oates holds,[12] the minister should always consider the relationship with and awareness to the 'third person' in any relationship (the presence of God). The person is never to be considered as a case or a thing, but rather in an I-Thou relationship. Pastoral care and counseling is therefore, a ministry to the total person, preventive and curative, therapeutic and nurturing. Gerkin's method of pastoral care is worth noting:

1. First: **Pastoral care as proclamation**, in which the person in crisis is simply reminded by prayer and sacrament, by use of the biblical language of faith in God that the infinite God is present and active on behalf of the person in whatever crisis of situation may exist.

2. Second: **Pastoral relationship as analogous to the relationship** of Jesus as the Word incarnate in finite human existence. The pastor seeks to be a little Christ to the other. That is the implicit gospel in all the therapeutic relationship.

3. Third: Pastoral care as engendering of an **incarnational style of tending** to present life experience. Pastoral care is that relationship to the other person seeking to open God's presence, to engender the quality of God's disclosure.[13]

Gerkin's view is similar to that of Frank Lake's (1988)[14] who links the human individual's life of crisis with the humanity and passion of Christ – "the study of the adult life of Christ as God's 'demonstration man'". Lake holds that, Christian doctrine of man and woman and their redemption is at every point illuminated by depth psychology and this theologically based ontology and psychodynamic model of human is a useful resource in clinical pastoral training.[15]

We have seen both Gerkin and Lake linking pastoral care with Christ and the Gospel. This is in line with what we have seen in the earlier section, about ministry as an attempt to make God's Shalom available on earth, or that the purpose of the ministry is to increase among humans love of God and neighbours. This work is done by Christ's representatives and as, the modifier 'pastoral' is validated. A pastoral care should always be informed by the Word and the tradition of the church. The Bible pictures humans as created in the image of God (Gen. 1:26; 2:7), but they rebelled and fell (Gen.3:6), but God won them back and now they have hope in Christ. Roger Shinn points out that Christ's twofold commandments sets man in three-way relation - with God, with neighbours and with self (Mk 12:30-31). Humans, according to Shinn, are not things as secularism may say. S/he has the God-image, neighbour-image, and self-image.[16] His/her relation to all these is an I-Thou relationship.

It is true theology does not deal only with individual persons. Pastoral care is concerned with the lost individual but also with the ninety nine sheep- that is the family, institutions and the society to which the individual is related. In other words Pastoral care is concerned with the biosphere within which the individual exists. H.J.Clinebell, developed this subject in one of his book.* Chinebell even talked of eco-therapy in which he relates the wholeness of the person as rooted in the person's healthy relation with the created world- the eco –system in which the person lives.** Why we have used the individual here is a model of how pastoral practice is related to its faith reflection, especially in relation to the individual, the dominant focus of pastoral care.

5:2 Theology, Pastoral Counseling and Pastoral Psychotherapy

The list of ministries commonly referred to in the New Testament are, Romans 12:6-8; 1 Cor. 12:7-10; 27-30; Eph. 4:11; and Phili. 1:1). Pastoral

---

* Growth Therapy .....Abingdon Press, 1979.
** (Eco-Therapy.... Fortress Press, 1996.

care and counseling can come under any category of ministry like teaching, exhorting, helps, services and healing, mentioned in these lists. All ministry is a sharing in Christ's ministry. The many ministries of the people of God are one. Each is a distinctive form of the single ministry of Christ (Pattorn). Pastoral Care is one of these distinctive forms of ministry. Gospel terms like, care, feed, or tend, are again more relevant to the work of pastoral care. Repentance, forgiveness and re-conciliation etc. are other important themes of pastoral care. The inaugural address of Jesus, the so-called 'Nazareth manifesto' had the background basis of Isaiah 61:1-2. However, in Is. 61:1-2, there are two significant phrases relevant to pastoral care like, 'to bind up the broken hearted' and 'to comfort all who mourn', which were not quoted by Jesus (Lk. 4:18-19). The text implies the coming of Jesus as a realised salvation rather than salvation as a future event. The 'poor' in the text, according to Walter Pilgrim,[17] refers to the captives, blind and the oppressed in collective terms.

The *Constitutional Papers of British Association of Pastoral Care and Counseling* quotes the lines from Luke 4, as Jesus' ministry implying two-fold aspects: "To proclaim the Kingdom of God and heal."[18] It is a totalistic approach or proclamation and therapy. Leslie Newbigin,[19] sees these words of Jesus *related to the ministry of care,* "Go and tell John what you hear and see: the blind receive their sight and the lame walk, lepers are cleansed and the deaf hear, and the dead are raised up, and the poor have the good news preached to them" (Mt. 11:4-5). Healing is closely related to salvation. The same Greek word is sometimes translated 'save' and also 'heal'. Nearly 1/3 of the N.T. reference of salvation (and its verbal form) and so in O.T. references denote deliverance from specific ills, such as captivity, disease and devil possession. Jesus is saviour and healer. Of Mk. 2:1-2, 2:17, 3:27, also, 2 Tim. 4:18. Healing the body was also a forgiveness of sin (as in the case of the paralytic). Healing was the centre of Jesus' work. Healing was also the sign of the presence of the saviour. This strong link between salvation and healing can be seen also in the work of James Lapsley. "Salvation and Health: the interlocking process of life" (1972).

As a result of the above said unity of body and soul in humans, the interlocking process of salvation and health, the talk about marriage of theology and therapy is on the increase. Doughlas Lewiss (1964)[20] talks of nearing the end of honeymoon period of that marriage and now being confronted with the day-to-day give and take relationship of the two. Tillich spoke of psychology as humans way of healing humans, and theology as God's way of healing humans. He says, "a theology which is influenced in all three directions by psychotherapy is a better theology than a theology without such influence. Thus the theologian would do well to remain in contact with the psychotherapeutic movement."[21]

Pruyser thinks that the greatest contribution of psychology to pastoral theology is "the elucidation of the dynamics of crisis situations to which the clergy is bound to address itself."[22] The reciprocity of theology and psychology has enriched each other. The only danger the Christian ministers have to be aware of, is the oft resounded loss of identity of the ministers by the overdose of the psychology. William Hume observed that "in former days the pastor's counseling was oriented in pastoral theology; today it centres in pastoral psychology; that the impetus of the movement has come more from the laboratories of psychological sciences than from the scholarship of the theologians. It is a psychologically oriented *seelsorge.*"[23] The over inclination towards the therapeutic aspect may lead to the sale of birthright of pastoral counseling.

On the other hand a stubborn emphasis on the faith tradition, even where it is irrelevant to the person in crisis is the other side of the danger. C.F.I. Horne rightly observes, "All too frequently the church has been too moralistic and judgemental in its approach. In making its moralistic approach, the church has often aggravated rather than help heal emotional illness. That psychotherapy should mistrust the church is not strange."[24]

Tillich and Oden are among theologians who see rapprochement of theology and psychology in healing humankind. Tillich, in his "Impact of Pastoral Psychology on Theological Thought" (1960)[25] has spelled out what he saw as the church's abortive attempt to heal human problems. Tillich's contention is that the church's insistence in the rigid and arid doctrines failed to communicate the divine acceptance of the people. The church's responsibility is to communicate this acceptance, but she failed in this mission. Ironically, what was failed by the church is carried out by the secular therapists by their unconditional acceptance of the people. The Christian mass in search of acceptance go to the therapists rather than to the judgemental ministers. A similar observation was made by Hume when he said, "Successors of the great churchmen of the past have too often communicated the doctrine of the church in a legalistic fashion that has little relation with the dynamics of human personality. The result is an over-intellectualised religion that is unable to reach the deep emotional conflicts of life: Such a religion plays in the hands of those who would rather rationalize than resolve this conflict."[26] The point here is, the church's insistence on retaining the pastoral identity by not over-involving in the secular tools sometimes steps into fundamentalism or stereotypic presentation of the religious resources. This sometimes goes to the extent of completely negating the psychological insight in understanding humans. That displays an attitude of "Christ against culture", especially among the evangelical Christians.

To Oden, healing through therapy is as good as healing through the gospel. He says, "What is therapy searching for other than wholeness, health, authenticity, to be a real man ? So far as therapy achieves this the church can only rejoice."[27] For, "there is no reason for the church to be embarrassed by the presence of the Holy Spirit apart from the church, or for the theologian to rush to the therapist and tell him he cannot accomplish this healing without Christ.[28] Oden speaks of 'Christ formation, in the world without the gospel being consciously heard and understood. In context of theology and therapy relation, Oden would believe in the unity of Christ formation, in the world without the gospel being consciously heard and understood. In context of theology and therapy relation, Oden would believe in the unity of Christ and culture.[29]

Theology, as Hume assumes, gives structure of religion. He says, "It tells the how and the why as well as the what. It is the solid stuff that lends character to religion and stability to the religious personality...it should therefore be a valuable tool to pastoral counseling." (Hume, *op.cit.,* p.15). We have seen also the idea of reciprocity between theology and therapy in Tillich. It is not that theology be pushed into a therapeutic relationship. They are synthesised by itself. The surprising coincidence is that the principles of counseling which has grown out of the science of dynamic psychology have also been expressed in religions. For instance, the therapist's positive regard of the individual, the pent up emotion and cathartic experience; the concept of acceptance and the doctrine of divine justification of the sinner; the concept of disciplined listening and the idea of God as a patient listener. On listening D. Bonhoeffer writes, "Anyone who thinks that his time is too valuable to spend keeping quiet will eventually have no time for God and his brother, but only for himself and his follies... he who can no longer listen to his brother will soon be no longer listening to God either."[30]

We have seen how principles of human relation are often expressed in religions. The pastoral practice is influenced by the church's theology. Clinebell is right in saying that biblical truth informs, guides pastoral practice and the truth of it the gospel incarnated in the arena of human struggle and growth. In this sense, pastoral care and counseling is 'doing theology'.[31] Quentin Hand[32] continues, "Pastoral counseling is the practice of theology by a minister in his or her interaction with one or more persons in the quest for wholeness of relationship with God, world and others, and in the quest for integrity of the persons involved."[33]

According to Richard Niebuhr and associates, the purpose of the church is to increase among men love of God and neighbours. Steward Hiltner sees the aim of the church and the aim of Pastoral counseling as same. Love is communicated in pastoral counseling situations. The person helped must realize God's shalom through the pastoral carer. Bill Kylle, says that the most apt scriptural description of the attitude of a counselor is given in 1Cor. 13.[34] If so, whatever the pastoral carer does is an incarnation of the gospel in human relations.

Pastoral ministry is often misunderstood as 'applied theology' which will simply make pastoral ministry a passive application of certain theological formulations. It is alright to say that what we believe is experienced practically in pastoral relationships but pastoral ministry is something more than that. Pastoral ministry is an activity of theologising, it contributes insights to theology from its experience with life's reality. In the words of Anton Boisen, pastoral ministry is a research with "living human documents" which can predict vital facts that should influence theoretical formulations. Seward Hiltner, in the same way showed how the body of divinity is of two foci - theory and practice, reciprocally influencing each other (see his *Preface to Pastoral Theology*). Paul Tillich, greatly admired insights from psychotherapy which influenced systematic theology to a great extent (see Pastoral Psychology Feb. 1960). Pastoral ministry is therefore an integral part of psychology and theology. Recently Jenning has proposed that the relationship between theology and psychotherapy be not merging on the ground of commonality but that of complementary to each other. This means the two disciplines will remain distinct and contribute insights to each other even as theology and philosophy are distinct disciplines though they enrich each other. And if theology and philosophy can enrich each other why not theology and psychology do the same? (see T.W. Jennings, Jr. in *Dictionary of Pastoral Care and Counseling*, Hunter edited, 1990, p. 862f.).

5:3 Conclusion

To state the main thrust of the section in a nutshell, the focus of pastoral theology is the individual person who is created in the image of God and lives as a child of nature. Besides the revealed Word, the pastoral carer uses insights from the whole divine milieu in nurturing, in healing, sustaining and guiding the person to reconcile the person to God and neighbour. The minister's use of both theology and psychology is also, due to the Holistic understanding of the person as a composite of body, soul and mind. The case of a young mother at Winston-Salem's North Carolina Baptist Hospital illustrates the theme of this paper : Her baby had been killed in a car smash. Her own injuries did not seem serious enough to be fatal, but she was sinking rapidly. After the surgeon had done all he could, he called in a psychiatrist, and said to him, "There is no medical reason why she shouldn't recover. But she wants to die – and she will unless her attitude is changed." Then the psychiatrist's careful analysis uncovered the root of the woman's problem : the baby killed had been born as the result of an extra marital affair. She had been able to live with her secret as long as the child was alive, but now nothing the psychiatrist said could shake her guilt-ridden interpretation of the accident's meaning. "I've got to die," she kept on repeating. "It's God's punishment for my sin. I deserve it." Then the psychiatrist summoned the chaplain, and told him, "This case calls for theological answers I haven't got." The story goes that the chaplain's ministry to the woman opened way to the experience of God's forgiveness that **changed the will to die, to a will to live**. Then the medicine began to work in her body rapidly, leading to healing.[35] Spiritual therapy is considered by some as 'modern medicine's newest ally', Today's resource persons in the healing team are drawn from the fields of social science, the science of human behaviour and the faith tradition of the church. The insight from these fields in knowing the person (and the human predicament) should be corrective of each other. An insight from a pastoral situation should also be able to correct the traditional theological position of the church, so that there is a constant mutual enrichment between the 'logic-oriented theology' and the theology born out of pastoral praxis.

ENDNOTES

1. Paul W. Pruyser, *The Minister as Diagnotician*, Westminster Phila, 1976, p.132.

2. Seward Hiltner, *Preface to Pastoral Theology, Abingdon*, 1958, p.68.

3. Paul Tillich, 'The Impact of Pastoral Psychology On Theological Thought' in *The Ministry and Mental Health* (ed.) Hans Hofman, Association Press, 1960, NY, p.13.

4. C.F. Horne, 'A Theology of Counseling' in *Pastoral Psychology*, Nov. 1968, p.30.

5. Doughlass Lewiss, 'Do Psychology and Theology Speak the Same Language?' in *The Journal of Pastoral Care*, Fall 1964, p.165.

6. Wicks, *et.al.*, (eds.) *Handbook of Pastoral Counseling*, p.8.

7. Newton Maloney, *Wholeness and Holiness : Readings in Psychology/ Theology of Mental Health*, Baker Book House, G. Rapids, 1983, p.41.

8. *Ibid.*, p.47.

9. *Ibid.*

10. *Ibid.*, p.46.

11. Holifield, *A History of Pastoral Care in America*, Abingdon, Nash, 1983, p.58.

12. Wayne E. Oates, *Pastoral Counseling*, Westminster Press, Phila, 1974, p.9.

13. Gerkin, *Crisis Experience*, p.36f.

14. Frank Lake, *Clinical Theology*, Abingdon, 1986, p.12.

15. *Ibid.*

16. Roger Shinn, 'The Story Of Man And The Image Of Man' *Wholeness and Holiness, op.cit.*, p.36.

17. Walter Pilgrim, *Good News To The Poor, Wealth and Poverty in Luke-Acts*, Augsburg Publ. Minn. 1981, p.67.

18. *British Association of Pastoral Care and Counseling. A Constitutional Papers* (n.d.).

19. Leslie Newbigin, *The Good Shepherd*, William Eerdsman, 1977, p.68.

20. Doughlass, *Journal of Pastoral Care, op.cit.*, p.161.

21. Tillich, Impact of Pastoral Psychology, *op.cit.*, p.19.

22. William Pruyser, 'The Impact of the Psychological Discipline on the Training of the Clergy' *Pastoral Psychology*, Oct. 1963, p.22.

23. William Hume, *Counseling and Theology*, Muhlenberg Press Phila, 1956, p.1.

24. C.F. Horne, *Pastoral Psychology, op.cit.*, November, 1968, p.29.

25. Tillich, 'The Impact of...' *op.cit.*

26. Hulme, *Counseling and Theology, op.cit.*, p.8.

27. Thomas Oden, 'Theology and Therapy' in *Wholeness and Holiness, op.cit.*, p.206.

28. *Ibid.*

29. Thomas Oden, Contemporary Theology and Psychotherapy, Westminster Press, Phila, 1967, p.62.

30. Clebsch and Jaekle, *Pastoral Care in Historical Perspective,* Prentice Hall, Englewood Cliff, N. Jersey, 1964, p.53.

31. H. J. Clinebell, *Basic Types Of Pastoral Care and Counseling,* Abingdon, Nash, 1984, p.50.

32. O.L. Hand, 'Pastoral Counseling As Theological Practice' *Journal of Pastoral Care,* 1978, p.1000f.

33. *Ibid.*

34. *British Association of Pastoral Care...op.cit.,* p.77.

35. R.K. Young, *et.al... Spiritual Therapy,* p.25, Hodder & Stoughton, London, 1960.

CHAPTER 6

Church Organisation and Administration

6:1 Should the Church be Organised?

The church today is a society of a complex organisation. It is organised and administered worldwide like any other human organisation. It is often asked whether the people of God in the Bible were organised and administered like we do today, or whether Jesus really intended his church to be organised. The Old Testament has enough evidence to show that God found it useful to organize Israel into tribes, groups and families with their respective commanders, heads, guides and servants. Power and authorities were delegated to the deputies by leaders like Moses, Gideon and Joshua. Looking to the New Testament again, we find Jesus and his disciples being organised in some way (though may not be intentional), Peter as a spokesman, Judas as a treasurer and James and John among the members of the inner circle. Jesus organised the seventy into two each and sent them with proper instruction, too. The earliest church in Jerusalem and the churches planted by Paul have the marks of organisation where responsible persons like bishops, elders, deacons (pastors and deacons), prophets, teachers and others worked in co-ordination.

In India, the question raised by the Madras Rethinking group whether it is a must for the converts to join an organised church or they should be free from any institutional formalities to allow them a spontaneous touch with Christ is resounded often. It is true that no human institution can stand in the way of the individual Christian from seeing Christ directly. It is true also that the organised church which these intelligentsia were attacking was the hierarchical church of their time. Even among the free churches of today it is not uncommon to hear certain evangelists saying they are not attached to any particular church. That can mean either that the church is oecumenical, or, negatively, that one is negotiable to join any denomination. The other possibility is that one is simply a follower of Christ without attachment to any particular church.

It is not necessary for the church to seek biblical warrant for every word and action as it continues to be the body of Christ today. Today's situation is different from that of Christ's or Paul's. The body of Christ should be structured to meet situations today. This is to say that, even if the Bible does not give a model for Church structure the need of the context requires a properly organised and administered church today. And that is purely for the greater efficiency of the Church as it ministers to the present society.

No human group can work without proper organisation and the church is one such human group. Big institutions like schools, hospitals or a firm are intentionally organised and administered. A tribe, a village and a family is not organised intentionally but naturally bound by heritage and commonality that functions like organised groups. Organisations arise from human need – the need to *maximize effectiveness.* In a tribal village the individual farmers organize themselves in to a labour exchange group to work as groups to each others in fields in turns. This is necessitated by the individual's limitation in achievement by working alone. Organisation, is therefore, a device to co-ordinate effort for achieving common goals from which the individuals also experience greater effectiveness. Some working definitions of organisation are as under:

6:2 Definitions of Organisation

An organisation is the rational co-ordination of the activities of a number of people for the achievement of some common explicit purpose or goal, through division of labour and function, and through a hierarchy of authority and responsibility.[1]

or, Organisations are social units (or human groupings) deliberately constructed and re-constructed to seek specific goals.[2]

or, An organisation is the breaking down of the responsibility of the group as a whole into parts which can be assigned to individuals and committees.[3]

The above three sample definitions may suffice to get an idea of what an organisation is. The second sample, which is of Talcott Parson, has an avenue of change in the structure of the organisation when required. Many churches today have their structure and pattern of ministry so archaic that they lack relevance to the modern world. The church today has been criticised to come out of her "Morpholo-gical Fundamentalism" to make her presence felt by the world today.

6:3 Administrative Insights from the Public Administration

In as much as the church in her personnel management borrows insights from the science of human behaviour, she also borrows from the science of administration in her administration of the church. One such useful concept from the public administration is abbreviated POSDCORD. Each letter of the memory aid represents as follows:

Planning   : to decide in broad outline the scheme of work.

Organising   : to give an orderly structure of organisation with a view to complete the work.

Staffing   : to recruit and train suitable personnel for running the machinery of government.

Directing   : to provide leadership in the operation of the organisation.

Co-ordination : to establish a link and interrelate the various parts of the organisation.

Reporting   : to submit report to the chief executive by the administration.

Budgeting   : to accomplish a work in the form of fiscal planning, accounting and auditing.

The Church can also use such a pattern of administration to maximize its achievements.

The existing organisational types and Church polities are briefly described below for comparison with the structure and polity of one's own church. The model organisations are from Max Weber's typology placed here to compare with our existing church organisations. Church organisations seem to fall in one or more of these five model organisations at any given time. Sometimes the vested interests of the church leadership as well as the need of relevant adaptation by the church may lead the church structure to oscillate between these types.

6:4 Organisational types from Max Weber

Type 1:   *The Traditional Theory of Organisation:* This type of organisation has a continuing life of its own, following the same path as before with a prospect of unchanging course in the future. *The leader* here has his/her place among the elite of elders, and the leader's task is *to maintain a tradition.* S/he is not the initiator of traditions but the embodiment of it, the living example and expression of it. S/he expounds the tradition and nurtures the people in it. It is non reflective because there is no alternative to choosing against what has been done before. *Decision making* in this organisation, the role of the leader, and the decision making process are all derived from the tradition which cannot be changed.

Type 2:   *The Charismatic Theory of Organisation:* A charismatic leader is one who pursues intuition, in the form of inspiration, a flash of enlightenment, a revelation, or may be an expression of a mere whim and fancy. Such a leader acts upon what s/he perceives. Usually the leader announces the content of the intuition by words and the people understand it by intuition. Both the leader and the followers have to obey the content of such perceived utterance. The decision making is thus an instantaneous perception, and the outcome is announced in definitive and discreet terms by the leader. The charismatic approach cuts at the roots of the past and will have the 'overthrow formalism' and can articulate the forces of social change. All members, all procedures, and all structures are subject to the judgemental authority of the leader. His/her adherents will withdraw when the intuitive power or charisma is no longer in the leader.

Type 3:   *The Classical Theory of Organisation:* This type of organisation is built on the theme 'running a machine'. Here, organisation is conceived as a mechanical structure, and is on the lines of pyramidal chart. Each part is distinct but linked to each other vertically till it reaches the apex. The important person is the one at the apex since the activity of the organisation depends on his or her initiative or drive. The decision making process consists of a series of highly rationalised steps; the decisions are expressed as orders which are issued to the subordinates. The members of the organisation are subject to coercion, and their response is that of obedience to instructions, and it springs from their contractual relationship with the superiors. The Roman Catholic Church, the Army and the Civil Administration are some examples of this type.

Type 4:   *The Human Relation Theory of Organisation:* This is a democratic type with its key phrase as 'leading groups'. The organisation of this type is the small group gathered together on the basis of their common interests. This organisation is a network of personal relationships within and between groups – intimate and informal. The leader is permissive and non-directive. The leader here helps people to draw out what is in them; he prepares the way for them to find the fulfilment of their inner desires. The decision making process in this type of organisation is essentially that of coming to a common mind within a group. All members participate in formulating the common goals and all respond in their attainment. The acceptance of the goal by the group leads to participation in their attainment. The sensitivity of members to the feelings of others is an important element in the communication process.

Type 5:   *The Systemic Theory of Organisation:* It is based on a system which may be described as a complete entity which consists of, but is greater than, the sum of its constituent parts, which parts retain their own identity though they are interdependent. The internal pattern is governed in part by the purpose for which the system exists and in part by the environment in which it lives. The organisation is in a state of continual adaptation to the world around it so that the expression of its purpose is always relevant to the environmental change.[4]

Of the above five types of organisations the Traditional model represents the organisation of a tribal village in which the source of authority is the tradition itself. In this, the question of change is a threat to the status quo. The Charismatic model is one to which the members of the Traditional and the Classical model with their long experience of subjugation and repressed spontaneity may often run and burst out their pent-up voices. This is taking place in the revival movements of the North-Eastern Indian churches today. The churches under the Classical model have tendency to interpret norms and guidelines in a rational-legal perspective. The prior concern in this model is to keep the system going which may push aside the human need. Most of the free churches will be found under the Human relation and the Systematic models. Humanitarian concerns, the rights of the individuals and flexibility are higher in these last two models.

6:5 The Polity (Government) of the Church

With the above introduction to the types of human organisations we now turn to the existing church governments.[5]

1. *Papacy*: This is an autocratic form of church government which is the form of the Roman Catholic Church. The idea is to consider one of the bishops as the infallible authority of the church who continues the authority of Peter, the first bishop of Rome. The Pope, whose claim is infallible stands at the head of a worldwide organisation. Under him is a graded ministry. The local congregation has little voice in the affairs of the church. They are told what they are to believe and what they are to do. Besides the RCC a part of the Greek Orthodox church has this form of government. In the organisational terms this polity will come under the Classical type of organisation.

2. *Congregationalism*: The Congregationalists and the Baptists follow this form of church government. They claim a strong New Testament support to such structure of the church. Based on the word of Christ that He would be in the midst "where two or three are gathered in my name" they claim that the Universal church is manifested in every local church existing by Christ's standards. They believe in the priesthood of all believers and that Christ gave authority to the whole church, not exclusively to the ordained ministry. While maintaining independence of the local church they co-operate with the organisations on matters of common interest. In a sense, we can say that this form of church government is the other extreme of the Papacy.

3. *Episcopacy*: This may resemble papacy in some way but it resists the claims of Rome. Here the status between bishops and elders are defined. They find in the bishop a successor of the apostles. They believe in the historic episcopate and would not co-operate with churches not so organised. Even within this set up there are some churches (like some Lutheran churches) who would not regard the "historic episcopate" as a must but as a helpful way of organising the church.

   The episcopals insist on the three-fold ministry of the church – bishops, presbyters and deacons. The Anglicans, the Eastern churches, Orthodox, Armenian, Coptic, Syrian etc., are episcopal in structure. The Methodist church, the Union churches of India have this form of government. The College of bishops make up the "superior clergy" and under them the "inferior clergy". Highest authority is vested in the bishops.

4. *Presbyterianism*: The midway between the Congregationalists and the Episcopals is the Presbyterian set up. The New Testament has some evidence of congregations forming a church as in Jerusalem, in Galatia,

which perhaps is the essence of this polity. The Presbyterians recognize real authority in the councils of the church – local, provincial, national and ecumenical. They accept the special function of the ordained ministry but insist that the whole authority rests in the whole church. The church session, composed of pastors and ruling elders has charge of the affairs of the congregation. Above the Session stands the Presbytery composed of the churches in a given district. Higher in authority than the Presbytery is the Synod. The highest authority of all is vested in the General Assembly.[5]

To these structural models of the church may be added the purposes of *church discipline* and of *church government.*[6]

6:6 Management of Office, Correspondence, Time and Personnel

6:6:1 *Office:* God who is the God of peace and orderliness brought order out of the chaotic state of the Universe (Gen. 1&2). The pastor's office (or the church's office) is often stuffed with properties like, secretarial tools, furniture, files and books. It is a part of the Pastor's administrative task to bring these jumbles to an ordered structure. Such will not only look decent but also display a spirit of stewardship. For instance, if the files are not properly arranged the papers will take you hours to retrieve them. It pays to be methodical than unmethodical.

Correspondence: Before the communications facilities came people had to travel miles and days to convey verbal messages. Now, much time, energy and money is saved by correspondence. Today, most of the administrative work is done through correspondence. Many responsible persons, including the pastors, legitimatize their laziness and irresponsibility saying, "I am not good in writing letters"! Such pastors often fail to answer urgent questions and timely messages awaited by the writers or people in need. Letters requiring prompt reply should be replied timely. Taking the Pauline method the pastors should write letters with their personal touch and caring expressions. However, in official letters, forms and formalities need to be observed and avoid sentimentality. Notices and fixtures should be administered on time and to all persons involved. Weakness in correspondence is a major mark of inefficiency in administration.

Time Management : Proper use of time in official appointments and other pastoral engagements is a mark of good stewardship. Irresponsible use of time is a great waste for a wanted person like the pastor. S/he cannot overspend time with one appointment and thus miss the next appointment.

It will be a poor show for the pastor to have the people gathered before him/her, waiting for his late arrival. S/he should arrive at the place first and wait for the people. Someone rightly remarked that when time is up nothing is left. Time is a valuable, limited, passing and non-renewable resource. St. Paul rightly advised all to make the most of the given time (Eph. 5:15). Use of diary and engagement pads to remind oneself of the daily appointments will enhance one's time management. Time saved is money saved, and even life can be saved.

Personnel Management : It is easier to manage things than persons. The church, which is the Body of Christ, is a composite of numerous individuals with varied experiences in life, different temperaments, different aspirations and world-views. Among the people are many who had business failures, unstable homes, relationship problems, emotional hurts and spiritual maladjustments. There are some leaders who have inborn insights in recognising presence of tensions in the people they meet. There are others who need proper information in gaining such insight. The pastor's familiarity with the basic knowledge of human behaviour will help greatly in this regard. For instance, a simple reading in Transactional Analysis will help the Pastor to discover the fact that people behave from one or two of the three main ego states in each of them (see T.A. section in chapter 9). These days many executive officers of government and NGO organisations go to counseling centres to learn the dynamics of human relations. Even to gain the skill of 'disciplined listening' from such exposure will equip the pastor with an immense resource for personnel management.

The maxim 'things are used, people are loved' is a living reminder of how the pastor may deal with people in Christian perspectives. Love, as St. Paul says, does not insist in its own way, and seeks the interests of the other, too. The pastoral administrator as a manager of people should not insist on his/her own way nor be bossy in dealing with them. This applies to all pastoral works ranging from a one to one counseling situation to chairing the board of deacons. The temptation to dictate or manipulate the people should be avoided. The pastor should recognize the feelings of the people and deal with them gently. S/he should recognize the rights and privileges of the people, recognize their contributions and talents and utilize them constructively. S/he should avoid partisan spirit and be the catalyst in reconciling polarised situations.

6:7 The Purpose of Church Government[6]

1. *For the edification of the Church:* (Eph. 4:12): Edification means building up. The church should be build up to a maturity in Christ. Through the common worship, observance of the ordinances, teaching and preaching of the pastors and other workers the church increases in strength and fulness of life. But the Church has also a task to Proclaim (Mt. 28:19-20). To fulfil all these tasks the church needs a proper organisation, administration of resources, personnel for an orderly fulfilment of the church.

2. *For the selection, ordination and supervision of the ministers:* The personal conviction and the sense of call for the ministry should be acknowledged by the believers' community (church). The New Testament shows this kind of ordaining and authorising by the church as necessary, e.g., Acts 6:1-6; 14:23; Titus 1:5.

3. *The needs of discipline* : calls for some kind of government. The reformers believed that one of the marks of the church is the 'right administration of discipline'. Paul showed such a need in the church (1 Cor. 5:1-7).

4. *For the determination of the maintenance of sound doctrine:* The church is called the 'pillar and bulwark of the truth' (1 Tim. 3:15). That means, the believers' community is responsible for examining strange and new doctrines and see whether or not such doctrines are in line with the central truths of the Gospel. For example, the early church faced Judaism which taught that it was not enough to believe in Christ for salvation but one should also be circumsised. The church at Jerusalem settled this by the council of Jerusalem. (see Acts. 15).

5. *For providing the poor with daily needs* : The early church gave away their goods and shared them with those in need. But this was to be done in proper orderliness. They appointed the deacons of Jerusalem (Act 6). There is also a need to organize for the collection and sending of the gifts, as in 2 Cor. 9. Today we can think of the resources of the church for mission and how they are administered. (from William Stewart, The Church and its Ministry).

6:8 The Purpose of Church Discipline

William Stewart shows at least three reasons why the church needs discipline:

1. *To determine who are to be enrolled as members of the church. An atheist cannot be a church member, for example:* Among the Baptists, only those

baptised in their adulthood are taken as members. They also have discipline to discontinue the membership when the member comes short of the norms of the society, should determine who can be the bonafide members of the church.

2. *To do its work in an orderly and purposeful manner:* In a church an individual cannot just claim freedom to do or say as s/he likes. There is some kind of orderliness required. God is a God of order who brought orderliness out of chaos, as we see in the book of Genesis, ch. 2. A worship meeting can be degenerated to confusion when there is no regulation by some kind of discipline. Saint Paul dealt with such problems as we see in 1 Cor. 14:33.40.

3. *For the benefit of the members:* The church maintains discipline for the sake of the members. It is not to punish the wrongdoers but to warn them in love against wrong conduct and to win them back to the right. The church should remember that the law is made for man, not the other way around, Ezekiel 33:4-6 clearly describes the kind of discipline the church needs - that is, to warn against danger.

Recognising these above needs the church exercises discipline to maintain a standard of admission in the church. The church should not follow a forcible conversion, for Jesus himself was against such practice (Mt. 25:15). Rather a person willing to be baptised should be examined properly and thus the church has some rules of testing the sincerity of the candidate for baptism. It also exercises discipline for *Orderliness of Business* and for the *Discipline of the church members.*

6:9 The Life of an Organisation

This section is included to alert the pastor to keep watch over the group (or organisation) to keep it alive and active. The pastor as the overseer, the motivator and director of the organisation should know whether the organisation is stagnant or dynamic, whether the institution, including the Church, is ascending or descending the ladder of its life. The following two models of the life-cycle of an organisation warn the pastor to be vigilant, to do the needful not only to sustain its life but also to maximize its achievements. Incidentally, these life-cycles take place not only in the life of the institutions, corporations, councils, associations, and the church. Such a cycle of events are experienced in an individual's life, for instance, in one's spiritual pilgrimage along the high and low experiences of the journey.

Model-One[8] : The stages of the organisational life-cycle. It is a cycle in the sense the organisation can be revived from the stage of crisis to get back to the original zeal and purpose with which it first began. If not revived the organisation ceases to function or exist.

1. *Organisational stage:* With a great sense of the community's needs the organisation comes into being with certain promises and goals.

2. *Consolidation stage:* The organisation begins to meet the needs of the people and the people begin to appreciate the organisation. The goals and procedures of the organisation enlarge and have meaning. The structure of the organisation becomes gradually enlarged and elaborate. Boards and committees formed to reach the goals. The organisation reaches a stage of efficiency.

3. *Ritualisation stage:* The institution becomes more concerned about maintaining order than the primary goal. Programmes and procedures become the end in themselves. The officers become functionaries. They become more interested in earning than fulfilling the goals of the organisation. The officers become bureaucrats, protecting their own interests alone. Here, the people become disinterested in the organisation, and they withdraw activities and memberships.

4. *Crisis Stage:* (a) Re-organisational stage : This is a period to make decision what to do. The people recognize their failures, affirm change and decide for the future. The members remember the original goals with which the organisation began. Here the organisation gets back to the first stage, re-affirms the original goals and gets into the cycle again. (b) The Stage of Death : When the stage of re-organisation, as above, does not take place, the organisation becomes defunct or dead.

Model-Two : The four Ms of an organisation.[9]

Olan Hendrix, a management expert, talks of the inevitable trend in an organisation in terms of four 'M's as MAN, MOVEMENT, MACHINE, MONUMENT.

1. A *man,* with a vision and a burden starts an organisation.

2. When he associates himself with enough other men and develops an organisational structure, it becomes a *Move-ment.*

3. When more people join the movement, the organisation becomes a *Machine* (lifeless and automatic functioning).

4. When the organisation enters this mechanical life it loses its dynamism and productivity and becomes, *Monument.*

No wonder many organisations today have become Monuments, existing for the sake of existence. Some organisations have lost their direction and become sidetracked. Howard J. Clinebell's use of Theodore O. Wedel's parable, "Life saving station" to preface one of his books on pastoral ministry is a clarion call to the inactive, insensitive, and the unintentional pastors. Christian workers, and for that matter, the pastors, cannot remain just functionaries watching their institutions and organisations deteriorate, and finally die out.[10]

ENDNOTES

1. Edgar H. Schein, *Organisational Psychology,* Prentice Hall, N. Delhi, 1979, p.9.

2. Amitai Etsioni, *Modern Organisations,* Prentice Hall, N. Delhi, 1978, p.3.

3. H.W. Byrne, *Christian Education for the Local Church,* Zondervan, 1980, p.33.

4. See Peter F. Rudge, *Ministry and Management, 1967 and* Max Weber, *The Theory of Social and Economic Organisations,* 1947.

5. For Church Government, See Clyde Turner, *The New Testament Doctrine of the Church,* Convention Press, 1971, and William Stewart, *The Church and Its Ministry,* CLS, 1951.

6. *Ibid.*

7. *Ibid.*

8. The present writer could not trace out the main source of this information as it is a reminiscence from class Seminar with Hunter P. Mabry, 1982, On Church and Society.

9. Olan Hendrix, *Management and the Christian Worker,* ELS, Madras, 1970, p.22.

10. *Basic Types of Pastoral Care and Counseling,* Abingdon, 1984, p.13 (see also 1967 edition).

CHAPTER 7

Re-Vitalising Pastoral Ministry in India Today

7:1 The Ministry is Pastoral

God is by nature Life, Light and Love. He wants to extend the nature to His creation. God is actively engaged in giving life to those perishing, light to those in darkness of various kinds, and love to those unlovables. When God's creatures are denied those three Ls due to human sins, He adds another L to liberate them to allow His creatures to enjoy fulness of life in Him. This activity of God in the world is the MISSION OF GOD.

God's mission in the world re-creates life. He shares His creative work with His people by engaging them in His mission. Men and women who join God in this liberating and re-creating activity are called, collectively, the Church. Thus the Church has a partnership in God's mission. This is the ministry of the Church. The Church continues the ministry of Jesus, the Shepherd-king. Thus, the work of the Church is Pastoral. The word 'Pastor' or 'Pastoral' is derived from the nature of the Church's ministry that continues the work of the Chief Shepherd. The term does not apply only to the officially appointed ministers of the church but to all who do the work of Jesus the Shepherd.

Alister Cambell[1] urges us to re-discover the original intent of Pastoral care or shepherding. He takes David the shepherd as an ideal. David said to King Saul, "Your servant used to keep sheep for his father; and when there came a lion, or a bear, and took a lamb from the flock, I went after him and smote him and delivered it out of his mouth; and if he arose against me, I caught him by his beard, and smote him and killed him." (1

Sam. 17:34-35). Such kind of shepherd-king could have described God's care for people in the language of the shepherd Psalm (Psalm 23).

Shepherding today can be wrongly modelled after modern shepherds who work in peaceful farms free of wild beasts, thorns, rocks and gorges, storms and scorching heat of the sun. Bishop Newbigin, in the same way warns us that we should take into account both the tough and soft sides of Jesus the Shepherd. He says that the figure of the Good Shepherd is sentimentalised in the course of church history. Instead of taking Jesus as "a womanish figure apparently fondling a pet lamb",[2] he says we should correct this by reading the text in Ezekiel, which must have inspired Jesus' parable (Jn. 10). The shepherd in Ezekiel is more like a warrior. King David the ideal shepherd did justice, punished the wicked, leading God's people in warfare and peace. A new hermaneutic of shepherding will evolve in a major revitalising of its functions today, especially as the shepherds today have to fight against various such odds of the society where the 'sheep' are threatened, exploited and swallowed up. Such ministry would deserve to be called 'Pastoral'. Pastoral care in India should not only help people to grow in the fulness of and toward maturity in Christ but also safeguard against social injustice and exploitations. The pastoral careers should use Christian faith and wisdom and address people whose trouble arise from the conditions of poverty and plurality.

Re-vitalising postulates the inadequacy or fall of the status quo. Any organisation or system is said to undergo a life cycle as seen above - the first stage in which, inspired by the needs of the people, an organisation comes into being. The next stage is the stage of consolidation, where the goals and plans of the organisation enlarge, board and committees are created for effective realisation of the goals. The next stage is "Ritualisation" where the programme and procedures become an end in themselves. Here, the officers become functionaries protecting their own rights alone. People become disinterested and they withdraw their support. The next stage is a crisis period where the people either (a) recognize their failure and revive their commitment to the original goal, or (b) the organisation becomes defunct. When the functions of the church becomes 'ritualised' and 'luke-warm', re-vitalisation is the only choice for survival.

I would like to consider re-vitalising the pastoral ministry in India today from two sides: the Pastor, and the Church.

7:2 The Pastor's Readiness for Effective Ministry

1. The pastor should have a genuine **commitment** to suffer with Christ in re-creating the broken humanity. Besides one's intellectual and professional readiness, one should be spiritually prepared to be a partner of Christ in the mission of God. One has to examine oneself if the call to the ministry is caused by an incentive of mammon, or God. One who can argue so much for his/her rights and comforts cannot be an ideal minister. Our zeal for community concerns alone does not make us Christ's disciples.

2. The pastor should have **the mind of Christ**, leaving no room for boasting or arrogance whether for reasons of birth, intelligence or status. S/he should be open to people's criticism, be humble to be able to listen to the people's story, face situations and respond to them through love, without persisting in his/her own way. Many pastors persist to hang on to the job even when most people dislike them. When this happens, one way to re-vitalize is to quit. The mind of Christ, 'to serve, not to be served' should always be the ministerial attitude. Going back to this seed of Christian ministry will be a stride in revitalising ministry.

3. The pastor should be one who **lives what s/he preaches.** This contradiction of belief and practice is the point of public-criticism of the civil servants, too. Recently, an editorial of a local paper had a headline 'OF SERMON AND DEEDS' speaking against a ruling party which reportedly, forgot to fulfil the promises made during election. This remains true of the pastors who are reportedly involved in court cases, drunkeness, exploitation, corruption, and immoral acts. Everybody preaches against the evils of society but no one likes to live out the ideal preached.

4. The pastor needs an **adequate training to meet the needs** of modern people. The curriculum for pastoral education should include areas like societal analysis, legal education, the nature of political parties, fundamental rights of the citizen, parliamentary procedures, first aid and pastoral psychology, etc., as compulsory subjects for at least functional knowledge. The pastor should also be trained to meet the needs of the special people like, the floating population of the cities, the addicts, the working people, the poor, the youth, the university students, etc. The present courses like 'Introduction to Pastoral Care and Counseling' offered to those who opt for it are not enough. Such specialised courses may be offered not to students but also to those

in pastoral ministry, through in-service trainings or occasional trainings.

Besides, pastoral training may also include first Aid, simple electronics, operation of household appliances, preliminary knowledge in keeping livestock and tailoring etc. Such knowledge will not only benefit the pastor's family but also help the poor people from being exploited in such simple matters.

5. **The pastor's support** is one hidden agenda that pervades all the thinking and activities of the pastor. The society considers it taboo if the pastor speaks of his/her own needs. S/he is on a 'sacrificial service' they say. The parishioners fail their duty with the pastor with the excuse "God will take care of you". Rollo May[3], a pioneer in counseling observes that a religion overdosed by the idea, **"God will take care of you"** is an unbalanced religion. For in such situations the adherents overdepend on God and forget their human responsibilities. When the pastor goes to the market s/he is not permitted to pay only half the approved rate of the market, nor can s/he pay only half the school fee for his children. Surely, the church is not one of the poorest institutions but sometimes she seems to lull the ministers by such ideologies (God will take care of you; or sacrificial ministry etc.). When "rats desert pastor's house"[4] the pastor lives in a very low psychology. What vital ministry can be expected of him/her? We may continue to value asceticism as a mark of spirituality. At the same time our care for those who minister the gospel to us is not the least of spiritual duties.

6. The pastor's **humanity is often forgotten** by the people. Some people claim the pastor's 24-hour dedicated service. They also say the pastor's house should remain open for 24 hours a day. The fact is, the minister is overused. S/he has no time to be with the family, no time to meditate or reflect. Some churches wisely leave a day free for the pastor every week, for the pastor's recreation and family life. Such a secret place in the life of the exhausted minister will re-vitalize the minister's resourcefulness. Some of the congregation members should make a regular pastoral call to the pastor and his/her family. H.J. Clinebell describes this age as that of a 'touch-and-run' culture. If the pastor is overused and most of the work s/he touched are of 'touch-and-run' nature, there lacks quality. The pastor should be relieved from the present excess committee works, at least when such work can be done by the others in the congregation. Though pastoral ministry has

administrative responsibilities, most of his/her time should be assigned to the caring and nurturing ministry.

Without re-vitalising the life of the minister we cannot revitalize the ministry.

7:3 Church Structure

If, as we affirm, the church does not have any readymade agenda for the world (for the agenda arises from the need of the given context)[5], neither should the church have any fixed structure that fits all situations. Dr. Premsagar reviewed the existing pastoral literature in India (1975) and found no suggestions for renewal or restructuring the church and her ministry in those books on pastoral ministry.[6] Perhaps this remains true to a great extent. The present writer's town church had to be re-structured to meet the needs of the scattered members of the growing membership. It was done by organising sector churches in which new pastors were appointed but not without the strong note of attachment to the 'mother-church'. In any attempt to re-structure the traditional church set-up there is the apprehension of undermining the strength and unity of the original church, or of the jurisdiction of the incumbent ministers. Church structures are either "come-structure" or "go-structure". The term "go-structure" was used by a WCC study group on a structure for a missionary congregation (1968). The opposite would be a "come-structure" in which the church expects people to come and join the church. In "go structure" the church refuses to engage in proselytism.[7] The study also warned us of the heresy of morphological fundamentalism.[8] When required by the need of the world the church should re-structure itself to reach the homogenous groups, the professional groups, the working groups and the institutional inmates to create a sense of identity and belongingness to the human community. To revitalize its ministry the church should make its form and the mode of presence adjustable.

7:4 Forms of Ministry

Another morphological change may be made on the pattern of ministry. The relevance of the three-fold ministry in Indian context is always questioned. If the ministry belongs to the whole people of God, our pattern of ministry should fit that belief. Such need of change simply become topics of seminars. As mentioned earlier Late Henry Devadas, a churchman of the episcopal tradition strongly confesses that the three-fold pattern of ministry is "unsuitable for conditions in India." He says, "After a good deal of thinking I am driven to the conclusion that the episcopal system is not suitable either for the CNI or the CSI, and we may have to abolish the episcopacy altogether and re-think the whole question of the three-fold ministry."[8] He also questions why the church should channel salvation through the church's rituals administrated by ordained ministers only, and says such rituals are more of psychological and therapeutic nature than discipleship to Jesus of Nazareth.[9] (quoted above, too).

7:5 Collegiality in Ministry

Related to Team Ministry are collegiality and co-responsibility. The principle of collegiality can be traced to the Triune God in whom exists co-existence, parity and co-responsibility. Jesus, in his ministry together with the disciples had the spirit of collegiality. Jesus the Shepherd sought to turn the small flock accompanying him to shepherds themselves. He did not behave bossy to them, he rather served them, loved them and died for them. He called them "friends" not "servants" and revealed to them all that the Father made known to him (Jn. 15:15). Judas, who came to betray him in Gethsemane was his 'friend' still, and he died for his friends, the whole humanity (Jn. 15:13). A friend is one with whom we can share our private life whether joy or sorrow, pain or pleasure. A friend is one with whom we can walk hand in hand, looking at each others' eyes without having to fear or suspect him/her. Jesus wanted that his followers love and serve one another. There should be no feeling of superiority or clericalism among the ministers of Christ. Even the terminologies in the division of labour among the ministers like bishop, elder, pastor, deacon or such other identifications should not create the feeling of status. In the story of the development of PAPACY one of the bishops of Rome, Gregory, was among those bishops opposing the idea, is reported to have declared: "I speak with confidence, for everyone who calls himself or desires to be called universal priest, is by his pride, a forerunner of Anti-Christ, because he acts proudly in preferring himself to others."* He is reported to have said also, when men spoke of his own right to order: "This word ORDER I beg you to take out of my hearing, for I know who I am and who you are; in station you are my brethren, in character my fathers."** Bishop Gregory was reported to have called himself 'servant of the servants of God'. Here lies the spirit of collegiality among the co-workers in the vineyard of God.

7:6 Team Ministry

Team ministry is often suggested as an innovation against the traditional clericalism. In Team ministry there is the spirit of collegiality, shared ministry with the whole people of God, and it is feasible in both rural and urban situations. Team ministry involves every man and woman of the church including the professionals like social workers, psychiatrists, physicians, lawyers, counselors and chaplains. A true story quoted above enlightens us in this team work: Let us read the story again as it explains team ministry so well.

> "The young mother in the emergency ward... was sinking rapidly. Her baby had been killed in a car smash, but her own injuries did not seem serious enough to be fatal. After the surgeon had done all he could, he called in a psychiatrist. 'There is no medical reason why she shouldn't recover,' he said, 'but she wants to die - and she will unless her attitude is changed.'
>
> The psychiatrist's careful analysis uncovered the root of the woman's problem: the baby killed had been born as the result of an extramarital affair. She had been able to live with her secret as long as the child was alive, but now nothing the psychiatrist said could shake her guilt-ridden interpretation of the accident's meaning. 'I've got to die' she kept repeating. 'It's God's punishment for my sin. I deserve it.'
>
> The psychiatrist summoned the chaplain. 'This case calls for theological answers I haven't got,' he said."[10]

The story continued that the chaplain's assistance brought back her will-to-live that became conducive to the body's receptivity for the medical treatment. The above story speaks not only of division of labour among the people of God but also endorses the idea of the divine knowledge, or instrumentality of all creation. The story also reminded us of the complexity of the cause of human problems that requires careful diagnosis. D.S. Browning has rightly stated that,

> "The major new development that has motivated the founding of the pastoral counseling movement has been the insight that most human problems are various mixtures of both conflicted human freedom and moral and religious discernment. This partially explains the new interest of the part of the professional minister in combining psychological-developmental understandings with moral and religious perspectives on human behaviour."[11]

In re-vitalising the pastoral ministry in India we need more saints to be equipped for the ministry. Men and women, each according to the measure of charisma bestowed by Christ. Lay people engaged in such ministries should be oriented to the nature of the work by the trained ministers. Thus the equipping ministry is one important function of the pastor. Fear to involve other people in the ministry will hinder God's purpose.

7:7 The Kingdom Values

Teaching the kingdom values: lawlessness and meaninglessness in life mark the people of our time. "The world seems to turn its back to whatever is true, right and good. The untried imparting of the gospel value should be a cardinal function of the church today. Bishop Gorai[12] observed that, "the greatest challenge the church is facing today is from the erosion of moral values." The church is often allured by emotional preaching that may touch only the 'affective' part of the person. Both Kerygma and Didache are important functions of the church, but more importance should be given to the latter for more lasting cognitive input of the values of the gospel. Besides the existing Sunday Schools, Bible study groups for all ages should be organised, and lessons prepared, keeping in mind the social situations and Christian response to such situations. The teachers should be able to demonstrate by their lives that following the kingdom value is the best policy to be happy in life. It is often said that teachers who say "do as I say" have lesser followers than those who, like Jesus, say, "Do as I do." Pastoral care is understood as the *application upon human troubles the wisdom, the resources, and the authority of Christian faith and life). (Clebsch and Jaekle)*[13]. One of the three moments of Christian ministry, according to Dr. K.C. Abraham, is "faith-reflection" where, "the scripture and the heritage of faith is studied and interpreted in the light of the experience of the people."[14] Pastoral care is the application of the Christian message to life situations. Therefore, a systematic teaching of the value of our faith at the right time of the person's life will prepare the person to have Christian response in all situations.

7:8 Shepherding Attitude

A ministry with shepherding attitude: Pastors always do things in a caring attitude. They should not behave bossy or arrogantly like some servants in public counters. Pastors are servant-friends who are accessible to all people. People in general, including those who do not believe in God any more, are afraid of divine judgement on their lives. Sometimes the pastors themselves become the embodiment of such divine judgements. Their sermons are packed with condemnations and judgements of those, who

---

*William Stewart, *The Church and its Ministry*, CLS, Madras, 1951, p.109.
**Ibid.

in their opinion, are less holy than them. Some people change the course of their walk when they see pastors heading towards them. Paul Tillich, speaking on the impact of pastoral psychology on theological thought, remarked that many troubled people avoid their judgemental pastors and go to secular therapists from whom they experience warm acceptance. Tillich was alarmed to find that the ministers of the gospel, of divine justification to all people, failed to convey that message to the people.[15] The unconditional acceptance of God in Christ to all people is the fundamental right of all Christians. Christ's acceptance of all people in spite of their unacceptability should pervade the caring attitude of the pastor. This spirit of acceptance in Christ should transcend human differences of race, caste, creed and status.

7:9 Pastoral Care and Religious Fundamentalism

When we think of pastoral problems posed by modern Indian living we cannot overlook the religious factor. In some way or the other, people relate their problems with the Ultimate concern. This is done covertly among the educated people and overtly among the backward communities, though, in fact, all people are equally haunted by the sense of the sacred. We heard of Jim Jones of Johnstown (1978), Ayodhya of India, and more recently, David Koresh of Wacco, and other phenomena in the Gulf and Eastern Europe. Religious fundamentalism and fanaticism disrupt the harmony of living everywhere. Many cases of communal conflicts have religious connections. What I want to underline here is the need of teaching mature and healthy religious beliefs. Beliefs that are liberating, life-affirming, growth enhancing and beliefs that are inclusive in nature. It is the duty of the pastor-teacher to inculcate universal values that promote co-existence. Clinebell, rightly calls such teaching of matured religious beliefs as, "theological repair work."[16] He writes, "Destructive theological beliefs, attitudes, and feelings feed many people's neurotic fears, superstitions and guilt feelings." To him, clearing away such theological debris is a major and essential step in spiritual growth for many people.[17] The best way to clear such theological errors is to teach healthy faith from the early life of the person.

The caretakers should not be literalists in their use of religious resources including the scriptures. Fundamentalism in our use of the religious resources will simply land us up in foolhardiness and fatalism rather than these resources helping us to resolve our daily hurdles. For, the scriptures are made to promote life, not vice versa. The caregivers should not give unrealistic assurances based on religious resources. This is because the ultimate concern of humans in God and if we make promises based on God and their failures lead the persons to mistrust God it will be a disaster. The caregivers should deal with the situation humanly, accepting the reality of life rather than try to escape saying, "don't worry, God will take care of you" or, "don't be afraid, she will not die". The caretakers should instill faith in a realistic God than superficiality.

7:10 The Girl Child

Pastoral care and the 'girl child': It will be of no use repeating the oft reported messages of the parents to the 'girl child'. Some of the messages are reportedly, "you are not wanted" or, "you are a burden to the family." Besides, there are acts of discrimination in the family in matters of education, recreation and in times of decision where the boy child is treated as priority. Such treatment at home may result in inferiority complex of the female child (why is shyness said to be a traditional Indian women's modesty?). Pastoral care movement has a message of hope for the rejected girl child, to give her dignity by conveying the message of acceptance. The girl child is bombarded with negative strokes by the parents and the society. This vicious circle in the girl child should be unlearned in caring context. The pastoral care ministry should spearhead in the church's ministry of reconciliation and God's acceptance. How can the church preach wholeness when half of the church remains the 'girl child'?

The Indian Church is not only patriarchal but also pre-dominantly episcopal where the girl child has not gained entry into the ministry. It is good to know that the Church of England has started ordaining women for ministry. In India, all the meals are served by the girl child, so it will be more indigenous to India if she serves the communion meal as well. When more of this girl child joins the ministry, the ministry of the Indian Church will be greatly revitalised.

7:11 Pastoral Care Groups

Pastoral care is generally understood in three modes: pastoral care in general, which includes all that the pastor does; pastoral counseling that concerns more structured ministry to the specific needs of the individuals; and pastoral psychotherapy, similar to the pastoral counseling but it takes place in a more structured and isolated form from the general atmosphere, helping those unable to make decisions freely. Here the trained minister uses relevant psychotherapeutic approaches to help the person. The caretaker should not be literalists in their use of religious resources including the scriptures. Fundamentalism in our use of the religious resources will simply land us up in foolhardiness and fatalism rather than these resources helping us to resolve our daily hurdles. For, the scriptures are made to promote life, not the vice versa. The caregivers should not give unrealistic assurances based on religious resources. This is because the ultimate concern of human is God and if we make promises based on God and their failures lead the persons to mistrust God it will be a disaster. The caregivers should deal with the situation humanly, accepting the reality of life rather than try to escape saying, "don't worry, God will take care of you" or, "don't be afraid she will not die." The caretakers should instill faith in realistic God than superficiality.

There is a growing need of counseling ministry, but even the introductory courses in counseling are still new to the Indian Church. The people in general are shy about seeing counselors. So, the pastoral departments of the church should re-consider the need of counseling ministry, making its training compulsory for all ministerial students. No pastor of today can be considered qualified without at least one course in counseling. More counseling workshops and seminars should be conducted for the pastors in service and other lay people of the church. These lay people with introductory courses in pastoral counseling can form care groups and help the pastor in reaching the people in their localities and other homogenous groups. An equal number of women counselors should also be trained for the work.

The concepts, attitude, and the purpose of pastoral counseling are fitting for human growth and healing. But in so far as the people in general are still shy about going to counselors, the church may also present these concepts to the mass through text books of religious nurture. For instance, the concept of acceptance, the respect for the other, the need of patient listening to the other's story, or even the need of confidential respect – all these dynamics of human intimacy remain in counseling relationship.

Why can't the Church incorporate these gems of human relationship in the text books and teach the community about healthy relationships? For, these dynamics are not mere counseling techniques but vital keys of everyday human interactions. They should be learned by all people in the community for applications between persons, groups, inter-communal and inter-racial relationships. Such ideas should also inform the international relations.

Re-vitalising pastoral ministry, therefore, will include identifying the people's special needs arising from today's Indian situation. It will include realisation of the goals of the Church's ministry, the ministers' rededication of their lives and continued training for relevance and competency, mass education in pastoral values and extension of pastoral services to more people by training the laity and involving them in the ministry.

ENDNOTES

1. Alister Campbell, *Rediscovery of Pastoral Care*, Westminster, 1983.

2. Leslie Newbigin, *The Good Shepherd*, Eerdman Publ. Co. 1977, p.14.

3. Rollo May, *Man in Search of Himself*, W.W. Norton, NY 1953, p.197.

4. From the Writer's Conversation with Dr. Gnana Robinson, 1986.

5. WCC Study group, *The Church for Others...* Geneva, 1986, p.20.

6. Indian Journal of Theology, July-December, 1976.

7. *The Church for Others... op.cit.,* p.19.

8. *The Church for Others... op.cit.,* p.19.

9. Henry Devadas, *Christ Inspires Human Struggle for Freedom and Justice,* ISPCK, Delhi, 1993, p.13.

10. Young and Meiburg, *Spiritual Therapy,* HOUGHTER AND STOUGHTON, London, 1960, p.15.

11. Capp et.al. edited, *Handbook of Pastoral Counseling,* Poulist Press, 1985, p.6.

12. "The Creative Role of the Indian Church in the present day Indian Society" *NCCIR*, October, 1993, p.526.

13. *Pastoral Care In Historical Perspectives,* Prentice, Hall, NJ, 1963, p.4.

14. "The Mission and Ministry of the Church in the Present Day Indian context: A liberationist Perspective" *B. Theol. Forum*, Sept. '89, p.46.

15. *Pastoral Psychology,* Feb., 1960, p.17.

16. Clinebell, *Growth Counseling,* Abingdon, 1979, p.152.

17. *Ibid.*

CHAPTER 8

The Task of Interpreting the Scriptures

A pastor may have sources of information from the varied fields of study beside insights from his or her ministerial experience. However, the Bible is the most important source of guidance for a pastor as well as the people. Besides, the interpretation of the Word of God and feeding the people with the living Word of God is an important aspect of pastoral ministry. Visitation, comforting, leading in prayers and worship alone though these are important pastoral tasks, is incomplete. The task of interpretation and appropriation of the Word to the present lives of the people is the most important task of a pastor.

The language of the Bible is sometimes not as simple as it appears. The words and expressions in the Bible are to be interpreted in their original senses and understood in today's equivalence. Random and free-lance interpretations of the Bible in the past have landed the Church to untold miseries including division of the Church. There are certain accepted principles to keep in mind as guides in interpreting the Bible. A distinct discipline of hermeneutics is developed today for deeper search of the truth about God and His purpose as recorded in the Bible. Not many pastors may get time to plunge into serious hermeneutic work but the following are some simple principles, which every student of the scriptures should keep in mind.

8:1 The Life of the Interpreter

The interpreter or reader before the text is a very important factor in understanding the Scriptures. Unless the reader is spiritually regenerate and searches the word with the spiritual eye it will be difficult to understand the Bible (see also 1 Cor. 2:14). A person willing to study the Bible as a literature or history only will miss its deeper and saving meaning. Unless the reader believes in the Word of God first he or she cannot teach the Word. The reader should communicate the Word only as a testimony of what s/he has believed. The reader's willingness to believe what the Word says to him/her and dependence on the guiding Spirit of God who will reveal the meaning of the Word to the reader are requisites for understanding the Word.

8:2 The Best Reading (version)

The method of ascertaining the best reading is called "textual criticism". Criticism here does not mean discrediting the Bible but it means reaching certain judgement or findings. Before our Bible came to be a solid book as we have today there were thousands of pieces of writings in Hebrew and Greek which were copied by hand and further copied by other scribes and copyists. Such copied manuscript of the New Testament is also called as *codex vaticunus,* a term familiar to students of biblical interpretation. The task of textual criticism is to ascertain the accurate meaning by identifying the original text from among the multiple texts. The work of textual criticism continues even today as more discoveries are made. For example, among the English translations the King James' Version, translated 400 years ago does not have many of the light shed on the translations as a result of modern discovery of better manuscripts. Even many of the English expressions of the King James Version requires retranslation to modern English to make the Word of God intelligible to the modern readers.

8:3 Determine the Exact Meaning of the Text

The words and phraseology of the text should be understood from the original context. Tools of interpretation like Bible dictionaries, commentaries and various versions of English Bibles are required in this task. The reader should always ask, **is this text or phrase a figurative expression or literal? Is this a question for seeking opinion or statement of a fact?** And, **Is this absolute or qualified?** When figures of speech are translated literally the result can be quite different from what the biblical writer meant. The Revised Standard, for example, has some italicised words, which were not found in the original texts but added by translators to complete the sense for better understanding.

8:4   The Importance of the Context

A verse or a passage cannot be isolated and interpreted without considering the total context of the story. This procedure is true also in explaining any passage of literature, like English texts. The setting of the text (some referred to as *Sitz em lebem)* is very important to consider in reaching the accurate meaning of texts. This can be done even by asking few of the questions beginning with W, thus:

Who wrote this passage and to whom?

What subject in what life situation?

When and where was it written to address?

What problem? What is its relevance today and

to the total message of the Bible?

A Bible teacher, H.P. Colston*, warns us of common mistakes of taking the face value of the expressions in the Bible and interpreting them to suit our own purpose. For instance, Colston says, the Word Study in Timothy 2:15, which has been exclusively used to mean *'study the word of God'* has no connection with the word study. The word in those days (1611 AD) meant just *'do your best'* and so modern translations like, GNB, RSV, NIV etc. have changed that "study" to "do your best".

Another example is the expression, "Touch not, taste not, handle not" (Col. 2:21) has been often used to mean temperance and total abstinence against which Paul was saying that Christians need not become ascetics. Originally this passage was not meantfor abstinence. The point is, the Bible is in favour of temperance but this is not the right text to support it. For among many such cases of interpreting the Bible at face value, the above two cases from Colston are mentioned to remind us to do justice to the text. When the passages of the Bible are interpreted without reference to the specific context of the text and without considering the central message of God recorded in the Bible the result will be disastrous. Beside the importance of the immediate context the central message of the Bible as, God is love, just, holy and forgiving should be in command to guide us to interpret any individual passages. We cannot take out passages in the Old Testament about polygamy or circumcision and practice it today or the regulation on the conduct of the Corinthian women in the New Testament and apply it today. For we know the central message of the

**Preparing to Teach the Bible*, Convention Press, Nashville, 1959.

Bible will advocate a single spouse and that the Bible teaches equality of sexes before the eyes of God. Considering the central message of the Bible should be one important hermeneutic principle.

8:5 Keep in Mind Customs, Practices and Thought Forms of the Biblical Time

Understanding the Sematic culture, expressions and circumstances will help in interpretation of the Bible, e.g., marriage and family, architecture, occupation, food habit, rituals, festival and pleasantries of the time. In this regard books like introduction to the O.T., or the *Background to the New Testament* (keybook), G.C. Weiss's, *Insights into the Bible* and Freeman's *Manners and Customs of the Bible,* Alpha Book Centre Vishakapatnam, etc. will be useful for pastors.

8:6 Literal and Figurative Language Expressions

The Bible has many figurative expressions, which should not be interpreted in a literal sense. In the tribal communities of Northeast, even the expression. *The Lord is my Shepherd* (Ps. 23:1) is reported to have been interpreted to mean *The Lord keeps my cattle* in certain dialects. Also expression like young shoots *from the stem of Jesse* (Is. 11:1) is often translated in the botanical terms rather than in the language of Jesse's generation. One form of figurative expression is called *hyperbole,* which the speaker deliberately overstates for emphasis. Jesus' reply to Peter, seventy times seven (Mt. 18:22) does not mean literally 440 times but means many times. One may also keep in mind the Hebrews way of saying one thing in double lines (parallelism) especially in the Old Testament, for instance, Psalm 70:1 says,

> "Make haste, O God, to deliver me;
>
> Make haste to help me, O Jehovah."

Again, Gen. 1:26, has, "let us make man in our image, after our likeness." Scholars sometimes debate what *image* means *and* what *likeness* means. It is probable that both the words mean the same. For the second verse of a parallelism says the same thing in a varied statement.

The parable of Jesus is generally agreed by the scholars that the story has one central point to make and that the story should not be interpreted in allegorical manner. For instance, one point interpretation of the LOST SON (Lk. 15) would mean *the father's love.* If it is interpreted allegorically, the father represents something, the younger son means something, and the elder son represents something. That manner of interpretation will have no end and sometimes the central teaching of the parable can be obliterated. In an attempt to make the word of God most effective in the lives of people of all generations we can hear today talks of looking at the scriptures from the perspectives (or hermeneutics) of the poor, the tribals, Asians and women etc. All those innovated hermeneutics should explicate the living word of God for maximum human benefit and for God's glory.

We began this section with the person before the text as a very important factor. It will be relevant to close this section with the person before the text as interpreter. Humans have the tendency to seek self-interest and even a vested interest can influence biblical interpretation. A text can be interpreted in a self-fulfilling manner, or to charge some other people. Such personal or sectarian bias should be ruled out from the interpreter and seek the guidance of the Holy Spirit to reveal to humans what the word of God says.

CHAPTER 9

Pastor and Basics of Communication

It is the same way with lifeless instruments that produce sound, such as the flute or the harp if they do not give distinct notes, how will anyone know what is being played? And if the bugle gives an indistinct sound, who will get ready for battle? (1 Cor. 14:7-8).

The pastor's main task is the communication of the good news of God's salvation in all human situations. The urgency of that task is said to be like a dying person communicating to another dying person. When the pastor communicates the people wait anxiously to hear what precious direction will come out of the pastor's communication. Many such anxious listeners are often disappointed, unfortunately, as a result of improper communication by the untrained pastor. Some pastors seem to just discharge their routine duty without caring if the congregation or the people see, hear and understand what s/he communicates. Many large village congregations suffer loss due to lack of understanding what the pastor communicates. This is true also due to inadequacy of Public Address System and power irregularities. Tribal mind with the sense of awe and fear towards God and God's ministers will not mind remaining uncritical or non-reflective concerning the Holy. Preachers, leaders of worship, and even those who make regular announcements in the church do not make themselves clear. These speakers think when they hear their own voice it is loud and clear enough for the last benches of the huge church as well. Look on such speakers when the congregation thinks mystery should always shroud the manifestation and proclamation of God and that people should not send feedback to the servant of the Holy. But such speakers are what is referred to as trumpets with indistinct sound.

The pastor's acquaintance with some basic principles of homiletics or public speech will do away with the above malady. Besides, the following few basics of communication (esp. verbal and non-verbal communication) may be noted.

The pastor is always busy and so does not have time to speak in elaborate narratives or superfluous expression. Such can be done when the pastor is in leisure and on holidays. While on official work s/he may keep in mind the common advice, *be ABC* - that is be Accurate, be Brief and be Clear. This will also save time because the pastor is a steward of time beside being a steward of many other things. *Simplicity* of thought and language is very important in communication. This means do not mystify what you express nor use jargon that will block the comprehension of the simple mind. This is especially true of communication to tribal people whose thought and cognition is simple. Be *concrete* in expression. The common people and especially the tribal people do not enjoy abstract ideas but would demand concrete symbolisation. Jesus' use of figures and parables were an attempt to bring out the abstract ideas of the Kingdom of God to concrete terms for the simple Galileans. Jesus therefore drew examples from the people's daily experiences. When *illustrations* are required use them keeping in mind those rules of using illustrations. Rehearse such stories and tell them to help understand your main point better, not for the sake of laughter or even for surprising the listeners with new or strange stories. Such illustrations always defeat the purpose of illustrations. If your talk does not require it do not simply decorate your talk by telling irrelevant things. Attempt also to find out from the people if they understand you when you communicate. Be willing to welcome any constructive feedback from the listeners.

When you know people cannot get what you communicate it will be helpful to analyse your way of communicating and how disturbances occur in the process of communication between you and the listeners. The science of communication is rapidly improved these days and there are pastors who are well trained in modern communications.

Among the technical terms that occur often in communication language are the *SOURCE* (the communicator), the *CHANNEL* (the various symbols or media used to transfer the message) and the *RECEPTOR* (the receiver of the message). The source *encodes* a message and that message goes through the channel and the receptor *decodes* the message to understand it. Communication is sometimes defined as, a *behavior designed to exchange meaning between organisms* (J.H. Hellens). Communication can be *VERBAL* or *NON-VERBAL*. The word communication comes from the Latin word *Communis* (meaning, "to impart that which is common"). Communication is the art of transmitting information, ideas and attitudes from one person to another. (Emery-Adult-Agee). Like verbal communication, non-verbal communications express meaning, attitude, feeling or intent. Non-verbal language may include posture, facial-expression, limb movements proximity to others, orientation toward other person, dress and non-verbal sounds (para-language, like laughter, cough, giggling or sigh etc.). It is said humans communicate verbally 30% and non verbally 70% of the intent (thought). It is not alarming to know that while language can conceptualize only 30% of what we are thinking, 70% of it is expressed non-verbally and perhaps without our being aware of it! It is also said, "non-verbal language (or body language) seems to be a more direct link between psyche and symbolic encoding". (Hellens[1]). Many a pastor may not know this amazing fact of communication when they stand before people to communicate. One can learn more about this non-verbal communication in counseling trainings.

Barriers to Communications

The distraction that takes place in the process of communication effecting the message to be distorted is called, *NOISE. C.R.W.* David,[2] a communication teacher, has underlined four important types of NOISE as *mechanical noise, physical noise, linguistic noise and psychological noise.* Pastors who are not well trained in communication can also learn from such analysis for improving effective communication.

1. *Mechanical noise,* refers to the distraction caused by the electronic communication like, telephone, public address systems, satellite, televisions, acoustic defect of the auditorium and such other defects.

2. *Physical noise,* refers to a wrong or bizarre posture or gesture of the speaker, distance structure between the speaker and the audience, body motions, idiosyncrasies, including the speaker's reactions to the audience behaviour.

3. *Linguistic* (or Semantic) *noise,* refers to synonyms (polisemy), wrong choice of word to express ideas, wrong grammar or construction of sentences, mispronunciation, repetitions or slang, names of places, things not indigenous to the audience though the speaker may know. Defining the difficult words, therefore, helps getting rid off semantic noise.

4. *Psychological noise,* refers to the emotions, anxieties, prejudice, and apprehension of the individuals that influence one's ideas. This is applicable to both the speaker as well as the receptor (audience). The listeners see or hear what their mindset dictates them to hear. Listeners may hear but retain only those lines with their interest. The attention span of the audience will also matter. One should discipline to be appropriate in responding to the stimulus. This psychological noise will be detrimental in communication process among people of different communities, especially if the speaker and the audience are from different communities, sexes, age groups, political parties and religious groups. Prejudice and apprehension about others is human nature and such feelings disrupt communication. One factor that can eradicate such human feelings toward the others is the fact of oneness in Christ, before whom one should love the others as oneself. Such new attitude in Christ alone will clear the psychological noise to let intimacy and love reign in human relations. The pastor as the communicator of the gospel should know these pitfalls of communication and maximize clarity and effectiveness of imparting the word of God.

ENDNOTES

1. Dict. PCC, *Dictionary of Pastoral Care and Counseling,* R.J. Hunter (ed) Abingdon, 1990.

2. *Communication and Theological Education.*

CHAPTER 10

Evangelism and Mission

Evangelism is the task of telling the good news to the world that God in Christ has demonstrated His love for humans and the whole creation irrespective of what they are to Him. The word *evangelism* is a transliteration of the Greek word *evangelion*. From the very beginning of God's dealing with humans, He told Abraham, "in you shall all the nations be blessed" (Gen. 12:1-3). The perennial task of the people of God is to continue to proclaim this message of blessing to the generations. Jesus came preaching the gospel of God (Mk. 1:14). The gospel writers are often referred to as *evangelists,* meaning good news. Paul urged Pastor Timothy to do the work of evangelist (2 Tim. 4:5).

One of the placards hanging on the trees of the Writers College campus is that of D.T. Niles definition of evangelism, as "a beggar telling other beggars where food is available." Perhaps Niles wanted to rule out the significance of the messenger, so that the content of the message originated from God the giver not from the messenger. However, it is also significant to relate Christ the living bread to whom all the living should go for feeding on the bread of life and satisfaction. The task of pointing people to this bread of life is the task of the evangelist. Delos Miles, defines evangelism as being, doing and telling the gospel of the kingdom of God, in order that by the power of the Holy Spirit persons and structures may be converted to the Lordship of Jesus Christ.[1] This is a good definition in that it requires believing and living the message by the evangelist (being), putting in practice the good news (doing) and communicating the good news (telling). Miles finds such a definition corresponding to what we call the cardinal characteristics of the church, namely, Koinonia, Diakonia and Kerygma – the love-bound fellowship of those who have accepted the gospel, the service of extending that love, and the public proclamation of that love in the power of the Holy Spirit. This proclamation is done through both living out the message and telling out the message. Every Christian therefore, is a living sacrifice, a story or a letter to be read by others.

Mission is God's attribute. The nature of the Triune God is missional. God the Father sent His Son Jesus Christ, and the Father and the Son together sent the Holy Spirit. God is by nature Love and out of His love God sent Jesus Christ to redeem the world and give abundance of life. Jesus the Saviour tells those saved by him, thus, "so send I you". The followers of Jesus Christ (the Church) join hands with the mission of God. The purpose of the Church is to go into all the world and extend this love of God. As the Church's reason for existence is to be the instrument of God in God's mission (missio-dei). Brunner rightly observed that mission to the Church is like burning is to the fire. Based on texts like Matthew 28:19-20, Acts 1:8, the Church feels burdened by this Great Commission from the Risen Lord to go to all the corners of the world to tell the good news of Salvation brought about by Jesus Christ. The word *missio* connotes sending, and the Church's task of making God known to the world is called mission. Mission is a term covering a wide range of the Church's task under which evangelism is an aspect of it. Evangelism is often understood as preaching of the gospel to people (anthropocentric). Mission covers the whole purpose of God for the whole creation. The task of mission is sometimes stated as "to establish Shalom in the created world". God's purpose in mission is to establish peace and harmony in the creation.

The entire life of the church is missionary. The church is for others. The people in the church are called *laos* of God, meaning the people of God for a purpose. The Willingen Conference of the IMC (1952) with a theme, *The Missionary Obligation of the Church,* affirmed that mission is rooted in the very nature of the Triune God and thus gave birth to the idea, *missio-dei*. Missionary activity is nothing other than "the manifestation of God's plan, its epiphany and realisation in the world and in history."[2]

"The Church stands in the service of God's turning to the world."

The *missio dei* concept was thus coined half a century ago (Hartenstein) to protect mission against secularisation and horizontalisation and to reserve it exclusively for God. The Church is privileged to work with God and "points to God at work in world history and name him there."

Bosch points out that the word "mission" in its modern sense was first used in the sixteenth century by Jesuits in Northern Germany to refer to their work of Reconverting Protestants to Catholism.[3]

Mission is sometimes defined as proclaiming the gospel, "where no church as yet exists, where the Lordship of God has never yet historically been proclaimed, where *pagans* are the object In so far as there are Christians who had become "pagans" again (living in post-Christian milieu) the proclamation of the gospel to those *neo-pagans* is considered "evangelism" and the proclamation to the pagans "out there" is considered "mission". This would mean mission is not only the first preaching of the gospel to the people of other faiths but also the reintroduction of the gospel to those neo-pagans.

Mission is not simply a proselysation of people of other faiths to our own religion. It is "alerting people to the universal reign of God" (Bosch, 1995). The need of reintroducing the gospel to the Christians who had gone back to paganism makes mission bipolar but not one directional such as from the christianiser West to the pagan fields. Some Christian thinkers today feel that the Western world can sometimes be tempted to think they no longer need to be evangelised and think that it is their (West) duty to evangelise the one-third World. Such modest thinkers even say that the idea of the 10-40 window of the globe is rather arrogant because of the fact that one part of the world singles out a section of the world as in darkness to be evangelised by the others. Of course it is true someone has to take the gospel first to a needy world but such torch bearers should not project darkness to the others only. As every human is in need of the gospel any time whether Christian or otherwise, mission should be considered a reciprocal activity among humans so long as God the Author of the gospel makes it available for all humans and the creation. Human nature is such that even in the people of this region (the North-East India) there are many communities who have the sense of urgency in sending missionaries to the people "out there" but fail to keep their own house in order. The mission in which the church is involved is the mission of God not the mission of the Church. This means God initiated the mission to establish Shalom on Earth. The Church participates in God's mission. Mission is not an obligation but an overflowing of gratitude so it is natural and spontaneous. The following are some points to remember in missiological thinking.

Among some of the asterisk marked are remembered from the writer listening to Ross Langmead, an Australian missiologist.

- Mission is incarnational, something that happens in our actual life not a theoretical formulation. Our living examples can be the greatest sermon in our lives.

- The gospel took the shape of Jesus at one time similarly it takes different shapes in different contexts. The gospel is neither a fixed shape nor culture bound.

- Mission sides the poor. It speaks for justice, responsible stewardship and liberation of lives from the bondage. (Douglas, John Hall).[5]

- Mission should be contextualised to the given culture (Richard Niebuhr)

- The positions the Church has taken throughout her history of mission are various.[6]

1. *Exclusivism* – The belief that outside Christianity there is no salvation, a belief based on the conviction that Jesus Christ is the sole criterion by which all religions are to be judged.

2. *Inclusivism* – The belief that salvation is to be found in all religions but that this salvation is ultimately from and through Jesus Christ. Christ, it is believed, is in some mysterious way present and active in all other religions.

3. *Pluralism* – The belief that all religions are equally valid paths to the one goal. The pluralists would say that Christianity is but one more way to God among the many that have appeared and are appearing in the world.

   - Mission involves also physical and structural development.
   - Every human society is both a channel and a recipient of the gospel at the same time.
   - True stewardship makes people mission conscious.

ENDNOTES

1. Doles Miles, *An Introduction to Evangelism*, Baker Book House, p.47.

2. David Bosch, *Transforming Mission*, Orbis, NY, 1988, p.390.

3. *Believing in the Future*, Trinity Press, Valley Forge, 1995, p.29.

4. *Ibid.*

5. Douglas Hall, *Mission as a Function of Stewardship*, Don Mills, 1980.

6. John Patrick Prennan, *Christian Mission in a Pluralistic World*, St. Paul Publication, Bandra, 1990.

CHAPTER 11

Some Aspects of Group Dynamics

The pastor as a worker with human groups should have some knowledge of group behaviour. The size of such groups may vary from family, clan, tribe, trade unions to the State. Humans have used such groups for various ends: for work, for fighting, for worship, for education and for decision making. Any simple villager of tribal communities knows well how the age group, the labour exchange group and the village, work and how the individual is physically, psychologically and socially rooted to such groups. When the church life came to the tribals as group life it was easily embraced by the group-loving tribal people.

What is a group? A group is not simply an aggregate of individuals. When two or more persons are engaged in any kind of functional relationship with each other it constitutes a group. One of the definitions of a group may be read thus:

> A group is a collection of two or more people identifiable by name or type, with a conscious identification of the members with each other, with a sense of shared purpose, with interdependence in satisfaction of needs, communicating with, influencing upon and reacting to one another, and with ability to act in a unitary manner. (abridged by the present writer).[1]

A *Primary group,* is that group in which the individuals interact in face-to-face relationships. In the *Secondary group,* the members' relationships are indirect and – frequently, simply because of the great numbers involved – assume a more structured and organised form.[2]

The word "dynamics" comes from a Greek work "dunamis", meaning "power" or 'force' as in dynamite. A dynamo in a machine generates power that keeps the machine running. As every individual has a distinct 'personality dynamics' there are also "group dynamics". Those dynamics are the forces or phenomena that occur naturally causing the individual or the group to behave the way they do. One of the characteristics of *dynamic* is that "it is always moving, doing something, changing, becoming, interacting and reacting". The name of a German Gestalt psychologist, Kurt Lewin (1890-1947) is known for raising the study of group dynamics to academic level.

The area of group dynamics is vast, ranging from the study of how an individual in a group setting behaves differently than when alone, how individuals respond differently to different styles of leadership, how a decision is reached in a group, and so on. The following are only a few aspects of group behaviour that pastors as group workers need to know. The following few tips are drawn from Malcolm and Hulda,[3] and modified where necessary for clearer understanding.

11:1 The Leader's Function in Group Building

i)	the leader *encourages* all the members, is warm and friendly, responsive to others, praises others and their ideas, agrees with and accepts the contribution of others.

ii)	the leader *mediates,* harmonizes the group, coordinates ideas of the members and reconciles differences of views and compromises.

iii)	the leader *enables and facilitates,* encourages every member to participate, saying, "we haven't heard from John yet", or setting a rule that talking be shared leaving time for everyone to be heard.

iv)	the leader *sets standards,* that is, sets standards for the group to use in choosing its subject matter or procedures, rules of conduct, ethical values.

v)	the leader *follows,* goes along with the group, somewhat passively accepting the ideas of others, serving as an audience during group discussions, being a good listener. Many leaders may lack this quality but it pays to be such a following leader at times.

vi)	the leader *relieves tension,* sometimes draining off negative feelings by jesting or throwing oil on troubled waters, diverting attention from unpleasant to pleasant matters. Leaders with a good sense of humour are cases in point.

11:2 The Leader's Task in Functions

i)   the leader *initiates*, suggests new ideas, or changed way of looking at the group problem or goal, proposing new activities.

ii) the leader seeks *information*, ask for relevant facts or authoritative information. The leader does not act on hearsay, nor bases on facts from one side.

iii) the leader *gives information*, provides relevant facts or authoritative information.

iv) the leader *clarifies*, inquires diligently for meaning and understanding, restating something the group is considering.

v)   the leader *elaborates*, builds on the previous comments, enlarges on it, gives examples.

vi) the leader *coordinates*, shows or clarifies the relationships among various ideas, trying to pull ideas and suggestions together.

vii) the leader *orients*, defines the progress of the discussion in terms of the group's goals, raising questions about the direction the discussion is taking.

viii) the leader *tests*, checks with the group to see if it is ready to make a decision or to take some action.

ix) the leader, *summarizes*, reviews the content of past discussion.

11:3 The Leader's Self-centred Behaviour

The purpose and interest of the group can be defeated when the leader behaves in a way that will benefit him/her personally. Among such factors are the following:

i)   such a leader *blocks*, interferes with the progress of the group by going off on a tangent, citing personal experiences unrelated to the group's problem, argues too much on a point the group has resolved, rejects ideas without consideration.

ii) such a leader is *aggressive*, criticizes or blames others, shows hostility toward the group or some individual without relating to what has happened in the group, attacks the motives of others, deflates the ego or status of others.

iii) such a leader seeks *recognition*, attempts to call attention to his/her self by excessive talking, extreme ideas, boasting, boisterousness.

iv) such a leader makes *special pleading,* introducing or supporting ideas related to her/his own pet concerns or philosophies beyond reason attempting to speak for the *grass-roots,* the *house-wives,* the common people, and so on. Such is an unethical way of touching the sentiment of the people for personal gain.

v) such a leader *withdraws,* act indifferent or passive, resorts to excessive formality, doodling, whispering to others.

vi) such a leader *dominates,* tries to assert authority in manipulating the group or certain members of it by 'pulling rank', gives directions authoritatively, interrupts contributions of others.

The members of the group who know basics of group dynamics may handle such leaders constructively because they see such behaviour as symptoms of deeper causes, like, valid personal need that are not satisfied constructively.

To this may be added some behaviours that may destroy the group. These behaviours may be seen more from the members of the group though the leaders may sometimes do the same. The present writer collected these ideas from his memory of reading a local paper a decade ago.[4]

11:4 To Destroy a Group

i) we should not attend meetings. But if we do so, we must come late only to find fault with the office bearers and others.

ii) we should never accept any committee appointment. Then it will be easier for us to criticize without responsibility and doing nothing.

iii) yet we should get sore if we are not appointed in a committee. But if we are included we should not attend meetings.

iv) if we are asked by the president to give our opinion about an important matter, we should say that we have nothing to say or keep quiet. But after the meeting we should tell everyone how things ought to be done.

v) we should do absolutely nothing. But when others volunteer their selfless service we should howl that the organisation is run by a clique.

vi) When a lunch or dinner is arranged we should tell everyone that money, which could be used for better purpose, is being wasted on frivolous things.

vii) when no lunches, dinner or any other entertainments are arranged, we should say that the institution is dead and needs vitalising.

viii) we should keep our eyes open for anything wrong, and when we find one, at every opportunity we should pick holes and threaten to resign and get friends to do likewise.

ix) after the vote for proposition at the meeting we should go home and do the opposite. We should agree to everything at the meeting but disagree with it outside.

x) always we should delay replying to communications from the group or better still, we should not answer at all.

Lastly, but most important, we should not actually resign, else we would lose the opportunity to kill the group (NE Times Ghy 1993).

The above examples are quite ironical but they have points to teach us to become more sincere and honest in our interactions. Infact, there are many organinsations, including the board of deacons of the church ruined by such ill-mannered members. Now we turn again to Malcolm and Hulda, cited above, for more insights on leader-role in a group[5]:

i) Authoritarian-led groups tend to produce a greater quality of work over a short-period of time, but experience more hostility, competition, and aggression – especially scapegoating, more discontent beneath the surface, more dependence and less originality.

ii) Democratically led groups, slower in getting into production, were more strongly motivated, became increasingly productive with time and learning, experienced more friendliness and teamwork, praised one another more frequently, and expressed greater satisfaction.

iii) Laissez-faire groups did less work and poorer work than either of the others, spent more time in horseplay, talked more about what they should be doing, experienced more aggression than the democratic groups but less than the authoritarian and expressed a preference for democratic leadership.

To this may be added the findings of J.Z. Clark[6] that greater satisfaction of members is experienced under democratic leadership than under autocratic leadership. It is also found that leaders under stressful situations tend to behave in a more authoritarian manner. Leaders with the habit of constructive communication even in the face of negativity directly influence group cohesiveness.

ENDNOTES

1. Malcolm and Hulda Knowles, *Introduction to Group dynamics*, Association Press, New York, 1959, p.39ff.

2. W.W. Meissner, *Group Dynamics in the Religious Life*, St. Pauls Publication, Bangalore, 1979, p.14.

3. Malcolm and Hulda, *op.cit.*, p.57.

4. A Gauhati daily, 1993.

5. Malcolm, *op.cit.*, p.57.

6. Clark, "Group dynamics" in *Dictionary of Pastoral Care and Counseling*, Edited, Rodney J. Hunter, Abingdon, 1990, p.481f.

Part - Two
Introduction to Pastoral Counseling

1

CHAPTER 12

Introduction to Counseling[1]

Originally the word 'Counseling' referred basically to an advice giving by informed and experienced persons to people in need of information, education, and insight for a practical living.

Among the Israelites of the Bible, the wise men, who, out of their life long experience and inspiration had gained some practical wisdom and moral insights were considered the prominent counselors. The Book of Wisdom of the Old Testament, especially the book of Proverbs is a collection of such practical wisdom. Those admonitions and advice are often referred to as 'proverbial counsel' and many of them remain useful even today.

Among other religious communities there are sages, *rishis, gurus*, and *mullahs* to whom people go for their advice in life crisis. Among the tribal people, the parents, the elders, the priest, the witches and the respectable members of the community were consulted for their advice in times of confusion, sickness, and life plans, any member of the tribe who disregards such seasoned advice is considered unwise and socially aberrant person. When a tribal member is considered uncounseled or nonaligned in the mores of the tribe such persons are reconsidered wayward or misfit.

In the secular world people use the word 'counseling' for visa applications, job applications, interview preparation and such other activities to get *instructions* but call it counseling. Such use of the word counseling should not confuse the student. For, counseling as understood today is *not advice giving or instruction* sessions where the client has nothing to do but obey.

Such authoritarian direction does not occur even in the secular counseling where people go with some kind of personal or relational problems seeking direction from the professional counselors. The counselors are cautious in the areas of advice or instruction that becomes imposition of their whims to the counselees. The counselors just provide the required relational atmosphere to help the counselee to dig within self to discover the best option available to him/her to cope with that situation. It is true there are situation where the counselor gives insight for vocational options and educational counseling but even here the trained counselor avoids the temptation of coercing or imposing the counselor's own position. Counseling as a distinct discipline whether of secular or religious nature is understood to be a service of *helping the counselee to help himself /herself*

This is a constant factor in counseling across various approaches, that the center of decision making is the counselee.

It is true there are counseling schools, each emphasising in a particular aspect, viz., the behaviorist will seek behavior modification in the counselee, the human potential oriented counselors will seek in identifying the person's potentiality and develop it to start with, the analytic schools would dig back the past and the present inner world that troubles the person, the logo therapist would emphasize in helping the person find meaning in living, the rational emotive therapist would help the person to avoid those irrational imaging in their attitude. Counseling in Christian ministry is often referred to as pastoral counseling and so the term here will be used consistently when it refers to Christian counseling. The word Pastoral refers to the work of the church as distinct from other counseling. Pastoral Ministry in general refers to the entire activities of the pastor, including organising, administering, teaching, preaching, visiting, leading worship, evangelising, administering sacraments, etc., Pastoral counseling refers to a specific situation involving an individual or a family, or a group. Seward Hiltner's[2] simple analogy is to the point here: Pastoral ministry in general refers to taking care of the 100 sheep involving the above stated areas of work. Pastoral counseling is a more narrowed activity directed toward an individual, like the lost seep which the shepherd seeks leaving the 99 sheep in the fold. Though the shepherd oversees the 99 his/her attention is concentrated in the one that is lost for that moment. Here, the individual may be going through depression, frustration, bereavement, loss, sickness, and relational problems with God or neighbors. The pastor here attends to the situation of the individual much like the Good Samaritan giving his whole attention to attend to the needs of the wounded man.

Pastoral Counseling came as a vital part of the church's ministry by the beginning of the 20th century, initiated by people like Anton Boisen of USA. Later pastoral theologians and counselors like Paul Johnson, Seward

Hiltner, Caroll A.Wise, Wyne E.Oates, Rollo May, and others followed to develop it more as a discipline. The era of the church before these pioneer was described by Wyne E. Oates, as 'one way traffic' where the clergy with their authoritarian advice made the parishioners to follow without reflections or clarifications. Many of such priestly advice were considered judgmental, using directions from the scriptures and the faith tradition. By the time of these pioneers in pastoral counseling initiated the conversation between the clergy and the parishioner appeared as both ways traffic. These new batch of clergy were enlightened also by the science of human behavior (psychology) in diagnosing and helping to solve the problems. These pioneers did use the resources from their faith tradition but they were also oriented with behavioral science of the psychoanalytic tradition and other related schools of personality. The discovery of the unconscious, catharsis, defense mechanisms, the role of rapport, respect, understanding, and confidentiality- all theses greatly facilitated the counselee to search themselves and come up with constructive decision.

There are other pastoral counselors who insist that the scripture alone is the text for counseling advice. Jay E.Adams of Westminster Theology Seminary is one example. Adams insists that psychological insights are worldly wisdom and that the scriptural command is the final rule of human life and action. Such position may sound like the preachers and evangelists can do the work. Our concern is that we used behavioral insight to help us understand the scriptures better even though religion is not always the prominent figure in counseling conversations. Like the other counseling pastoral counseling attempts to see the emotional dynamics that prevails in the counselee and makes the judgment and decision making difficult.

Rather than looking at the counselee as a case or an object the pastoral counselor sees the person before him as a person of value, of God's image, temporarily weighed down by life burden. Thus the pastoral counselor always remembers, as W.E. Oates observed, that there is a third person present unseen in all counseling relationship of two. This fact helps the counselor to avoid exploitation and misuse of the person or the counseling situation. This is so even through the pastoral counselor, like other the counselors, uses insights from culture, faith tradition, human science and personal experience. Use of religious resources becomes only one aspect of the repertoire of counseling wisdom of the pastor.

12:1   Introducing Counseling, Christian Counseling, and Pastoral Counseling

Counseling services are available everywhere, run by different individuals and organisations. The purpose and the levels of such counseling vary depending on the need of the counselee and the motto of the centers. Counseling that is attached to the Church and its ministry is called Pastoral Counseling. Pastoral counseling often uses insights and resources from the Christian Faith tradition. In secular counseling situations God-talk is not important unless the counselee initiates the agenda. In pastoral counseling the counselor always conveys the good news of Jesus even though it is not overtly proclaimed. In secular counseling there are chances of the counselor tempted by the counselee in respect of unfair economic gain or sexual exploitations. Secular counseling requires high fees of moderate amount. The redemptive message of Christ that every person is accepted without merit is best communicated by the pastoral counselor when s/he communicates as unconditional positives regards and respect of the counselee. Counseling relationships are not necessarily for judging, moralising or confronting the counselee who at times can be beyond the regions of faith, rationality or right response to stimuli. It is a moment when the counselor as the representative of Christ communicates compassion, understanding, a walk by the side through the rough weather faced by the counselee at that moment and mutual-burden-bearing.

12:2 Biblical /Theological Foundation

Healing is the goal of God working in a broken world. The Bible makes it clear that God is in search of bringing healing, a holistic healing to the groaning creation. Healing was an important mode of the ministries of the priests and the prophets. Jesus gave such importance in healing the body and soul, healing the broken relationships between God and human, human and human. When a person is said to be healed that state of healing refers not only to the body but its effects goes beyond the body. People often speak of dying as a healed person. Healing is a strong synonym of salvation too. James Lapsely, in his book, *Salvation and Health* has brought out this relationship of healing and salvation. Theology would see the human as a whole person, composite of soul, body and mind that God wants humans to present themselves to him in perfect whole-body, soul and mind. Healing is therefore an essential part of making the broken person whole. God's attempt to establish his shalom in the world can be experienced only if the person is healed from all round brokenness.

Seward Hiltner spoke of what occasions healing and said it could be due to defect, invasion, distortion, schedule and direction. Defect will refer to deficiency in the physical, mental, intellectual aspects of the person that disable the person. Invasion would refer to viral infections; unjust intrusion by other members of the humans in the life of the person causing brokenness etc., Schedule would refer to breach in the ordered time for proper functioning of life. Distortion can include discrimination, marginalisation and betrayals by humans.

A. Healing in the Old Testament

B. Jesus and the healing ministry

C. Healing through counseling as Redemptive Experience

12:3 Selected Models of Counseling from Depth Psychology

As mentioned earlier, some conservative pastors insist that the Bible is enough to draw insights for solving any human problem and guiding for life and action. They disregard other sources of healing like, psychology, as worldly and that pastors should discard such secular wisdom. We should not forget that the science of human behavior is within the milieu of God's wisdom. There are cases of how scriptures and science find each other a profitable ally in healing the human. Most pastoral counselors, therefore, use insight from human science. Among the frequently used schools are Psychoanalysis, Transactional analysis, Gestalt Therapy, Client-Centered-Therapy, Logotherapy, Rational Emotive Therapy, And System's therapy. Depth psychology refers to the method seeking the cause of problem in the unconscious level of the person as in Psychoanalysis and Jungian therapies. Depth psychology is often symbolised by a spade due to the fact that it digs back the past experience of the person. The belief is that whatever the person experiences from birth, positive or negative impacts from the society around remains ingrained in the soul of the person. They talk of the formative years of a person, the first five (or even seven) years of anyone's life. They believe in the harmfulness of suppressing strong emotions in the persons, such as, the urge to cry, to rejoice, to ventilate anger, and including the sexual urge and hunger. The society's treatment (especially the parents while young) of the young life is vital in informing a positive or a negative worldview of the person. When the negative messages are too strong and response to such a feeling is prohibited by culture or religion the person represses the emotion, which remain very powerful influences in the unconscious level of the person. Other than the depth psychology there are many other schools that help in caring situations. Among them are Gestalt School, Behaviorist School Rational emotive Therapy, Psychosynthesis, Reality Therapy etc. which the counselors employ.

A. Psychoanalysis

B. Client –centered –therapy

C. Transactional analysis

D. Logotherapy

12:4   Essential Elements in Counseling

In elementary science we read about the three conditions necessary for germination of a seed, oxygen, moisture, and sunlight. In a counseling relationship, if healing should result, there are important elements/ conditions working together to effect healing as listed in the contents. Each of the elements is vital and contributes to result healing. Rapport opens the gate of relationship, a disciplined listening makes the counselee pour out the content of the heart's burden, respect, an empathetic understanding of the counselor assures the counselee that someone cares for the latter, confidentiality assures the moment of trust and security, and genuineness on the part of the counselor itself is a source of healing. There is no strict rule that these elements should appear in certain moments of counseling only. They are present in all moment of relationships though some of them come to the forefront in certain stage of the session, for instance, Rapport normally comes at the very beginning of the sessions. (See Chapter 17 & 18 for more on these elements)

- Rapport

- Acceptance

- Listening

- Empathy

- Genuineness

- Concreteness

- Respect

- Facilitative Self –disclosure

- Confrontation

- Referral

- Facilitating Action.

12:5   The Process of Counseling

In Stage-I,   the counselor establishes a rapport allowing the counselee to express freely. The counselor then listens to the story using both verbal and non-verbal communications. It is often said that a person communicates 70% by verbal symbols. The counselor responds using both the means of communication.

In Stage -II,	the counselor facilitates the counselee for self exploration to see if the causes of the problem is partly through his/her behaviors, or how the problem was seen before, whether the counselor has unused potentiality to solve the problem was seen before, whether the counselee has unused potentiality to solve the problem, or if s/he had a strong defense in making the problem surface.
In Stage-III,	Here the counselor helps the counselee to review the counselee's past modality in handling the problem, to see if an attitudinal change is required in the counselee, to re-examine the kind of worldview one had. All these should lead to a new view to the old resulting in constructive solutions.
In Stage-IV,	The counselor helps the counselee to put in action whatever new outlook they both had discovered. If the sessions do not lead to a helpful action on the part of the counselee the counseling session did not help.
In Stage-V,	Here the formal sessions may be discontinued but the counselor keeps observing and monitoring the situation and reinforce helpful action. Chapter 24 has more on the stages.

12:6   Faith Resources in Counseling

Christian counselors often become ambitious in referring to their faith resources in counseling. When faith resources are used appropriately they are very effective. An indiscriminate use of faith resources do more harm than good. There are times when the counselee is in rebellion with God due to seeming failure of God to answer prayers. When the Bible itself tells us not to throw pearls to swines we should not use the valuable scriptures where it is not welcomed. When the counselors use these faith resources they should be used with proper rehearsals and readiness to apply effectively. These presentations should never appear artificial or exploitative. If, in the course of counseling the counselor can instill a strong gospel value in the counseling it will strengthen the latter in forgiving, bearing of life burden as essential part of life, and still maintaining the hope in Christ. However, this can be done in an appropriate time and occasion. (See Scripture texts at the end of book for use in different occasions).

A. Scripture

B. Prayer

C. Sacraments and Rituals

D. Community Resources

E. Singing

F. Counseling the sick, the bereaved, the overjoyed, the disabled, and those with life threatening sickness

12:7 Counseling during Developmental Crisis

One of the highway placards reads, "be gentle at my curve". Human developmental have many curves or stages of development from birth to death. Such stages, if not handled gently will break the person. Pastoral counselors are carefully watching the growing person throughout the stages of childhood, puberty, marriage, vocational decisions and such other crises events. A good pastoral care service in these crisis points leads to a more need-satisfying outcome from crisis. On the other hand, if the growing person is left to struggle alone through these changing phases of mood, physics, and social issues the outcome will be negative and growth can be constricted. For instance, a child in *Oedipus/Electra* complex, on entering puberty later, preparing for mate selection, facing death and loss, should be guided properly. As the child enters the psycho-social growth it needs careful guidance. Children should be rightly stroked for their psychological health as they grow. Negative strokes constrict their growth. *The adolescents* enter a stage where their interest in opposite sex increase and their physiology show their urges. Sex education should be given properly so that adolescent should not experience unhealthy sexual life. Sex in all stages of life should be taught to be taken as God's gift and used properly and in need gratifying manner. Guidance on such crisis points of life prepares the person to face life courageously because such guidance attempts to minimize frustration and trauma inherent in many stages of development. Young people intending *for marriage* should be properly guided in the decisions and preparation for marriage. Many parents today are informed with the basic caring skills during such transitional periods and parents are the best counselors in such times. *The aged persons* are in the wane of their social relationships and productivity, which make them feel less important. Supportive counseling is required to encourage them to live on. Continue with the following:

A. Counseling children

B. Counseling adolescents

C. Premarital counseling

D. Counseling the aged

E. The Marginalised

F. The Person with disabilities

In family counseling in India one has to keep in mind the dynamics of the family relations. Most families live in a joint family where the older mother (mother-in-law) is the key person to whom the husbands pay their homage. There are advantages and few disadvantages of living in a joint family. Modern Indian brides prefer living separately than in a joint family. This will also create tensions. Dowry question can also create tensions. It will be quite the opposite in a tribal family. Although many tribal youth have been exposed to modern livings they are still obliged to abide by the traditional authorities. Many of them will respect parental values and direction as in the case of marriage. The counselor should be aware of these sensitivities. They should see that they are not biased after listening to one party. They should listen both the sides before making decisions.

BIBLIOGRAPHY

(A) Required Reading

Antony, D.John   *Types of Counseling,* Anugraha Publication, Nagercoil.

______________.,*The Skills of Counseling, Anugraha* Publication, Nagercoil.

Ashbrook David J. .*Minding then Soul: Pastoral Counseling as Remembering,* Fortress.

Atkinson D.J. *New Dictionary of Christian Ethics and Pastoral Theology,* IVP Illinois.

Ausburgs D. *Helping People Forgive,* Westminster.

Capps D. *Biblical Approach to Pastoral Care and Counseling*, Westminster.

Clinebell, Howard *Basic Types of Pastoral Care and Counseling*, Abingdon.

_______________,*The Intimate Marriage*, Harper & Row.

Collin G. R. *Christian Counseling*.

Currie Joe *Barefoot Counseling*, ATC Bangalore.

Dyringer, Richart *The Heart of Pastoral Counseling*, Binghamton.

Dossey, Larry *Prayer is Good Medicine*, Harper & San F.

Egan, G *The Skilled Helper*, Worthsworthy.

Fuster, J *Personal Counseling* Bandra.

Feider, Paul *Healing and Suffering*, London, Dalton.

Fullmer and Bernard *Counseling: Content and Process*, Thompson, Delhi.

Garkhuff, R.R.   *The Art of Helping*, VII, Amhesrst, HRD Press.

Glasser, William Reality Therapy.

Gerard K& D *Counseling Adolescent*, Delhi, Sage.

Hiltner, Seward *Pastoral Counseling*, Abingdon, Nashville.

Humphery, G.M&Z *Bereavement*, Sage, New Delhi.

Hunter, Rodney, J *Dictionary of Pastoral Care and Counseling*, Abingdon.

Jacob, Michael *Still Small Voice*, London, SPCK.

Swift Small Heal, London, SPCK.

Kazdin Alan, E, *Encyclopedia of Psychology*, Vol. 1-8, Washington.

Nelson Jones, R, *Introduction to Counseling Skills*, Delhi, Sage.

Olsen D.C, *Integrative Family Therapy*, Fortress Press.

Prashantham, B.J.*Indian Case Studies in Therapeutic…*Bangalore, ATC.

Satir, Vir *Conjoin Family Therapy*, Palo alto.

Taylor, Charles, *The Skilled Pastor*, Fortress Press.

Kirkwood, N.A. *Pastoral Care in Hospitals*.

Kennedy, Eugene *On Becoming a Counselor*.

_______________., *The Pain of Being Human*, Mumbai.

Kakar, Sudhir *The Indian Psyche,* OUP.

__________., *Mystics, Doctors...Indian Healing Systems* OUP.

Lucas E. *What Can we believe,* London, Lunx.

Lapsley, James *Renewal in Late Life through Pastoral Counseling,*. Paulist P.

Murry, E. *An Introduction to Pastoral Care and Counseling,* ISPCK.

Pearson M. *Christian Healing: Old Tapan N.J.Chosen books.*

Ramsey, H. *Pastoral Diagnosis,* Minneapolis, Fortress Press.

Reinner & Wagner *The Hospital Handbook,* Harrisburg, Morehouse Publications.

Stone, Howard & Clements *Handbook on Basic Types of Pastoral Care and Counseling,* Abingdon, Nashville.

Varma, V. *Managing Children with Problems,* Cassel, London.

Yeo, Anthony *Partners in Life,* APECA, Bangalore.

__________., *In the Shadow of Death,* APECA, Bangalore.

Wicks, Robert P. *Clinical Handbook of Pastoral Counseling,* vol. I & II.

CHAPTER 13

Definitions:
Pastor, Pastoral Care, Pastoral Counseling

13:1 Pastor

This word came from the Shepherding Culture of Palestine. A herd, in Greek is *poimen* from which the word 'Poimenic's comes. Poimenics, is the study of pastoral work (pastoralia). *Poimen,* is a flock of sheep or herd. One who tends or cares for the flock is Poimenas or Pastor, (Eph.4:11), or *Poimen* (Jn. 10:10). The word 'Pastor' in its adjective form 'pastoral' refers to the life and work pertaining to tending and caring in general, for instance, 'pastoral tribe' would mean a wandering community that follows their herds in shifting grasing areas. Thus, a 'Pastoral Prayer' is the prayer for others in a caring way (Intercessory Prayer). Hence, pastoral work or a pastoral prayer can be done by any (Christian) person with Christly attitude of care, service and sacrifice. Sometimes a pastor is also referred to as *'minister'* in a Latinised form. The basic work of a minister is selfless service rendered to people. The other Greek word for service of this nature is *diakonia,* referring to menial service done to serve the other, like those waiters at the table. The work of Christ, and for that matter, all Christian work can be referred to as *diakonia* (deacon's work). Although there are church workers appointed for full time, called, pastors, deacons, evangelists and other officers, other Christians can also be engaged in such pastoral, ministerial (or diaconal) work. Thus pastoral counseling can be done by any Christian who does the work of that nature. Clebsch and Jaekle have defined the ministry of pastoral care as consisting of, "helping acts done by representative Christian persons, directed towards the healing, sustaining, guiding and reconciling of troubled persons whose troubles arise in the context of ultimate meanings and concerns."[1]

13:2 Pastoral Care

As Pastoral Counseling is a branch of the general pastoral care a brief definition of 'Pastoral Care' is in order:

Pastoral Care is a broad term that refers to all that a pastor does, including organising, shepherding the people and communicating the gospel to them. S. Hiltner identified three important tasks of Pastoral Care: Healing, Guiding, Sustaining (1958, preface to Pastoral Theology). In 1964, two church historians, William A. Clebsch and Charles R. Jaekle[2] added 'Reconciling' as another cardinal task of pastoral care.

To these four traditional functions of pastoral care, Howard J. Clinebell,[3] added 'Nurturing'as another vital function of Pastoral Care (1984). Thus, they are the *Healing task, Guiding task, Sustaining task, Reconciling task, and Nurturing task*. If, as often mentioned, the task of the church is four-fold, (like the four corner pillars of a church building) Teaching, Proclaiming, Fellowship and Service, we can also say that the task of Pastoral Care revolves around these four traditional functions of the church.

13:3 Pastoral Counseling

Pastoral Counseling is a specific task within the umbrella of Pastoral Care. Pastoral counseling arises from a crisis situation of the people. It is a caring ministry centred around an individual or group focused on a specific problem. It is a pastoral ministry extended to a person seeking special help under conditions of agreed time, place, contract, and even fees where applicable. There are also avenues of informal and short term counseling.

In Counseling ministry a Pastor is trained in human relation courses that makes a Pastor understand his/her own dynamics of growth and how one can help others in the same experience. In the training, the pastoral counselor is trained to use insights from the religious resources, the science of human behaviour, the prevailing cultural values and other dynamics of human relationships.

In defining Pastoral Counseling, Hiltner's definition is precise and to the point. His book, Pastoral Counseling,[4] has a sub-title "How every Pastor can help people to help themselves".

Dr. Mascarenhas[5] would define Counseling as *helping a normal person who is unhappy or anxious.* Counseling includes varied range of help required - from educational guidance to vocational counseling.

J.N. Fuster, in his book defines Counseling as, "a procedure which consists of a relationship between the client and the counselor, in which the client, aided by the counselor, examines the causes underlying the growth of his problem, and learns a new and more satisfying way of adjusting himself to his real environment" (personal counseling).

It is useful to refer to the renowned Pastoral Counselor Howard J. Clinbell, who defines Pastoral Counseling as, "the utilisation of a variety of healing (therapeutic) methods to help people handle their problems and crises more growthfully and thus experience healing of their brokenness

13:4   The General Principles of Pastoral Counseling

Of many guiding principles Robert Lee has summarised into following four dominant principles:

1. The counselor should in no way make efforts to manipulate the person seeking help whether psychologically, morally, or religiously. When the counselee asks information may be given on certain matters as requested and advice may be offered if it is necessary but not authoritatively but as an expression of the counselor's opinion without coercing to accept it. The counselee must be led to make his/her own decision to which the counselor may support.

2. The counselor must show his/her full acceptance of the person seeking help. The counselor's affectionate relationship should help the person to heal up broken relationship of deprived affection in the past life of the counselee. The counselor's genuine love, trust and acceptance without any condition is an important principle of counseling.

3. The counselor should not take his/her own agenda to put forward in the counseling's conversation. It is the counselee who is the most important person in such a relationship and therefore the counselee's agenda are followed. There can be a time when there will be a two-way traffic of the conversation but the counselor should always keep his/her needs and motives in the background and give important to the counselee to express without disruption, to explore and make decision.

4. The pastoral counselor must remember that God gives the freedom to everyone to choose his/her own way of ordering life rather than simply

conforming to the custom that may appear unproductive to the counselee. The pastor should also remember that God also gives everyone the faith to come to the good sense and recognize the good and the right to choose. The counselor is there only to assist in this choosing that may bring the best of satisfaction. The pastoral counselor sees that his /her function is to discover the innate healing forces of the counselee and to stimulate and foster it to discover the innate healing forces of the counselee and to stimulate and foster it as the counselee strives to experiences fullness of life.

(modified from an item by Robert S.Lee, Principles of Pastoral counseling S.P.C.K, London, 1986).

13:5   The Goals of Pastoral Counseling

The following goals are common to pastoral counselors even though they may not achieve all of them in a counseling occasion and even though the counselee may not need or experience all these in one counseling event.

1. *Reduce undue tension:* Most counselees come to a pastor with some tension. It is important for the counselor to help the parson drain off their emotion and reduce their anxiety. This is called catharsis, meaning, cleansing the inner pent –up emotion. In many cases the counselee experience this catharsis before the understanding listener is all that bring them to the pastor.

2. *Resolve harmful conflict:* Counselees come to pastors with relational problems and conflicts with their spouse, children, co-workers. Unresolved and uncontrolled hostility can be destructive to self or others. It is alright for humans to be angry but proper dealing with it is important.

3. *Improve insight and self –understanding:* The pastoral counselor helps the person to gain deeper insight in self-understanding, understanding the situation s/he is in to help making appropriate decision.

4. *Increase self –acceptance:* Most counselees find difficult to accept themselves as they are. They have a poor self-image and feel incompetent and even feel rejected. Acceptance comes not by persuasion but by the pastor's acceptance of them and helping them have a positive understanding to their own needs and problems. It is the pastoral counselor's task to communicate God's acceptance of all humans even when we were yet sinners and the cost by which God redeemed every individual created in God's image.

5. *Release internal resource*: Humans have potentialities within themselves, which need be identified and affirmed with the help of the counselor (educative guiding).

    A bit of encouragement, support, or reassurance will enable them to master their own ego strength and cope with their own problems.

6. *Provide information:* The information that the common people have on certain matters may be faulty, limited and confused by emotion. Without clarifying confusion some problems cannot be solved. The counselee cannot reach a decision if the information is not adequate. The counselor therefore is, at time a facilitating teacher (or friendly teacher as Kemp puts it).

7. *Make realistic choice:* The counselor should neither give unrealistic promises nor allow the counselee to have such unrealistic expectations. It may help to adopt the S.M.A.R.T. method of decision-making even in counseling.

8. *Attain self-fulfillment and self–actualisation*: The pastoral counselor seeks not only to resolve conflicts but also to help the person to move to higher state of attaining one's potential, growth and fulfillment. It is a continuation of the task of the Chief Shepherd who taught people to transcend the perishable and the temporal realm and experience the incorruptible and the eternal. It is exactly the model of the Samaritan woman's encounter with Jesus for her temporal concerns. Jesus led her from the need of the temporal water to the plenty of the eternal water of life that quenched her thirst forever.

    (cf: C.F.Kemp, Pastoral counseling guidebook, Abingdon, Nashville, NY, 1973).

13:6 Know your Emotions to Handle them Better

Counseling is an encounter with human emotion. If a stitch in time saves nine, a wise dealing with emotion in time will save lives.

WHAT IT IS	OVERCOME IT
Anger Anger could range from mild irritations to full-blown tantrum, rage and resentment. Being insulted, intense disappointment,	Politely communicate your norms and expectations without blaming other people. Or just leave the place, take a few deep breaths, listen to

feeling vulnerable or threatened can make one angry. It is often a projection of displeasure with ourselves.

music or just walk a few paces to quell the ceaseless train of hostile thoughts.

Sadness

Sadness could mean being overwhelmed by sorrow, grief, depression or a feeling of helplessness. Things that happen seem random and beyond one's control and a feeling of defeat and pessimism engulfs one.

Re-evaluate your priorities and deal with them individually. Resurrect dreams buried in the past to avoid failure. Visualize turning your best dreams into reality and think how you would feel it you could fulfill them.

Fear

This emotion spreads across feelings from low-grade concern, apprehension, worry, anxiety to absolute fright and terror. It tends to convey the need to prepare to cope with undesirable happening that we are anticipating.

Take possible action to prevent the dreaded from happening. Consider the precaution intended but then do the very thing that you fear to do. Do it more often in spite of a violently pounding heart.

Resentment

It is the feeling of having been deprived or having received less than what is fair or just. Resentment makes one withhold one's love for others but it also keeps one from getting it from others.

"Resentment is like taking poison and waiting for the other person to die," someone said. Don't blame others for not giving you what is your due. Take responsibility for giving yourself other things that you can.

Frustration

Frustration is the wall between efforts and the result that we are expecting out of them. It therefore conveys the need for reviewing and looking for more powerful strategies, may be with some help.

Stop comparing your efforts with those of others. Accept yourself and, more importantly, cultivate patience. Make sure you aren't setting unrealistic goals for yourself. It results don't show, move on.

Guilt

Guilt represents regret and remorse. It conveys that you have just violated an important value in your life and warns you not to transgress it again as you are meant not to break it but to uphold it.

Begin with acceptance, mentally relive the episode with all details that caused you to feel guilty and replay the whole episode upholding the value that got violated earlier. Do this exercise every day till confidence is restored.

Disappointment

Disappointment strikes when you get less than what you were expecting. It's an offspring of ambition, a state when hope flickers, snubbing out the desire to face future plans.

Evaluate to see if you are unreasonable in setting the goals. Leave the past behind and being afresh by setting more appropriate goals that are immediate and within reach.

Worry

Feelings of uncertainty and lack of courage when taking risks causes worry. Often lack of preparation or readiness can cause worry. But no amount of foresight and planning for the future can completely keep worries at bay.

Worries will continue to persist until the experience is gone through or the deed is done. Visualising yourself doing what you want to do every day will help build confidence. Then you will be better able to face situations.

Jealousy

Jealousy represents a feeling of being less fortunate than other, the fear of losing what we possess, or of being insecure because of the lack of a sense of worth and self-esteem. It stems from a sense of mistrust and ingratitude.

Trust the fact that everything that happened or is yet to happen is ultimately going to be in the best interest of everybody. Trying to know the person you are jealous of will often show your fears to be unfounded and uncalled for.

Self-pity

Self-pity has its roots in our hunger for attention as a child. Since you feel you've been denied,

Seek out your hurts and write them down. Then look for the closest people to share it with, if you still feel the need. Besides, focus on you mollycoddle yourself excusing your errors while getting hostile about those of others.

getting and giving attention to positive things.

Self-Hatred

It lowers our faith in our intrinsic capabilities and leads to constant self-depreciation. Some of us become depressed, withdrawn and passive, thereby curbing our potential or negating it altogether.

Give yourself credit and evaluate your positive qualities. When you identify the root of this detestation, try expunging it. Instead of magnifying inherent shortcomings and failings see what is positive and learn to love yourself.

Inadequacy

Unworthiness comes when we fail to handle something. It conveys the need for more competence, understanding, knowledge and confidence that you are currently doing without.

Strive to strengthen the area you're meeting failure in check if your expectation from yourself are unrealistic, considering the inputs you have made so far, and then assess the output.

(Courtesy – Life Magazine)

ENDNOTES

1. Clebsh & Jaekle, *Pastoral Care in Historical Perspectives*, Premtoce Hall Ins. N. Jersey, 1964, p.4.

2. *Ibid.*

3. H.J. Clinebell, *Basic Types of Pastoral Care and Counseling*, Revised, 1984, p.43.

4. S. Hiltner, *Pastoral Counseling*, Abongdon, 1949, 1981.

5. Marie Mascarenhas, *Family Life Education*, CREST, Bangalore, 1993, p.295.

6. Basic Types of... *op.cit.*, p.26.

CHAPTER 14

The Biblical Understanding of Counseling

It is not necessary that every Christian behaviour is documented by the Bible. For what God wants His people to do is a lot more than the Bible could contain (cf. John 20:30-31; 21:25). However, counseling activities today can be rooted in some of the New Testament concepts. For the believer, the Holy Spirit is the ever present Guide, whose *still small voice* is always felt by the believer at every crossroad. The *parakletos* of Jn. 14:16, 26; 15:26; 16:7; 1 Jn. 2:1, whose presence will assist, console, comfort or compensate the absence of Christ himself, is an example. Such functions of the counselor is also found in the Pauline writings like, 2 Cor. 1:4 and 15:13.[1] 2 Thessalonians 5:14, has at least five terms that would correspond to the work of counseling: *exhort, admonish, encourage, help* and *patience.* The *Neutheto* of 1Cor. 4:14, Col. 3:16, Rom. 15:4, is translated by the RSV as *admonish* or instruct. Counselors like, Jay E. Adams, would take pastoral counseling as basically 'neuthetic' (instruction with the scripture), a direct confrontation of the person in error or in need with the biblical injunction for the situation. However, there are other counselors who would make use of religious resources like the scripture only if the situation demands. In any case, the pastoral counselor's task, even without announcing the scripture text, is to bring to a living experience to the helped what the scriptures promise. Besides, they believe that the wisdom from the word of God, whether of science or arts, or human insights, are meant to lead God's people to happiness and fulfilment. Pastoral counseling, by its essence, focuses on the spiritual element of the person by use of religious resources without neglecting its holistic approach in understanding persons.

S. Hiltner[1] has rightly observed that the aims of Pastoral Counseling is same as the aim of the church. The purpose of the church, according to Richard Niebuhr, is "the increase among men the love of God and neighbours."[2] This is also the theme of both the Old and the New Testaments. It can also be stated as reconciliation to God and fellow beings. Reconciliation to God is reconciliation to life itself, adds Niebuhr. "Love to the Creator is love of being, rejoicing in its existence, and its source, totality and particularity. It is loyalty to the idea of God when the actuality of God is mystery; it is the affirmation of a universe and the devoted will to maintain a universal community at whatever cost to the Self."[3] S/he is the "Companion whom I am commanded to love as myself, or as I have been loved by my most loyal neighbour... He is the near one and the far one; the one beside the road I travel here and now. He is my friend, the one who has shown compassion towards me; and my enemy, who fights against me. He is the one in need, in whose hunger, nakedness, imprisonment and illness I see or ought to see the Universal Suffering Servant."[4]

Someone observed that God's aim of relating Himself with the created world before the fall was to maintain His good relationship with Adam and Eve with the host of other living creatures and the Universe. Then God had a shift in the goal of relationship after the fall to regain the broken relationship with His creation, especially humankind whose disobedience made the creation subject to futility. Jesus Christ became God's instrument or mediator in this task of reconciling the lost world to God. When Saint Paul declared, "God was in Christ reconciling the world unto himself" (2 Cor. 5:19) or, "Christ loved the church and gave himself up for her" (Eph. 5:25), Paul was referring to this fact that the task of reconciling the broken world to God is left to the followers of Christ - the church.

C.W. Brister affirms that the actual practice of ministry by the church is with, as, well as to or for, persons moving through life's passages and perils, and that pastors and people, in "Working together with God," transcend solidarity struggles and powerful forces in order to advance his kingdom (cf. 2 Cor. 6:1).[5]

The Protestant church understands Pastoral ministry as being authorised to the whole people of God. The pastor is a servant of servants. She/he is there to train the people for the work of ministry (Eph. 4:11-12). If the pastor is a shepherd, the task of the shepherd is to turn the whole flock into shepherds as Jesus did with the disciples. The minister has no room to idealize himself/herself as the shepherd, raised above the level of others in goodness, to consider the rest as a flock of sheep under his mercy. She/he is always reminded of his/her own wounds as S/he ministers to the wounded humanity. In Henri Nouwen's term, S/he is a wounded healer.

He also raised the ego of those people with low self-esteem, like the widow who offered a mite, Zacchheus, the corrupt tax collector, Matthew and the immoral Samaritan woman. He also relieved the guilt ridden heart of the woman caught in adultery, Peter who denied him, and the criminal who repented on the cross. Thus Jesus' ministry was a ministry of healing, guiding, sustaining, reconciling and nurturing. These are the five traditional tasks of Pastoral Care which is drawn from the ministry of Jesus. Every ministry we do is a sharing in the ministry of Christ (1 Cor. 12:12-13).

ENDNOTES

1. Hiltner, *Pastoral Counseling, op.cit.,* p.19.

2. Niebuhr & Williams, *The Purpose of the Church,* Harper & Bros., 1956, p.31.

3. *Ibid.,* p.37.

4. *Ibid.,* p.38.

5. Brister, *Pastoral Care in the Church,* Harper & Bros., 1964, p. IX.

CHAPTER 15

Jesus as a Model Counselor

15:1 Jesus and the Samaritan Woman (John 4:7-42)

Jesus, as a model counselor had a deep psychic insight to read human mind. On many occasions he revealed the hidden thoughts of the people. He could read the life of the Samaritan woman who later declared, "Come, see a man who told me all that I ever did. Can this be the Christ?" (Jn. 4:29). Jesus wanted to talk to this woman of loose character to help her find a life of lasting joy. But he did this in a very methodical approach as any counselor would do today. In any therapeutic relationship the first task of the Counselor is to *establish a rapport* with the counselor. Jesus did this by asking for a drink from the woman. This act may have a point in Jesus's humanity, but it has a significance in therapeutic relationships.

15:2 *RAPPORT*, in a counseling relationship is the atmosphere of relationship between any two individuals (or groups). Rapport is created by the counselor's disciplined listening and reflecting to the feelings of the counselee in an accepting attitude. This leads to a catharsis in the counselee (See more of this in Ch.6) Catharsis, is another vital process in counseling relationship relating to the counselee's cleansing (greek; "katharizo" means, I cleanse) of the emotional pent-up. One can relate this to the Christian idea of confession, too.

In the case of the Samaritan woman, to be asked for a drink by Jesus was a great surprise, an unbelievable event to arouse her ego. She knew Jesus was a man, a Jew and a holy man as against her being a woman, a Samaritan and an immoral woman!

With this affirmation that the ministry is with and for persons moving through life's passages and perils (Bristter), we are affirming that the ministry of Pastoral Care and Counseling is informed by the biblical focus on ministry as seen in the ministry of Jesus Christ. Christ's ministry was basically to the poor and the oppressed. Those in bondage of various kinds (Lk. 4:16-20), in bondage of moral laxity, physical deprivation, spiritual emptiness, human injustice and estrangement from God and fellow beings.

Jesus took the person as important, worthy of love and reconciliation who was created in the image of God and thus worth dying for. The person was redeemed of God and thus of more importance even than the law (the Sabbath was made for man, not the other way around, Mark 2:27). Jesus also saw potentialities in humans, He would ask them to be self responsible and do their part. He *respected* the freedom of humans. He would just knock at the door of their hearts if they would open to let him in. He also understood human frailty and treated them gently (cf; the woman caught in adultery, or Peter who denied him). Above all, He loved them, served them and died for them.

Jesus took the person in *wholistic understanding.* His main purpose was to reconcile them to God and give them the joy of life. Jesus took salvation as an abundant living that concerns the physical, social and spiritual aspect of the person. In His *preaching,* He brought the good news of God's forgiveness and liberation, giving hope to the blind and the lost. In His *teaching,* He guided them to the principles of active, godly living that concerned both in the purity of the individual and ethical living in the society.

Taking wholeness as complementary to holiness, Jesus' great concern was to heal the people of their physical and mental impairments. He fed the hungry, healed the dumb and deaf, the leper to let them gain social acceptance and enjoy fulness of life in the Society. He opened the blind eyes of the people-those blind to the beauty of God's holiness, truth and love, blind to the beauty of God's creation. He healed those physically weak, sick and deformed. He drove out the demoniac powers, evil powers of various kinds from the people with such bondage.

Different schools of counseling may see the encounter of Jesus and the Samaritan woman from their respective angles. Take for example, a logotherapeutic approach to help a troubled person.

15:3 Logotherapy is a system developed by Victor E. Frankl, a Vienese therapist. Logotherapy, seems to have originated from the Greek word, 'Logos', meaning 'word' or 'meaning'. Vienna had been important in Psychotherapeutic field. Sigmund Freud and his Psychoanalysis was the first school. The central focus of Psychoanalysis the "will-to-pleasure" of human and that frustrations arise due to unmet sexual needs. Alfred Adler and his individual psychology, centres on the inferiority feeling. The person with inferiority feeling strives to come to certain status or "Power" to compensate the inadequate feeling. This second Vienese School is said to centre in the human "will-to-power". The third Vienese School is the Logotherapy of Frankl, the "will-to-meaning" in human nature. When a person loses meaning in his/her existence that life is filled with boredom and depression that can lead even to suicide. Meaninglessness is said to be one great malady of modern living.

It is often said that Frankl developed this approach based on Nietzsche's observation, "One who has a why to live can bear with almost any how." Frankl endorsed this saying through his observation of his fellow inmates at a Nazi concentration camp during the second World War. He observed that the inmates of the camp who nursed a hope of living meaningfully inspite of the fact that the guards told them they would go out of the camp only as corpses, could survive the inhuman conditions of the camp.

In fact, many such optimists could wait till a time when they were released as Frankl himself was, Frankl's conclusion was that one who has a purpose (meaning) for living can face any situation in life.

We find Jesus, helping the Samaritan woman find meaning in life. She had started living without a purpose. She was trying to meet her existential need through temporal pleasures.

She had lost faith in the future, accountability of life and thus was living an irresponsible life. In the language of Robert G. Leslie,

> "It is where the search for meaning has been abandoned so that a vacuum exists that secondary goals become primary ones. In an attempt to fill the vacuum, goals that are inappropriate for humans take priority. Such was the situation with the Samaritan woman at Jacob's well."

Jesus, recognised that, she had tried to fill the existential vacuum with the pursuit of pleasure. He would teach that the ultimate took precedence of the penaltimate. He would teach that one should lose the one to find the other. In the same way, Jesus helped the Samaritan woman to experience self-realisation, to, re-orient her life for a lasting satisfaction. As Leslie puts it, Jesus would show her that, "Pleasure comes, not by seeking it, but by finding the satisfactions of filling one's responsible place in life."[3] For, she was living an irresponsible life.

The woman tried to change the subject in a subtle way, to draw the interest of the religious minded leader, namely, the question of the appropriate place for worship. Jesus had seen that the woman was entangled in a serious question in life and so he took the issue seriously.

Jesus established the rapport with her in a most appropriate and spontaneous behaviour – asking a drink from the person in search of water and a situation of hectic travel in the scorching sun.

The woman, a Samaritan and an immoral woman had strong defenses that prevented her to believe the man, the Jew and the holy prophet. She could not but hide herself behind the prejudices of her day. She therefore, could not accept the acceptance of Jesus.

Jesus accepted not only the immoral woman but also her defensiveness, however irrelevant they may be. She tried to reject and avoid him but He did not do so. He neither retaliated nor ran away from the situation. Jesus re-directed the irrelevant question of the woman to the area of personal relevance for her and the conversation led to the need of needs – God. Jesus made clear that an immoral or irresponsible life is detrimental to a true relationship with fellow human beings or with God.

Jesus comforted the woman only after she herself realised her need and asked for help - "Sir, give me this water, that I may not thirst, nor come here to draw." This is important in any effective helping. Counseling cannot be forced to a person. Self motivation on the part of the counselee leads to satisfactory counseling.

No counselor, at the final analysis can approve a person's behavior or life-style that is destructive to life itself. Jesus did not ignore the destructive life-style of the woman. He led the conversation in such a way that the question of plain water led to the living water. The woman could see in him a genuine interest in re-creating her and how he could perceive her inner life.

The woman's resultant experience of satisfactory interview led her to proclaim the discovery, inviting others to come and meet the counselor - Jesus. (R. Leslie)

15:4 The Walk to Emmaus: (Lk. 24:13-35): Cathartic Experience

This is one of the living stories of the world. The manner in which Jesus encountered the two men. They were perplexed by a situation which they could not explain. They were walking in sorrow and disappointment because their hopes and dreams had been shattered and buried.

He did not shock them by saying he was the resurrected Lord. He joined them in their walk in a most natural way though He knew He was the subject matter of their astonished talk. He did not cut short the process of their grief or frustration. He allowed them to express the pain. For the bottled up emotion needed cleansing or pouring out. We have seen that in greek, *Katharizo*, means to cleanse, from which word we have *catharsis*, a technical term that refers to cleansing out a painful emotion. It is healthy to vent a pent up emotion. Repression of strong emotions leads to bursting of the bottle like the soda bottle. Expression of painful emotion through words and tears heals.

Shakespeare is often quoted for saying "Give sorrow words." In the same manner Jesus wept when he was touched by the sorrowful scene of Lazarus' death. Paul advises us to weep with those who weep and rejoice with those who rejoice (Romans 12:15).

Sometimes crying is prevented by cultural conventions like the case of men in tribal societies who should not be panicky or lacrymous. Psychologists tell us that more men die from heart attack than women because the former hardly shed off sorrow. The latter are always ready to shed tears when they are emotionally disturbed. Sometimes crying is prevented by religious beliefs, as Christians do, saying, to cry is a sign of little faith. Counselors facilitate crying out when a person finds it difficult to accept a loss and to express it. What Jesus said of those who mourn has a significance here (Mt. 5:4), to be comforted.

15:5 Jesus' Respect for Human Freedom

Jesus did not confront or interrupt the flow of the story of frustration of these two men though he had to tell them later that Christ had to suffer. *Catharsis* had its significance in healing.

Another aspect of Jesus' approach was, like He would always do, He did not enter their homes forcibly until the two invited him to do so. He would walk further away if not invited, or stand outside the door of human heart and knock to see if the inmates open to him. This is the principle of 'respect' in counseling. Jesus respected the free-will of the people to choose if they would have him in. In other words he asked the blind person, "What do you want me to do for you?" (Lk. 18:41)

There is also a record of Jesus meeting Peter who had denied Him. He met him not to deliver Peter's sin of denial to him but to regenerate him in a manner that surprised Peter himself - without condemnation or accusation for the fault.

The two men who experienced Jesus went out to tell people about the helper. They were first satisfied and they shared that good news with others. For, the purpose of the healing is to turn people to healers.

We believe the scriptures to be a sound guide to understanding and solving life's mystery. There are some Christian counselors who insist that the Bible is the sole source of information for Christian life and conduct. However, many pastors today accept insights from the Science of Human behaviour as inevitable factors (if not complementary to the biblical insights) in understanding and helping people.

ENDNOTES

1. G.W. Allport, "Preface" on Man's Search for Meaning, V. Frankl's *Introduction to Logotherapy,* Better Your self Book, 1983.

2. Robert Leslie, *Jesus and Logotherapy,* Abingdon Press, 1965, p.49.

3. *Ibid.,* p.52.

CHAPTER 16

Psychotherapeutic Approaches in Counseling

16:1 Transactional Analysis (T.A.)

One of the theories of human personalities that Pastoral Counselors often borrow insights from is the Transactional Analysis (T.A.) developed by Psychiatrist, Eric Berne. It has been said that one day a friend dropped into his office and said he felt *child-like*that day. That remark gave Berne a thought leading to the development of Transactional Analysis. Among the concepts of T.A. are the following: 1) *Structural Analysis;* in this Berne Propounded that each person, irrespective of age has three ego-states. *PARENT EGO, ADULT EGO* and *CHILD EGO.* (The Parent Ego and the Child Ego are further divided into Nurturing Parent and Critical Parent, Free-child and Adapted child). A child as well as an old person can have these three ego-states at the same time.

Ego States

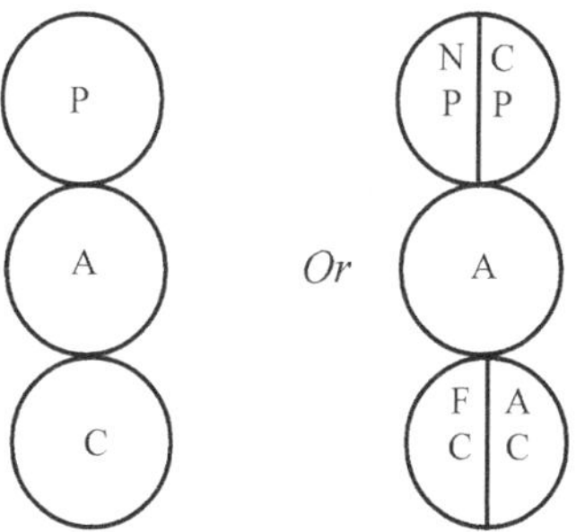

1. *Parent Ego:* Sometimes we behave like our parents or like those who brought us up. That part of parental behaviour can be at times critical and controlling, or at times nurturing and helpful or both at a given time. The parent in us uses languages like — must, should, don't, ought etc.

2. *Adult Ego* : The Adult in us is the seat of reason and appropriateness. It asks questions like who, what, or observes like practical, correct, fitting.

3. *Child Ego* : This is the seat of emotion.

The Child in you can be a Free-Child or an Adapted-Child. This part in you behaves in some way like you did when you were small. The Free-Child in you is the seat of creativity, spontaneous, imaginative and a fun-loving part. An Adapted Child in you is the seat of anger, withdrawal, rebellion. Its expressions are like, Waw, Won't, Can't etc.

This structural analysis tells us that when any two persons interact there are actually six different persons interacting (Each person with three different ego states). In Social interactions the Adult Ego of Mr. A may ask "what is the time" and Mr. B's Adult Ego may respond giving the exact time. This is called a Parallel transaction, thus.[1]

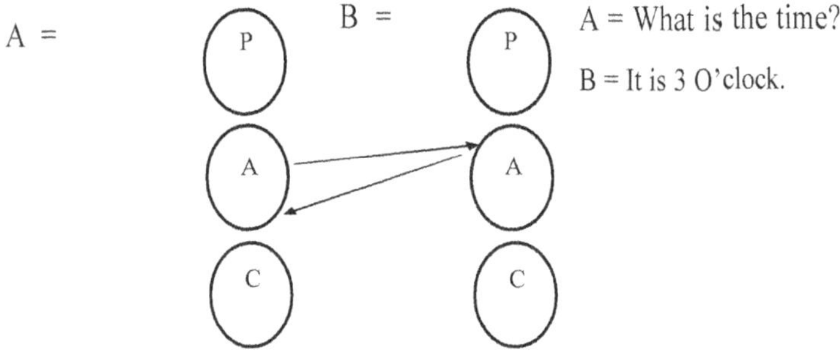

Figure: 1

If the parent of Mr. B becomes critical and responds "Why do you ask me the time?" This reply will be received from the Child Ego of Mr. A who asked for the time.

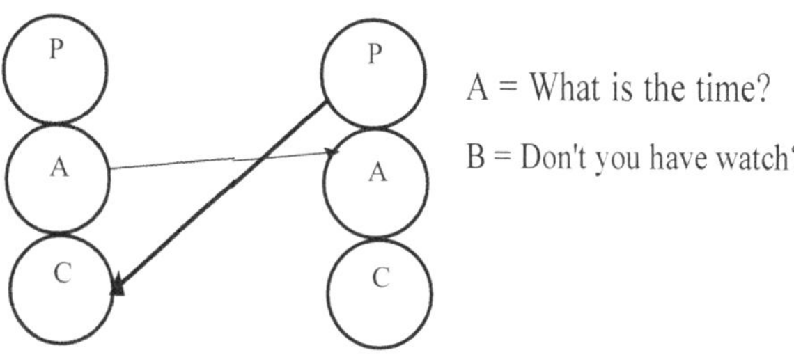

Figure 2

This is called a *Cross Transaction*. In a Social Transaction or (in a conversation between two persons) when the line of transaction is complementary or parallel as in Fig. 1. the relationship is healthy and the conversation can continue.

When the line of transaction is crossed as in Fig. 2, there is a clash and this relationship is unhealthy. Such conversations cannot continue long. All the three Ego states are important aspects of our personality. However, it is said that we must cultivate the adult in us and let it lead the other two. Then we can be reasonable with appropriate responses to stimuli in social interactions.

People with too much of the parent ego can turn to be critical and judgemental to self and others landing themselves in problems. People with too much of the child ego may like fun, pleasure, sentimentality more than required thus resulting in irresponsible behaviour. It should be the counselors task to make such persons aware of the ego-state which is dominant in the person and help find adjustment.

There are also what is called ulterior *messages* in transactions. When on one level the speaker may say one thing (Social level) the motive may be different. That ulterior message (Psychological level) can lead to playing psychological games. Games are ulterior messages used by those who have developed a negative attitude about themselves, "I am not OK, you are OK." Such "not OK" persons relate with people in an unhealthy way. They express through games to satisfy themselves by reassuring themselves of their decision (that they are not OK) by the pay off through games. When a person is found engaged in games the therapist helps him/her to relate with others in an open intimacy. By counseling one is helped to change the negative script to a positive one and to live a gamefree life.

A script is the decision one makes in early life about oneself which the person follows for the rest of his/her life. A person can formulate a script about himself in accordance to the messages she received (Strokes) from the parents and the society about him. One who is treated unkindly and told that he is not okay will decide to behave that way for life time.

Eric Berne defines script as, "an ongoing programme developed in early childhood under parental influence, which directs the individual's behaviour in the most important aspects of his life."[2]

As a script is a decision it can be changed by a new decision. A person's negative script can be replaced by a constructive Script (Counter-Script). See also p. 215-218)

Transactional Analysis : Eric Berne (1910-1970), an American psychotherapist was a follower of Freudian school for 15 years. When he applied for membership in Psychoanalytic Institute he was refused. He then branched out to a new school called Transactional Analysis (TA). Dualistic thinking like good and evil (God and Satan) or superior and inferior aspects of life inspired Berne to think of different levels of the ego states in different times. He identified at least three different primary ego states, like, *parent ego, adult ego* and *child ego* (these are different states of the *ego* in Freudian thought). The ego states are a coherent system of feeling with its related set of behavior patterns. The child ego recapitulates the feelings, attitude, and behavioral propensities existed in the child up to about 6 years of age. The parent ego represents an exact recording of parental (or God's) values, prescriptions, and advice along with varying degrees... The adult is the aspect of the person which acts as a computer, recording data and using its data as basis for computing expectancies regarding future events. A decision that it is safe to cross the street when there is no signal to regulate traffic is often given as an example of adult computer functioning. In any given situation one of the ego states is activated to become the operational center.

Eric Berne's first book was Transactional analysis in Psychotherapy (1961). He conducted seminars and consultations his findings beside writing articles in the *Transactional Analysis Bulletin* (later became *T.A. Journal*). When he published *Games People Play* in 1964, it became the best seller and people began to accept his theory ever more convincingly.

Basic concepts: Beside biogenetic drives relating to survival, TA tends to stress those basic human needs which are mostly directly related to everyday observable behavior. These needs include, *strokes hunger, recognition hunger, excitement hunger, structure hunger,* and *leadership hunger.*

1. Stroke hunger, is the continuation of the child's original contact hunger, his needs to be held, soothed, rocked and otherwise attended to be friendly and sympathetic persons. Another person's time and attendance are sufficient to satisfy stroke hunger, although physical contact, the warmth of human body constitutes the best form of stroking.

    Stroke, plainly speaking refers to the positive messages humans give to one another in communication. Humans began receiving strokes non-verbally through the mothers milk from the very early stage of life, and then through verbal appreciations such as 'you are beautiful, or handsome' or, 'you are a wonderful addition to our family of love' or, 'you did very well'. These are the expressions of the peoples' recognition of the person addressed as acceptable and lovable. The negative strokes are the opposites we often give to others, such as, 'you are not lovable, you are good for nothing, or you are a burden to us.' As strokes are vital factors in human growth their absence is said to constrict the growth. It is even said that the child who does not receive positive stroke at all can literally become hunch. It is also said, 'negative strokes are better than no stroke at all.' This means when the person cannot get recognition by positive strokes s/he will seek even a negative stroke to draw the attention of the people to him/her. The hotel waiter dropping the tray and breaking the contents on the floor thus attracts the manager's attention and probably those present in the hall. The scolding of the manager and the accusing state of the people present there to the waiter is the negative stroke received by the waiter.

2. *Structure Hunger:* This refers to one's use of time - what to do with 24 hours a day. A person may devote most of his time in biogenic functions like, eating, sleeping, finding supply for sustenance, such as food, shelter, clothing and so forth. Good leaders are those who can best help people structure their times. Consciously or unconsciously people are said to structure their time everyday in one or two of the following ways:

    i)   Rituals: Some part of the day we are engaged in doing the common things done by all everyday which are not necessarily important, like brushing teeth, washing, or even greeting each other. They are not expressly required but just done as regular feature of everyday life.

ii) Timepass: As often heard from the peanut seller we pass time by eating peanuts, telling stories, gossiping, attending to the media and talking of the current issues in the society, etc.

iii) Activities : This is when we are engaged in goal achieving and fruitful work like attending an interview, studying for examinations or attending to family and personal needs.

iv) Games: At times we are engaged in psychological games, living in future or the past and not in the present reality of here-and-now. This is an activity from the child or the parent ego of us (not from the adult ego which is in touch with reality) without our awareness. We are said to play games to receive *kick me* pay off or negative strokes. In playing games we seek to relate with people not by intimacy or love but by ulterior motive. Such a way of relating to one another is unhealthy.

v)   Withdrawals: This withdrawal can be both psychological and physical withdrawals as when we are physically present but psychologically on excursion, in loneliness, sleeping etc. even though we are in the midst of people. No social interaction or friendly communication can take place when one is withdrawn.

vi) Intimacy: This is when we spend time in relating with people in genuineness, love and concern. Games have no place in intimacy. When there is a lack of intimacy we are engaged in one or the other five ways of spending time as above.

The Transactional Analysts would like all of us to pause from daily business from time to time and call to consciousness the time that we are engaged in that moment, or to spend time every evening on how we spent the most of our time that day. We may discover that we had spent a considerable time of the day neither helping others nor ourselves productively. We can check like that often and increase the way we spend time in activities and intimacy.

3. *Excitement hunger:* Other things being equal, the preferred ways of structuring time are those that are *most exciting.* Conversely the most distasteful ways of structuring time are those involving the least amount of excitement (as in solitary confinement). This is to say that we unconsciously structure our time following the line of our interests, or say directed by our *pleasure principle* (Freud).

Among most interesting ways of structuring time are those which involves getting strokes from other persons, from the simple strokes to the strokes involved in interpersonal intimacy and close physical proximity to another person. The lack of autonomy in human behavior is evident from the way the person follows the *script*. A script is a life plan decided upon at an early age by each person as a means of meeting his needs in the world as he sees it from the vantage point of that person's *life position* (see the four life positions given in this book). Scripts help the person to write his/her life position, like, *I am Ok, or I am not Ok.* etc. *Transactional analysis* and *games analysis* are other aspects of TA approaches in understanding human behavior, which are not underlined in this section.

16:2   The Four Life Positions (Transactional Analysis)

One of the basic tenets of transactional analysis is that we live our lives largely according to "scripts." These scripts are similar to dramatic scripts, complete with a list of characters and roles, stage directions, dialogue, and plot.

Our culture provides us with one kind of script. This cultural script provides us with guides to proper dress, rules for sexual conduct, roles for men and women, a value system pertaining to marriage, children, money and education, the concepts of success and failure, and so on. Families provide another kind of script. Family scripts contain more specific instructions for each of the family members–the boys should go into politics, the girls should get involved in social work: this family will always have its own business: this family may not earn much money but will always have adequate insurance: the oldest son takes over the father's business: the oldest daughter gets married first: and so on.

From our early experiences, particularly from the messages received from our parents (both verbal and nonverbal), we develop a psychological script for ourselves and, for the most part, follow this throughout our lives. Individual scripts are generally "written" by the age of three and provide us with specific directions for functioning within the larger cultural script. Should we play the victim or the persecutor, the slave or the master, the clown or the intellectual?

Some children, for example are told they will be a success. Nonverbally, they are given love and affection: verbally, they are reinforced for numerous actions. Some children are told they will never succeed. Statements such as "No matter what you do, you'll be a success" or "You'll never amount to anything" are extremely important in determining the script the child assumes in later life. Generally, people follow the scripts their parents have written for them. But such scripts can be broken we do not have to follow the script written for us by our parents. One of the major purpose of transactional analysis is to break the negative and unproductive scripts, to substitute positive and productive scripts in their places, and to prevent destructive messages from getting written into the script.

These scripts, which we all have, are the bases on which we develop what are called "life positions". In transactional analysis there are four basic life positions.

I'm Not OK, You're OK

This person sees others as well-adjusted and effective (you're OK) but sees himself or herself as maladjusted and ineffective (I'm not OK). This is, according to Thomas A. Harris, the first position we develop as very young children. This is the position of the child who sees himself or herself as helpless and dirty and sees the adult as all-powerful and all-knowing. This person feels helpless and powerless in comparison to others and withdraws from confrontations rather than competing. This life position leads one to live off others, to make others pay for their being OK (and for oneself's being not OK). Such people are frequently *depressed*: at times they *isolate themselves*, lamenting, "If only..." or "I should have..."

I'm Not OK, You're not OK

People in this category think badly of themselves (I'm not OK) as well as of other people (you're not OK). They have no real acceptance of either themselves or others. They give themselves no support (because they are not OK), and they accept no support from others (because others are not OK). These people have given up. To them, nothing seems worthwhile, and so they withdraw. Interpersonal communication is extremely difficult since they put down both themselves and others, and interpersonal communication does not seem particularly satisfying either. Attempts to give such people help are generally met with refusals since the would-be helpers are seen as being not OK.

Such people seem to have lost interest in themselves, in others, and in the world generally. Living seems a drag. In the extreme, argue Erics Berne and other transactional analysts, they are the *suicides* and *homicides*, the *autistics* and *pathological*.

I'm OK, You're Not OK

Persons in this position view themselves as effective (I'm OK) but see others as ineffective (you're not OK): "I am good: you are bad." These people have little or no respect for others and easily and frequently find fault with both friends and enemies. They are supportive of themselves but do not accept support from others. They are *independent* and seem to derive some satisfaction from interpersonal communication but reject *interpersonal* interaction and involvement. Literally and figuratively they need space, elbow room: they resent being crowded by people who are "not OK" Criminals come with disproportional frequency from this class, as do paranoids, who feel persecuted and blame others for their problems.

I'm OK, You're OK

This is the adult, normal, healthy position. This, says Eric Berne in 'What Do-You Say After You Say Hello?' Is "the position of genuine heroes and princes, and heroines and princesses." These people approach and solve problems constructively. They have valid expectations about themselves and others and accept themselves and others as good, worthy, and significant human beings. These people feel free to develop and progress as individuals. They enter freely into meaningful relationships with others and progress as individuals. They feel neither inferior nor superior to others. Rather, they feel worthy and feel others are worthy. This is the position of winners.

This is the position of the effective communicator, the one who views oneself and others positively, equally, sportively, empathically, and openly. This is the person who communicates with confidence, with a connectedness that is evidenced both verbally and nonverbally, with specific goals and relevant strategies for achieving these goals, expressively and with a view of and a focus on the other person.

Depending on the specifics of the situation (source, receiver, message, channel, context), each of the other positions lack several or all of these qualities of effective interpersonal interaction.

It is impossible to say how many people are in each class. Many pass through the "I'm not OK, You're OK" position. Few arrive at the "I'm OK, you're OK" position: few people are winners in this sense. Most probably the vast majority of people are in the "I'm not OK, you're OK" and "I'm OK, you're not OK" positions. These are, of course, general classes, and human beings resist each classification. Thus these four positions should be seen as areas on a continuum, none of which have clear-cut boundaries and yet all of which are different.[3]

16:3 Freudian School: Id, Ego, Super Ego

Id: The problem of society is to modify this primitive creature which can only need and desire, hate or fear, want pleasure and avoid pain, into a civilised being. The primitive aspect of mind which includes not only the innate drives of sex and aggression but also all those thoughts and emotions, is described as *Id*, and just because it contains this sort of material thought and emotions within it becomes or remains unconscious.

Ego: When an infant is born, its mind is all Id, but sooner or later the child is confronted by stern reality when it comes to realize that desires are not satisfied automatically. Sometimes it is wet and uncomfortable and has to wait to be "changed". All these events occur even to the most fortunate baby.

So, a part of the mind comes to be separated off from the primitive *Id*, whose function it is to deal with reality, and this part is known as the ego - the conscious mind as we know it in adult life. The basic function of the ego is to deal with life as it really is, not as we should like it to be.

Super-Ego: Still later, perhaps at the age of three or four, the child is faced by another problem, for it has to start conforming to the ethical dictates of society to what is ordinarily described as the *moral code.* A child has to learn what is done and what must not have been done, and so a further division in the mind takes place and part of the mind begins to specialize in moral control. This part is known as the *Super-Ego.* The Super-Ego arises in two distinct stages - first, the child comes to realize that, under penalty of punishment or disapproval, it must obey its parents. At this stage then, compulsion comes from outside.

Later, however, the child by a process of what Freud describes as *'introjection'* takes the parental standards within itself. One part of the mind, as it were, plays the role of moral parent in relation to the rest. This is a fully-fledged Super-Ego.[4]

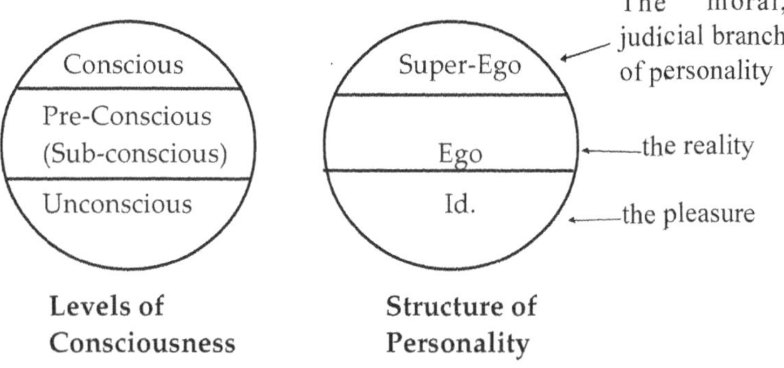

Levels of Consciousness   **Structure of Personality**

Clinebell, commenting on Freud's contribution to the discovery of the unconscious leading to healing and growth, wrote thus:

> It was his illumination of the unconscious that makes Freud the conceptual grandparent of all 'depth psychologies'. As he discovered, it is through the repressed memories, wishes, conflicts, and impulses in the unconscious that painful experiences and unfinished growth from the early years continue to cripple the ability of many people to live creatively in the present. He demonstrated that bringing these repressed elements into the light of conscious awareness often facilitates healing and growth.[5]

It may be mentioned that Freud's psychoanalytic therapy cannot be made useful by untrained pastoral counselors. For, the busy pastors can neither afford the time consuming process of therapy (even years) nor acquire the skill. Its inclusion here is for the purpose of conceptual information on human behaviour. In a survey like this one cannot leave out such a formative system from which many other healing systems grew. In fact, the study of some of the concepts even by lay persons is very informative in understanding human behaviour, like the instincts and drives, the defence mechanisms, repression leading to storing of explosives in the unconscious, and the psycho-sexual development of a person.

16:4 Psychoanalytic School

This school was developed by *Sigmund Freud* (1856-1939) of Vienna, Austria. There are two other psychological schools born of that historic city, *Vienna*(Alred Adler's and Victor Frankl's) but Freud's was the first. It is called *Psychoanalytic* school in the sense it is a study of the history of person's mental experiences from birth to the present that matters in the present functioning. It is a kind of digging the past experiences in depth to explain why the person behaves as s/he does at present. This school is sometimes called *Freudian School,* after the founder's name. Sigmund Freud is called the *father of modern psychology* as he attempted to study human behavior scientifically. Before his time, humans were believed to be a different being from animals by virtue of their having souls.

Freud lived in a time of the height of scientific discoveries such as the Evolutionary Theory of Charles Darwin. Darwin published his findings, *The Origin of Species,* in 1859, and *The Descend of Man* (1871) proclaiming that humans are nature too, nothing different from the rest of the animal world and that they were evolved from a stage of animal life. This meant that human behavior can be studied along naturalistic lines. Humans, thus became an object of scientific study. The other scientist who influenced Freud in his scientific thinking about humans was a German Philosopher, Gustav Fechner, who founded the *science of psychology* in 1860, demonstrating that mind could be studied scientifically and that it could be measured quantitatively. Gregor Mendel, was another scientist who investigated on the garden pea and founded the *modern science of genetics*. Hermann von Helmholtz, who formulated the principle of conservation of energy, leading to various studies of dynamics, had a great impact on Freud, who later created his *dynamic psychology*. Thus, with Fechner and Freud, psychology began to take its place among other natural sciences. Freud was a medical doctor but became more interested in scientific study of human behavior and in psychotherapy than in medical practice. Freud, is therefore, one of the founders of modern psychotherapy.

16:5   The Dynamic Psychology of Sigmund Freud*

Freud's wish to become a scientist was not possible due to lack of financial support for further trainings. He practiced medicine and began to think his relationship with the patients in psychological terms. His probing with the psychic factors of the patients revealed to him the *dynamic forces at work* that were responsible for creating abnormal symptoms that he was called to treat. He discovered that most of these psychic forces were *unconscious.* Thus, putting aside physiology and neurology he concentrated on the psychological investigation. Freud began to treat patients in his couch and talk-out method. The patient was asked to lie on a couch, all alone in a room and to say anything that comes into the mind spontaneously. Freud used to remain nearby listening to those words and tried to see how these words may have association with certain psychic forces in the unconscious mind of the person.

This approach was called *free-association.* Another method Freud used to reach the dynamic factors in the unconscious mind was his dream interpretation. He believed that those dynamic factors which the person cannot openly express in the waking life also finds freedom to surface in dreams, though in symbolic representations. Among his important publications are, *the Interpretation of Dreams* (1900) and *Civilisation and its Discontents (1930).* Freud called dreams *the royal road to the unconscious.* Other books of worth study by Freud include, *The Royal Road to the*

---

* Books referred: Calvin C. Hall, A Premier of Freudian Psychology (New American Library, London 1954).

Unconscious. The Psychopathology of Everyday Life (1904), *A Study in Psychosexuality (1947), Beyond the Pleasure Principle (1948),* Gustav Fechner had said that human is an energy system and that a human does not stand outside of science, and that human mind can be brought to the laboratory for scientific study following laws of physics. Freud was therefore, convinced by the radical view that human as a living organism is a dynamic system to which laws of chemistry and physics apply. Freud proceeded to create a dynamic psychology. *A dynamic psychology is one that studies the transformations and exchanges of energy within the personality.*

Sigmund Freud felt that the irrational forces in human are so strong that the rational forces have little chances of success against them. He also saw that the influence of human on the society and the society on human is a vicious circle from which only a few hardy souls can free themselves.

We as pastoral carers are neither trying to become psychoanalysts nor pretend to know much of Freudian thought. We simply attempt to borrow concepts from this pioneer explorer of human behavior to gain more insights in our understanding of humans whom we encounter in our daily ministry. We therefore select few of the concepts from Freudian school and explain them briefly as follows:

16:6 Topography of the Mind

Freud's earlier conception of the human mind was his division of the mind into three mental systems – *the conscious mind* (the present conscious thought of our mind, the pre-conscious mind (the memory that can be recalled), and *the unconscious mind* (the experience present in the depth of our being but cannot be re-called easily). This difference between preconscious and the unconscious mental activities is important in psychoanalysis.

16:7 The Structural Hypothesis

In his later attempt to study the mind Freud came to the conclusion that the mind consists of three functionally related structures – *the id,* the *ego,* and *the super-ego, as seen above.*

In general, the *id* represents the basic drives (instincts). This is the seat of what Freud called *'pleasure principle'* in humans. This irrational nature of our mind seeks all pleasure without pain and its gratification without respect for law, ethics, neighbors or God. Freud called this mental force of the exerted form the id as *libido.* Freud considered this libido to be the erotic drive (sexual) but later as the *life force,* the energy of the *Eros instinct,* which is not only the sexual drive but also the drive for procreation and preservation of the species. Later, as the person grows, a section of the mind begins to be in touch with reality and begins to think and see things more rationally. This second stage of the development of the mind, Freud called, *the ego.* This part of our mind is the mediator between the irrational demands of the id and the external reality of the world. Still later, a section of the mind is developed to contain the individual's moral precepts and ideal aspirations (the conscience of the person). This part of the mind (being above the ego in the diagram) Freud called *the super-ego.* The super-ego is the seat of the moral do's and don'ts mostly learned from our parental world.

16:8   Instincts

Since an instinct represents a bodily need the number of human instincts are said to be as many as human needs. An instinct is said to have a source, an aim, an object, and an impetus. Sigmund Freud recognised two major groups of instincts, those that are *in the service of death 'Thanatos instinct' and those that are in the service of life as 'Eros instinct'.* The aims of the instinct is to remove a bodily need after which the instinct disappears and the individual returns to a state of psychological quiescence. The hunger instinct, for example, aim to remove the physical condition of hunger. The Eros (or life) instinct aims at continuation and preservation of life. The thanatos (death) instinct represents that no particular living thing could live for ever. Life's ultimate destiny is always to return to the inorganic. The death instinct represents the aggressive and destructive nature of human. When this destructive instinct cannot find its target in the external world it can turn inward leading to suicide or narcissism. The death instincts are said to perform inconspicuously and so not so public. *The life instincts* on the other hand are said to work more publicly. They are the mental representatives of the bodily needs whose satisfaction is necessary for survival and for propagation. In psychoanalytic theory of personality the sex instincts are considered very important. The sex instinct is manifested in various parts of the bodily zones called *erogenous zones.* The mouth, the anus, and the genital organs are the chief erogenous zones through which the person, from the moment of birth, experiences sexual gratification through these zones.

16:9   Anxiety

Anxiety is a painful emotional experience caused by internal or external stimuli. When the person encounters excitation (internal or external) they are reacted upon by the automatic nervous system. For instance, when the person is excited his/her heart beats faster, breathes rapidly, the mouth dries, the palms and hands sweat automatically. Anxiety is synonymous with fear except that fear may sometimes be only caused by external stimulus. Freud identified three types of anxiety, *reality anxiety, neurotic anxiety,* and *moral anxiety.* In reality anxiety the source of danger is external (objective anxiety) such as snake. In neurotic anxiety, the threat resides in an instinctual object-choice of the *id.* It is an unrealistic fear or anxiety. In moral anxiety the source of threat lies in the conscience of the super-ego system. That is the fear of punishment for breach of the standards of the ego ideal in thought, word or action.

16:10 Frustration

Frustration is anything that prevents a painful or uncomfortabl excitation from being discharged. It is something that stands in the way of the operation of the pleasure principle. A person can be frustrated when the necessary goal object of a particular instinct is not found in the environment. Such a situation is called *privation.* On the other hand, when the goal object is available but taken away or withheld from the person who wants it, that situation is called *deprivation.* Privation and deprivation are both external frustrations because the causes are in the environment. When the frustration is caused by an intra-psychic factor that prevents the person from obtaining satisfaction it is a *conflict.* Personal inadequacy to achieve satisfaction or fear can also cause frustration.

The person is in a constant struggle to overcome or adjust with these obstacles. And the ways in which a person meets and attempts to handle these obstacles matters so much in shaping his personality.

16:11 Defense Mechanisms

The ego may try to solve the anxiety and problems faced by it through *realistic means* or by *methods that deny, distort or falsify the reality.* The latter methods are called defense mechanisms of the ego. Freud considered these defenses as unconscious phenomena. When these defenses are used consciously they are considered dishonest ways of copying with situations or relating with people. These mental mechanisms are many but few of the following are significant in our study here:

a. *Repression*: When the ego senses a threat (internal or external) one of its ways of dealing with it is to prevent the threat from entering into consciousness by denial, distorting the threat or falsifying the existence of the threat to the ego's safety. This way of adjusting or dealing with the threat (or id-cathexis) is called *repression.* In other words, the ego forces a dangerous memory, idea, or perception out of consciousness and sets up a barrier against any form of motor discharge. This is an attempt *to save the ego from anxiety.* Repression may be used to some extent even by normally functioning people but when someone depends on it entirely and exclude other ways of adjusting to unpleasant stimulus it becomes unhealthy. A repressed person may remain withdrawn, tense, rigid and guarded. For instance, one who is afraid of the sexual impulse and thus represses it continually may become impotent or frigid. Freud seems to have observed two types of repression, primal repression and repression proper, which may be studied in detail by those working on this topic.

b. *Projection*: When the ego is stimulated by anxiety prone feelings from the id or the super-ego the ego assigns its cause to the external world, not to itself. This way of adjusting or dealing with the unpleasant thought is called *projection*. When the person projects such feelings the expression becomes 'you are biased' instead of saying 'I am biased' or 'you hate me' when that person hates the other, in fact. All these are an attempt to avoid unpleasant feelings entering the consciousness and creating anxiety to one's ego.

c. *Reaction formation*: When one of the instincts creates an offensive impulse and thus creates anxiety the ego shifts to the opposite entity of that offensive impulse, for instance, feeling of hate will suddenly be changed to feeling of affection, or a destructive impulse may suddenly turn to constructive one, all these in attempt to save the ego by overcompensating it for the unacceptable feelings. If feelings of hate toward another person make the person anxious, the ego can facilitate the flow of love in order to conceal the hostility. But the fact that hatred remains underneath the surface relationship of love is deceptive. Love here is used as a mask only. Such a shift of feelings from one impulse to the opposite one is called *reaction formation*. Such is not an actual representation of the person's inner state.

d. *Fixation*: Psychologists tell us of how all people grow physically and psychologically from one stage to the higherstages. When physical growth of a person is arrested the person is *stunted*. When person's psychological growth is arrested s/he is *fixated*. Fixation in a person takes place as a defense against anxiety. This happens when the person becomes afraid of the risks involved in growing up to the next higher stages and decides to remain static in the same stage.

A child may become apprehensive on the first day of the school, students may become apprehensive about the impending graduation, and so any person in taking the first venture even though one may also see the reward of being promoted. This creates anxiety on the ego. The anxiety that one experiences on leaving the old and the familiar for the new and unfamiliar is called *separation anxiety.* When separation anxiety becomes too great, the person tends to remain fixated on an old way of life rather than advance to a new one. Fear of failure and thus being ridiculed or punished can also result in fixation. Calvin S. Hall's exact words in this regard are insightful,

"In addition to fixation upon objects there are also fixations in the development of the structure and dynamics of personality. Some people do not advance beyond the level of wishful thinking. Others never learn to differentiate clearly between the subjective world and objective reality. Still others live under the domination of a severe superego or exist in a strait jacket of childhood fears. Some people fixate upon a particular defense mechanism around which their whole personality revolves. Others remain at the level of impulsive, discharge behavior. There are all kinds and degrees of fixation, which prevent one from realising his/her fullest psychological potentialities. Nearly everyone is stunted psychologically in some way by fear. (A Primer of Freudian Psychology, p.95).

e. *Regression*: Related to fixation that remains in the same stage regression is a defense to retreat to earlier stage of growth for fear of certain situation. Any flight from a realistic and controlled thinking is regression. For example, a young married woman after her first quarrel with her husband may return to the security of her parents' home. Or, moral anxiety may cause a person to do something impulsive so that s/he will be punished as done when he was a child. Many people regress from time to time to reduce anxiety saying they need to blow off steam.

In brief, we should note that defense mechanisms of the ego are irrational ways of dealing with anxiety by denial (repression), by externalising one's thought (projection), by hiding the danger (reaction formation), by standing still (fixation), and by retreating (regression). Proper maturation in the person's life through the stages of growth alone can avoid such unrealistic ways of facing life as mental defense. For a proper upbringing of the person from childhood the environment in which the person grows should be conducive for such a result. Then only the ego will engage in more realistic and healthy means of adjusting with the realities of life. Parents and teachers should also be informed of the psychological principles in bringing up children.

Among the *psychopathological conditions* identified in psychoanalytic approach include the following (see C.H. Patterson, *Theories of Counseling and Psychotheraphy, Harper & Row, NY 1973*).

16:12 Some Psychopathological Conditions

1. *Anxiety neurosis* – Failure in important social or sexual relations is the precipitating factor, which results in regression to hostile and destructive impulses that threaten to become conscious. Anxiety, the fear of conscience appears in consciousness. The ego develops defenses against the anxiety, which subsides but may recur.

2. *Phobias*: Fears of specific situations caused by early anxiety-laden situations (see list of phobias, such as agoraphobia, hydrophobia, ergatophobia...)

3. *Obsessive*-compulsive state: Obsessive idea and compulsive rituals in the behavior of a person. Compulsive acts overdo the good to allay anxiety. The struggle is to maintain a balance.

4. *Depression*: this state is marked by the symptoms of melancholy, hopelessness, retardation of psychic processes, self-criticism, and sometimes suicidal impulses. Hostile impulses are directed inward, arousing guilt.

5. *The manic-depressive reactions*: The manic phase includes elation, self-confidence, flight of ideas, aggression, irritability, and unrestrained sexuality. It is a state of uninhibited pay, or overpays - for the guilt incurred in the manic phase.

6. *Neurotic character* (psychopathic personality): They are characterised by the irrationality and stereotyped behavior patterns arising from the dominance of unconscious factors, and by self-destructiveness arising from unconscious guilt. The guilt, stemming from repressed conflicts (usually from the Oedipus situation), is displaced to criminal behavior, which is less objectionable than the forbidden desire in the unconscious. The punishment for the former relieves the guilt for the latter. They require realistic activity, not fantasy, to satisfy their needs. Their adjustment to the social environment is based on faulty principles, established by early parent-child relations (Patterson).

7. *Alcoholism and drug addiction*: These habits are usually secondary to depression and character neuroses. Alcohol is an escape from depression, a means of overcoming inhibitions, and its adverse consequences *replace other forms of self-punishment.*

8. *Conversion symptoms*: the replacement of an emotionally charged idea by a physical symptom.

There are many more situations than listed here above as samples. These few concepts are given here to see how often we come across such situations. Often in our pastoral work although we are not competent to handle the situations as a psychoanalyst would, nevertheless we can notice the behavior and refer to those who can help beyond what we can.

16:13 Deviations from Freud in Psychoanalysis: (R.A. Harper)*

1. *Alfred Adler:* Unlike Freud, Adler maintained that neurosis is caused not by sexual impulse but by inferiority feeling. Alfred held that sexual fantasies were directed to masculine goal. Masculinity was considered power and femininity weakness in Adler's system. Masculine protest is common in both men and women but women do so as a striving for power. The power hunger in human motivates all actions. Everyone has an inborn inferiority feeling due to the long childhood dependence. This basic inferiority feeling can be exaggerated by: a) body and organ defect (whether imagined or real), b) having older and more powerful siblings, c) parental rejection and neglect, d) other factors. Adler held that the person's development is conditioned by his/her environment rather than biological forces and that the individual can be analyzed by the present purposes of life goals rather than his infantile past.

2. *Carl Jung* : Like Adler, also did not go to the psychological past but to the purposive, goal-striving interpretation of behavior. Jung visualised various collective life purposes (not individuals as Adler did). The disturbed person's symbolic presentation resembled those of primitive people. This led Jung to think that there must be an inherited portion of the mind that contained the imprints of ancestral experiences and hypothised a collective unconscious. Jung spoke of 'archetype' (primordial images) present in humans of which *animus,* the mate ideal of the female

---

* Robert A. Harper, Psychoanalysis and Psychotherapy: 36 System (Prentice Hall) Englewood Cliffs, 1959

psyche, and the *anima,* the mate ideal of the male psyche. Along with the collective unconscious Jung further divided the human psyche into *persona* (the social mask of the individual) and *the ego,* a deeper part of the psyche which is reflective of personal experiences and is partly conscious and partly unconscious. Emotional disturbances develop when there is disharmony between the *persona,* the ego, and the collective unconscious. Also when the anima is in conflict with the *anumus* there arises emotional disturbances.

3. *Karen Horney:* According to her, the determining principle for human behavior is the need of security (not sex as Freud said). Human inner conflict is developed by ten neurotic needs and also by attempting to cope with these needs by irrational and neurotic means: a) need for affection and approval, b) for a partner who will take over one's life, c) for restriction of life with narrow borders, d) for power, e) for exploitation of others, f) for prestige, g) for personal admiration, h) for personal achievement, i) For self sufficiency and independence, and j) for perfection and unassailability.

The neurotic person tends to create an idealised image of him/herself in which the contradictory trends presumably disappear (but are actually only repressed). This thought of *idealised self* usurps the person's best energies and makes the person unable to realize his/her potentialities. The idealised self is the godlike being bound to hate the person's actual being (*actual self*). The idealised being is the neurotic, prideful, glory-seeking aspect of the personality. The actual self is the whole personality of the individual as it actually exists at any point of time. Horney also spoke of *'real self',* meaning, the central inner force of the individual which Horney believed to be the source of free, healthy development of personality potential (only the first three of the deviations are mentioned in this section).

16:14 Psychosexual Development of a Person (S. Freud)

"The true instinctive moulders of human destiny, said Freud – were a kind of boiling reservoir of unfulfilled sex desires from infancy onward... every behaviour pattern of human has a cause, and it is most likely that the cause will be unconscious."*

---

* Robert A. Harper, *36 System: Psychoanalysis and Psychotherapy,* p.12.

Sigmund Freud, the so-called father of modern psychology based his study of personality development on the infantile sexuality. His theory affirms that the *libido*, or life force, drives the individual in search of pleasure. While this life force is primarily sexual in nature, it includes all feelings which motivate a person to desire a pleasurable contact with others or even with himself/herself. He held that the experience of pleasure without obstruction leads the person to maturity and similarly, its frustration leads the person to *fixate* his/her libido at any of the stages of growth and thus causes pathological conditions.

The first stage of sexuality is the *oral stage* (first year) during which phase the libidinal energy of the child is centered in the mouth and gratification is derived through the oral channel.

The second stage (1-1 ½ yrs.) is the oral stage, when the libido partially transfers itself to the anal zone, anal intense pleasures are derived from the retention and expulsion of faeces. The child's interest during this period is derived from himself (narcissism) and satisfactions are derived chiefly from his body (auto-erotism).

The third stage is the *phallic stage* (about 3 yrs.), during which the penis (clitoris in the female) becomes the focus of libidinal energy.

The fourth stage, is the *Oedipus Complex.* In the phallic stage interest in the penis (clitorist) is auto erotic, but soon sexual interest in the parents develops and thus the OC develops. This is the stage where the child is inclined sexually to the parent of opposite sex. It originated from a Greek legend where Oedipus killed his father and married his mother. Other complexes associated with this stage are the child's strong feeling of *anxiety and guilt,* the male child expecting punishment from the father (castration anxiety for loving his mother) and the girl developing an inferiority complex (penis envy).

The fifth stage, latency period, a period of sexual quiescence in the individual (about 7 yrs.) that lasts till puberty begins, (about 12-14 years). The increased activity of the genital glands heightens the libido which reactivates the old Oedipus interests. If the Oedipal Complex was successfully resolved the individual now directs the interest to persons of opposite sex outside the family and goes on to mature sexual fulfilment.

16:15 Rational-Emotive Therapy (R.E.T.)

This system of therapy was developed by Albert Ellis, a psychoanalyst who parted from the classical psychoanalysis and developed this system in the fifties. Ellis would trace his insight to the Greeks, a teaching similar to the statement of Marcus Aurelius, thus,

"If thou art pained by any external thing, it is not this thing that disturbs thee, but thy own judgement about it. And it is in thy power to wipe out this judgement now."[6]

In this therapy, the goal is to establish more realistic goals and to eliminate irrational beliefs. This is a congnitive therapy, based on a formula, A, B, C, in analysing the hurting situation as follows:

Stage A: *Actuating Event:* e.g. : Someone criticizes us harshly and unfairly.

Stage B: *Belief System:* that is, our perception of this event is coloured by the irrational belief that one's worth is dependent on others approval.

Stage C: *Consequent emotion:* that is, as a result we become depressed and feel worthless, as though a major catastrophe has occured.[7]

Or for example, a student met a teacher on the way and greeted "Good morning sir". The teacher with much preoccupation did not notice the student to respond and passed by. The student began to think that the teacher ignored her and many imagined and biased beliefs began to crop up in her mind. This made her withdraw from the teacher's presence and she began to question the teachers sincere care for her and became very disturbed.

A = The *Actuating event* here, is the meeting of the teacher who could not respond to the greeting.

B = *The Belief* (irrational belief) is that the teacher ignored her to insult her.

C = *The consequence* is the disturbed mind leading to frustration and withdrawal.

Here, the student would not have experienced frustration if she had placed the situation in a rational alternative: that the teacher did not ignore her but did not notice her nor hear her fearsome voice.

The rational psychotherapy makes the client ask oneself four basic questions:

What am I saying to myself? Is it true ? What is the evidence for my belief?

Wrong association of ideas is avoided in this therapy. Facts are separated from opinion, thoughts from feelings. The clients are taught to identify their irrational ideas, their "sane" versus "insane" statements.

Many people are troubled by their irrational ideas, the most common being,

Positive and negative exaggeration,

Rationalisation, Catastrophising, Absolutistic Statements.

Meaningless metaphors, lies, rhetorical questions and overgeneralisations.[8]

By argumentation or direct teaching the client is taught to challenge and replace the irrational thinking with rational alternatives. Then the client can also be given homework to visualize himself/herself thinking and acting on the basis of his new cognitions and the desired outcomes. This is called *Rational Emotive Imagery* (REI). The following is an illustration of how irrational ideas can be replaced by rational ones:

Irrational Idea	Rational Alternative
1. It Upsets Me	This is reality I upset myself by thinking about it.
2. I have to...	I don't have to do anything. I will consider only my long term interests.
3. I should get what	Everything is exactly as it should be. I may wish for, want, or desire what I want, but it is only *unfortunate* if I don't get it - not awful or a catastrophe!
4. My self-worth is defined by my	Behaviour is only a small part of my total self. I can rate performances, in order to increase my efficiency, but it is illegitimate to even attempt to rate myself.[9]

Howard J. Clinebell, has also listed some of the irrational ideas that disturb our feelings, perception, thinking and acting.

1. I must be perfectly adequate and achieving before I can think of myself as being worthwhile.

2. I must be approved or loved by almost everyone I know for virtually everything I do.

3. When I am very frustrated, treated unfairly, or rejected, I must view myself and things in general as awful and catastrophic.

4. My emotional misery is derived from external pressures, and I therefore have little ability to control or change my feelings.

5. I must preoccupy myself and keep myself anxious about things that seem dangerous or fearsome.

6. I must blame myself (and others) severely when I (or they) make serious mistakes or do something wrong.

7. It is catastrophic if I cannot find perfect solutions to the grim realities in my life.

8. It is easier to avoid facing difficulties than to take self responsibility and develop more rewarding self-discipline.

(From Ellis and Harper, A Guide to Rational Living: para-phrased by Clinebell. See Contemporary Growth Therapies, p.142).

Robert A. Harper, has also given some examples of people's irrational thinking that land them to frustration:[10]

Irrational Statements	Rational Alternatives
1. It is a dire necessity for an adult to be approved or loved by almost every-one. It is better to depend on others than on oneself, for a self sufficient person is a selfish person.	It is pleasant, but not necessary, for an adult to be approved or loved by others. It is better to win one's own respect than others approval. It is more desirable to stand on one's own feet than to depend mainly on others.
2. It is terrible, horrible, and catastrophic when things are not the way one would like them to be; they should be better than they are. Other's should	It is too bad when things are not the way one would like them to be, and one should try to change conditions for the better; but when this is

make things easier for one, help with life's difficulties. One should not have to put off present pleasures for future gain.	impossible, one had better become resigned to the way things are and stop pointless complaining. It is nice when others help one with life difficulties; but if they don't that is too bad and one can confront the difficulties oneself. If one does not often put off present trouble for future gain, one sabotages one's own wellbeing.
3. It is easier to avoid than to face life's difficulties, and self-responsibilities. Inertia and inaction are necessary and/or pleasant. One should rebel against doing things, however necessary, if it is unpleasant to do them.	The so-called easier way is usually the much harder way in the long run, and the only way to solve difficult problems is to face them squarely. Inertia and inaction are generally unnecessary and relatively unpleasant: humans tend to be happiest when they are actively and vitally absorbed in creative pursuits. One should do necessary things, however unpleasant they may be, without complaining and rebelling.

16:16 Reality Therapy

Both the Gestaltists and the Reality therapists reject the traditional idea that the person in need of help is 'sick' (medical model). The depth psychologists like Freud would dig the past life of the person to diagnose the present problem, believing also that an inner change will bring an outer change in the behaviour. But Reality therapists believe the other way around: change of unwanted behaviour can lead to change in attitude. William Glasser, the founder of the Reality therapy, gives much importance to *RESPONSIBILITY*. By responsibility, Glasser meant the person's change of hurting behaviour that can help self and others without depriving others (Clinebell). When the person changes the hurting behaviour, the therapist reinforces that change to a reality based behaviour. The therapist discourages the irresponsible behaviour of the person and shows new ways to behave responsibly. This approach is, in some way related to RET discussed in this section.

16:17 Gestalt Therapy

On the origin of Gestalt theory, Walter Kempler, affirms the there is nothing in Gestalt therapy that can be considered original. He says:

> All its theoretical considerations can be found throughout man's (sic) written history. Furthermore, there is nothing in its activity that has not been done by someone, somewhere, sometime.[11]

Kempler quotes Gen.3:7, how Adam and Eve were brought to their 'awareness' (as naked) by the tempting morsel in the Garden of Eden. Further, Adam and Eve also came to know the existence of good and evil- that is polarisation. Today, "Gestalt therapy postulates that coming to know one's own psychological polarisation is the first step toward psychological integration and consequently a higher state of awareness."

From the existing gestalt psychology, Gestalists like Frederick Perl (born 1893, Berlin), innovated a Gestalt therapy which brought a lightening information in therapy. The German word 'gestalton' which does not have an accurate English equivalent, can be translated as 'wholeness', 'configuration' or figure formation', a wholistic configuration that determines all its parts. A gestalt formation is very important in our perception. A face is seen beautiful because of this gestalt. A tune sounds beautiful because of this gestalt, and a scent (though its components may be distasteful) smells delightful because of this gestalt in our perception (Vatsayan).[12]

Gestalt therapy focuses on the *here and now* experience of the client rather than the formative past history. The therapist gives more importance to the awareness of the current experience by the client. The person is also seen as an organism living in close relation to the environment even as a figure is seen in its background. Gestalists believe that the person alone (without the environment) is only part. Therefore, gestalt therapists seek to help the person improve the quality of this relationship. Clinebell uses 'contactfulness' of the person there is an 'unfinished' part which is revealed by some obvious behaviour like the way the person talks, moves or breathes. The therapist helps the person to be aware of and be in touch with those obvious behaviours which experience will result gestalt formation in the person (wholeness experienced). To this may be added

Vatsayan's illustration, that, when a task is completed by a person there is a gestalt formation. People tend to think more about the unfinished task than the finished ones and they suffer from this lack of gestalt or completion. Hence, it is said that mental tension results from the unfinished gestalt. One aspect of gestalt therapy is the well-known "gestalt hot chair" this method helps in reconciling polarisation within a person and between persons.

The task of the gestalt therapist is, therefore, to fill in the gap in the personality 'created by the disowned or rejected aspect of oneself), to make the person whole again. The person is enabled to relive and finish the incomplete experiences that they carry from the past.

Another therapy *'Psychosynthesis'* developed by an Italian therapist, Roberto Assagioli, is similar to Gestalt therapy which also seeks wholeness in the person. Psychosynthesis synthesizes all aspects of the person, including spiritual aspect of the person in the spectrum of healing approach.

16:18   Behaviour Therapy

This has the root in the conditioning theory of the Russian Psychologist, Pavlov. Others in this school include J.B. Watson, O. Hobart Mowrer and B.F. Skinner. We have seen that Reality therapy believes in the change of behaviour before the change of attitude. Behaviour therapy believes the same process - change of behaviour, overt or covert is the primary focus. It rejects also the medical model of sickness or childhood experience influencing adult behaviour. It also discards insight therapy as the dynamic schools do. Behaviour therapy believes that the learned behaviours can be unlearned. The hurting behaviours can be unlearned and more wholesome behaviour learned. In this the therapist helps the person to identify the negative and the positive behaviours and encourage the positive behaviours while discouraging the negative ones.

16:19 Rogerian School: Client-Centred-Therapy

After a brief experience in China as a missionary, Carl R. Rogers returned to the United States and became a renowned psychotherapist. He is an important figure in the *Human Potential Movement* that recognizes an inborn capability in every human to develop and grow to maturity. Rogers, as if by his acquaintance with the biblical view of humans as *created in God's image,* changed his attitude toward human nature, that humans are worth respecting and accepting. Consequently, he changed his approach to human problem and its solution from a therapist-centred and advice-giving approach to a person-centred (or client-centered) and relationship oriented approach. He began to call the traditional approach of advice giving or exhorting as "museum peace of psychotherapy" and called his new approach as *Client-Centred-Therapy,* in which the person became the central focus, not the person's problem.

Rogers proposed a turn from such old methods to a newer Psychotherapy where the emphasis will be: (see his counseling and psychotherapy, p.87)[13]

1. Not on the problem but on the person. It aims at the complete independence of the person.

2. Therapy will not be a matter of doing something for the person but freeing him for a normal growth and development.

3. The new approach stresses upon the emotional elements, the feeling aspect of the situation than the intellectual aspect.

4. It stresses upon the immediate (now) than the individual's past.

5. For the first time this new approach stresses *relationship* itself as therapeutic. *Warm responsiveness leading to rapport, permissive attitude* of the counselor (acceptance, non-judgemental) and the *client's freedom* without the counselor intruding with his own idea, are the elements of therapeutic relationship in Client-centred-therapy.

The client's perception of this accepting attitude of the counselee will make the client dare to explore new ways of feeling and behaving. One of the cardinal principles in this approach is that the individual must be helped to work out his/her own value system, with the minimal imposition of the value system of the therapist. Rogers' three basic conditions for therapeutic relationship are: *congruence, acceptance* and *understanding* (see the section on these elements in this volume).

Rogers' basic hypothesis is that, "the individual has within himself the capacity and the tendency, laden if not evident, to move forward towards maturity. It exists in the individual and awaits only the proper condition to be released and expressed (Pastoral Psychology, Feb. '56, p.10). To Rogers, the person seeking help is not a dependent person but a responsible client (On Personal Power, 1977, p.5)[14]. So Rogers leaves the decision making in the hand of the client. He says, "The politics of Client-Centred-Therapy is that power and control is in the client. The decision making power is in the client). (see also Client-Centred-Therapy, p.159-160).[15]

ENDNOTES

1. Erio Berne, *A Layman's Guide to Psychiatry and Psychoanalysis,* p.277.

2. *What Do You Say Halo, Corgi,* 1989, p.418.

3. J.A. Dovito, *The Inter Personal Communication Book,* 4th edn. Harper & Row Publisher, Cambridge, 1986. Also, Thomas Harris, *I am Ok, You Are Ok.*

4. *Pears' Encyclopedia,* "Psychoanalysis", F.38.

5. H.J. Clinebell, *Contemporary Growth Therapies,* Abingdon, 1981, p.27-28.

6. David G. Bernner, (Ed.), *Baker Encyclopedia of Psychology,* Baker Book House, 1967, p.974.

7. *Ibid.*

8. *Ibid.*

9. Chinebell, *Contemporary Growth Therapies, op.cit.,* pp.142-143.

10. Robert Harper, *Psychoanalysis and Psychotherapy: 36 Systems,* Spectrum Books, Prentice Hall, 1959, p.123.

11. R. Corsini, *Contemporary Psychotherapies,* Peacock Publishing, Illinois, 1973, p.251.

12. Vatsayan, *History and Schools of Psychology,* Kedar Nath Ram Nath, Delhi.

13. Carl R. Rogers, *Counseling and Psychotherapy.*

14. _________________, *On Personal Power,* p.5.

15. _________________, *Client-Centred-Therapy.* p.159-160.

CHAPTER 17

Counseling Approaches

The two common approaches of Counseling are Directive Counseling and Non-Directive Counseling.

17:1 In Directive Counseling

In Directive Counseling, the counselor attempts to give his/her opinions of what the solution could be and advises the counselee to follow certain directions. In this approach there is a tendency to coerce, impose ideas by the counselor. This approach can be considered *advice giving or guru-shiksha* relationship where the helped has to accept the direction and follow it. This approach may also be equated with the proverbial counsels of the wisdom books of the Bible. In this approach there is also a tendency to consider the helped as a sick or weak person, incapable of deciding by himself. Such an attitude of the counselor towards the counselee can also be referred to as the *Medical View* of human problem, in which the helped is considered sick and sometimes considered a misjudgment of the value of the person created in the image of God. In the past, many authoritarian pastoral counselors had this approach, moralising all situations and sermonising their advice to the person.

From the counseling point of view, a decision initiated by the helped in the light of the varied possibilities the helper unveiled will last longer and prove more effective than a decision based on the helper's advice. A course of action suggested by the helper may prove impracticable to the helped, worsening the situation and leading to the one being helped trusting the helper no more.

17:2 In Non-Directive Counseling

In Non-Directive Counseling, an advice given at the right time is considered valuable but the attitude of the counselor towards the counselee is almost the opposite of the directive counselor. Here, the counselor does not consider himself/herself as the only source of wisdom in arriving at the solution of the problem. There is a high regard of the *potentiality* (Carl Rogers and the Human Potential Movement) of the helpee who is also a human with God given potentiality. An atmosphere of *acceptance, respect* and *understanding* of the helped by the helper prevails in a non-directive counseling relationship. The pastoral helper here gives up the role of a preacher or instructor, gives up the attitude of *'holier than thou'* and becomes a fellow-being rowing together in the same boat of human finitude. The helper is only a 'brother-man' (W.E. Oates) or a 'sister-woman' to the helped. In the language of Henry Nowven, the counselor is a 'wounded healer' to the wounded person.

In the case of directive counseling, the pastoral counselor alone speaks (monologue). In the non-directive counseling relationship the pastor allows the person to talk more on a sharing of views (dialogue). Oates, even quotes D.D. Williams, to say that the relationship is not only a dialogue but a trialogue, for God is always the *third person*[1] when two humans meet. This is perhaps something of the Christian counselor's prerogative, to recognize the Omnipresent God even in counseling relationship.

One important factor the pastoral carer should not forget is that the Spirit of God is at work in all human relationships - humans to God and humans to humans. Don Falkenberg, testifies that even some of the psychotherapists recognize the presence of the Holy Spirit in human relations. He writes, "if a psychotherapist can speak so freely about the Holy Spirit in the counseling process, may be it's time that pastors spend some time thinking on this power working through us."[2]

Flakenberg, proposes that we as human counselors should own up to our own humanness - our own finitude, and allow the Spirit of God to reveal and guide us to the truth. To Wayne E. Oates, both the counselor and the counselee are *incurably human* (Falkenberg, p.32). Even the acceptance that the counselor extends to the counselee is incomplete without the acceptance resulted by the Spirit present there. This is in line with Reuel Howe's idea that humans cannot love or accept perfectly (Howe, Man's Need and God's Action, p.91) This is why the human helpers should always recognize the working of the Spirit through human encounters.

Carl Rogers, would insist that the decision making centre is the client, not the therapist, and such is the basis of non-directive counseling. Similarly, Seward Hiltner, would use a term like *'educative guiding'*[3], to mean the wide spectrum of avenues the counselor may present for the counselee to choose from. The helper here, is a *fecilitator,* not a director nor a *'Listening Wall',* a term by which the extreme Rogerians are labelled.

Both the directive and the non-directive approaches are used helpfully in different settings. The helpee background may also suggest the kind of approach the counselor may use. Even the theological and denominational background of the counselor may determine the approach in some cases, as in the case of the counselor-responses (see below). However, we find that most pastoral counselors follow the non-directive approach. Similarly, the use of psychotherapeutic approaches is determined by the background of the counselee, and in accordance to the relevance at the given situation. No single, approach is THE approach. Rather, *an eclectic* approach is advisable. One important truth to remember, especially by the pastoral counselors, is that the human being, created with potentiality and value, is beyond all psychological insights or techniques of therapy. The person is the final document though some insights from the science of human behaviour can help us understand a person to some extent.

17:3   Types of Counselor-Responses

This item is available in other counseling books, especially, in Howard J. Clinebell' books. Nevertheless, having discussed the fact that one's theological tradition can suggest one's counseling approach, its presentation here will supplement the above statement. Our survey of the Transactional Analysis will also help us see from which ego-state we respond mostly. Clinebell, having listed EISPU of Elias Porter, adds A(Advising), making the acrostic: E+I+S+P+U+A *(Evaluative + Interpretative + Supportive + Probing + Understanding + Advising)* responses.

Evaluative Response is one in which the counselor will come under directive counseling discussed above. In such a response the counselor gives a judgement on the goodness or otherwise, appropriateness or rightness on the behaviour or the decision of the helped. For instance, 'What you have done is incorrect, you should have done this way' etc.

Interpretative Response may also come under directive approach in that the counselor tries to explain the causes and tends to teach or impart meaning to the helped. Eg. 'Your negligence caused it.'

Supportive Response may come under the non-directive approach in that the counselor supports the feelings of the helpee by reinforcing assurance leading to the helped catharsis (expression to defuse tension). For instance, 'It must have been hurting you'.

Probing Response can be dominant in directive approach but the non-directive counselor also uses it to clarify and probe deeper into the story. For instance, 'Tell me more about that.'

Understanding Response is basically of non-directive approach in that the counselor sees the situation from the point of view of (or the experience of the helpee) and understands the helped instead of criticising or being judgemental. This is also supportive. For instance, 'I can see how you have been rowing against rough weather and have been torn apart.'

Advising Response comes directly under directive approach. It tries to tell what the counselor thinks is correct and that the helped should follow that course of action. For instance, 'Your father being a pastor it will be good for you to go for theological training.'[4]

For a greater detail in this responses, see Clinebell's revised edition of the Basic Types of Pastoral Care and Counseling (p.95f). As said earlier, the last response is Clinebell's addition. Few lines are quoted from the book to show how, according to Clinebell, one's faith and tradition can influence the choice of the given response.

> I have found the EISPUA categories useful in helping pastors and students become aware of lopsidedness in their counseling responses. The counseling of many ministers consists almost entirely of *P* (probing) and *S* (supportive) and *A* (Advising) responses without their being aware of it. Moralistic ministers tend to major *E* (Evaluative) and *P* (probing) responses. Clergy with some exposure to abnormal psychology and psychodynamic theory often overemphasize / (interpretative) responses, involving theories about why people feel and act as they do. Those whose training have been mainly in Carl Rogers' approach may rely too heavily on *U* (Understanding) responses. Ministers with no training in counseling seldom use *U* responses.[5]

As suggested earlier in respect of approaches, the counselor should not be exclusive in one response or the other. All these responses are useful in different contexts of counseling. However, S and U responses with P when necessary can be considered indispensable in all types of counseling situations. In any case, the counselor needs to avoid responses that threaten or block the expression of the counselee.

ENDNOTES

1. Wayne E. Oates, *Pastoral Counseling,* Westminster Press, 1974, p.11.

2. Falkenberg, "The Holy Spirit in the Counseling Process" in *Pastoral Psychology,* Nov. 1964, p.11.

3. Seward Hiltner, *Preface to Pastoral Theology,* Abongdon, 1958, p.151.

4. Clinebell, *Basic Types...,* op.cit., p.94.

5. *Ibid.*

CHAPTER 18

Qualities of a
Good Counselor

There are born counselors as well as trained counselors. Some individuals are born with the natural dispositions much like the modern list of qualifications for a good counselor. Some are born non-judgemental, patient in dealing with people, insightful and ability to perceive other people. In many others these dispositions are acquired by learning. Any human person is always in need of the other for a meaningful living. No one has the complete know-how of solving life's reality with its problems large and small. No human person can see or understand oneself fully without the help of the other fellow humans. The well known *Johari* window of a person teaches us how, in a person there are regions *known to self and not known to others*, there are also region *known to others only and not known to self*, there are regions *known both to the others and self as well*, so also there are sections *not known to both self and the others*. Accepting this fact of each of us alone will lead us to associate with and live together with fellow beings in an interdependent existence. In such a human situation we are sometimes helpers and sometimes the helped as we live unveiling life's reality everyday.

The Hebrews gathered around their veteran sages who, from their experience of life, counseled the younger generation. The Wisdom books, esp., the book of Proverbs in the Old Testament is probably a collection of such counsels. Similarly, the tribal societies today impart wisdom for good living by the elders to the younger ones like the Hebrews did. The sitting stone circles in every sector of the tribal village, the working companies who sing and narrate the stories of their heritage, the senior members of the families who chant poetry to the younger ones or someone in life's crisis, the village religious officials who change the unwritten liturgy on the family rituals, and the peers and relations around the individual are all sources of insight and direction for the person in need of guidance and help.

The pundits, gurus, the seers and the other sages of Indian tradition and culture are sources of counsel. India has a highly developed spiritual tradition that provides an immense source of sustaining in life crises. Sudhir Kakar, a leading Indian psychoanalyst, has surveyed the traditional healing systems of the Indian society which have been the means of healing from time immemorial. The spiritual leaders of India are known to be good counselors.

All this is to say that human societies, from the primal stage to the present have been provided with natural built-in system for healing themselves through their religions, ideologies and the charismatic personalities. Most of these healing systems, though in crude maxims have been the source of comfort, alternatives, directions and regeneration.

Modern life's problems may appear more sophisticated with problems arising from the hazards of modern living that requires more analytical assessment of the situation and a healing approach. The helpers today need acquaintance with the doctrines, not only of religion but also of human behaviour. The field of the science of human behaviour is a wisdom from God which enhances our knowledge of ourselves and others. The pastoral counseling profession, in particular, has been greatly enabled by the insights from the science of human behaviour. Besides resources from the culture, the pastoral counselor, by his/her heritage has immense resources for healing from the Christian tradition. However, the appropriate use of such religious resources is also taught in modern counseling training. Therefore, the pastoral counselor today should have a comprehensive know-how in helping those wounded on the modern Jericho road.

The experts in the field of human relations have found some of the skills (or elements of healing relationship) inevitable for all types of approaches, as follows:

18:1 Ability to Listen

Listening in counseling is different from hearing. The Principles of Selectivity is applicable here. A person seeking help communicates in two ways - verbal 30% and non-verbal 70%. In counseling we speak about disciplined listening or genuine listening or Pseudo listening. To be a good listener a Pastoral Counselor has to consider the other as his 'thou' so that the relationship is 'I-thou' relationship rather than "I-it" relationship. The former is to treat the other as human in God's image. The latter is to treat the other as a thing, not human. (See chapter 9 above communication)

Listening is so important especially in Christian relationship that the German theologian, Dietrich Bonhoeffer said refusal to listen to each other is the beginning of spiritual death. He said we have the ministry of listening and of holding our tongues (see his book, Life Together). Howard J. Clinebell quotes Bonhoeffer, thus, "Many people are looking for an ear that will listen. They do not find it among Christians, because Christians are talking when they should be listening. He who no longer listens to his brother (or sister) will soon no longer listen to God either... ."[1]

Many people in the villages are looking for ears to pour in their sad stories, many more in the industrial world are looking for ears to pour in their stories of hurt and stress caused by modern living. Lack of listeners in today's world causes pastoral problems, causes suicides, mental disturbances. On the other hand, listening helps the burdened soul to experience catharsis. Listening would increase the output in industrial relations (like workers and supervisors relationship). One Bhaskaran, writing on listening in management said India's economy will boost if all managers and supervisors are trained to listen to the grievances of their subordinates and workers. Disciplined listening becomes so important in human relationship because, as the experts say human minds can think 600-800 words a minute but can speak only about 200 words. The gap between thinking and speaking makes the minds wander away from the topic. Hence, the need of attentive listening.[2]

18:2 Confidentiality

No counselor will be trusted if they go about telling out all that are confided to them in counseling relationship. Even to tape the counseling interview for educational purpose should be done with permission from the counselee. This requires the verbatim report to have fictitious names, too. Confidential respect is one qualification that a counselor should have.

18:3 Being Sociable

This is another important qualification of a counselor. This is especially true of pastoral counselor whose friendly contact with the people establishes the rapport. A pastor, by virtue of his/her office becomes friendly to one and all. A pastor's availability is one factor that keeps him in touch with people and their living conditions.

It is also true that a pastoral counselor is one who is in touch with his/her emotional life, and has become aware of his/own identity, strength and weaknesses. This makes him/her adjusted with all people in a sincere and mature manner.

A pastoral counselor, by his training is able to comprehend a given situation. She/he is sensitive to the feelings of people, perceives the trend of the dynamics of human behaviour and understands the seriousness of the given situation.

18:4 Humility

A pastoral helper is certainly not an arrogant or complacent person. This does not means s/he must have a low self-esteem. S/he should assert himself, be firm at times. But he is neither one who has a "holier than thou" (I + U -) attitude. He is after all human, like any other, with his vulnerability, fragility and finitude. S/he should have a high respect for the people he comes in contact. That will make him approachable. This makes a simple and exemplary life-style an added qualification as a helper.

ENDNOTES

1. Howard J. Clinebell, *Basic Types..., op.cit.,* p.72.

2. The Hindu (daily paper, Bangalore), Sept. 1, 1982.

CHAPTER 19

Conditions Necessary for Healing Relationships

Botanists tell us of the conditions necessary for germination of a seed as - water, sunlight and air. Human relation experts tell us of the conditions necessary for a healing relationship as - rapport, respect, acceptance, genuineness, understanding and confidentiality. These conditions are created by the counselor in the relationship leading to the birth of a new person. These conditions are briefly described below:

19:1 Rapport, is a friendly condition existing between two persons or parties. In some relationships rapport may exist due to earlier acquaintances between the parties. In some cases rapport is established there and then for special relationships. Whichever way it is established it becomes the foundation of the relationship. Among the tribals, it is customary to ask, 'Where are you going?' or, 'Have you had food?' when they meet. In Nagaland, offering a cup of tea (a cup of rice beer among the people of other faiths) becomes a rapport whereas in Meghalaya and Assam it would be a roll of betel-nut. Other communities in India have such other traditional pleasantries. Jesus' request for a cup of drink became his rapport with the woman of Samaria. Even among old acquaintances a rapport may become necessary to get on to a new topic or a sensitive issue. Rapport simply means to be in close relationship with someone. It is a condition necessary for creating ease and confidence in the helped who may have come to the counselor.

19:2 Acceptance, is an attitude in the counselor of an unconditional regard and acceptance of the counselee in spite of what the counselee may have been. The spirit of acceptance rules out prejudice, assumptions and past knowledge the counselor may have toward the counselee. It also transcends animosity, race and status differences. In brief, acceptance means the counselor's respect and trust of the counselee admitting the latter into a friendly relationship. Its opposite is rejection and condemnation. The counselor accepts the counselee as s/he is, without any preconditions. Thomas Oden, the theologian, would even point to what he calls God's grace in Jesus by which we are ontologically accepted. Oden makes the counselor's acceptance of the counselee as analogous to God's acceptance of all without any precondition. Taking the Christ-event as the accepting event, Oden says, "Its eventful character is Jesus Christ, and must not allow the event of divine acceptance to become vaguely dehistoricised into the general idea of acceptance, or the act of faith reduced to a genre of existentialist courage." Oden said this commenting on Tillich's idea of acceptance. The whole idea is that, if God in Christ has accepted us all we should not hesitate to accept each other.

19:3 Genuineness, sometimes called reality or concurrence, refers, to the counselor's need of honesty in his/her dealing with the counselee. S/he should not be phony or acting. The counselor should avoid role playing and professionalism but become genuinely human to the other human. Without the counselor's empathic concern to help the other by truly entering the counselee's world of experience the counselor cannot help.

19:4 Respect, is the counselor's regard for the right and freedom of the counselee to be. The counselor respects not only the person as a creation in divine image, but also respects the feelings and the experiences the person has. This principle of respect for the other rules out any possibility of exploitations by the counselor.

19:5 Understanding, is an indispensable condition for helping others. To Seward Hiltner, counseling proceeds from understanding. A moralising pastor will find it difficult to 'understand' the other because his/her yardstick will be only 'right' or 'wrong' and there will be no concession. On the other hand, an understanding counselor brackets moral issues for the time being and enters the world of the helped and experience 'walking in the same shoes' with the helped. This also refers to knowing the situation that made the person behave in that manner, not simply condemning the resentful behaviour.

(For the principles of Listening and Confidentiality, see also characteristics of a good counselor, above).

19:6 Referral

A Pastoral counselor works in the community of healing. S/he has the limit of jurisdiction and capability as a member of a healing team. Therefore, when the helped needs assistance that is beyond the capability of the pastor s/he should refer the helped to a more competent member of the team. These other members to whom the helped is referred to may be physicians, psychiatrists, psychologists, social workers or legal advisors, depending on the assistance required. This referral is a part of the professional ethics of the pastor that avoids encroachment in anothers' discipline. When referral is needed it is important to tell the helped in a way that will be acceptable.(see also chapter 24).

CHAPTER 20

Some Areas of Counseling

20:1 Counseling the Sick

When I was sick you visited me (Mt. 25:36)

Jesus the Healer and the Saviour came both to heal and to save. Healing the physically ill was one of his cardinal tasks during his ministry on earth. He came for those who needed a physician. Jesus' salvation is holistic and physical healing was indispensable in making the person whole. One of the criteria for the last judgement he said, will be whether or not the believers visited the sick. The community of faith is often considered a healing community in which the members bear one another's pain and suffering. The pastor becomes the initiator or co-ordinator of this mutual healing.

Those who have had the chance of serving in rural congregations will know the expected role of the pastors in human brokenness, especially, in sickness. The people are distant from the modern medical facilities and the village pastor is the only hope the people have even in acute sickness or fractures. Besides healing by prayers, the pastor's presence at the time of sickness becomes a source of comfort and courage. This is true of both sickness at homes and in hospitals. Therefore, it becomes necessary for the pastor to have some idea of the psychology of the sick person. The physicians tell us that, a person, when attacked by sickness or injury goes through stages of healing. It is important for the pastoral visitor to know those healing stages to minister to the sick relevantly.

20:2 The Healing Stages

About the first three days of the sickness or injury is the *INJURY* phase when the body fights the infection or injury by using much blood sugar and the blood sugar becomes low in the process. The adrenaline from the body system mixes with the blood to prepare the person for 'flight or fight', For want of more glucose the body tears down the proteins (gluconeo-genesis). Consequently the person loses weight, becomes weak. The person's sex drive and hunger becomes low. As a result the person is weak, discouraged and becomes negative in attitude. This can also be called a negative phase where the patient is not much in a position to have visitors to talk politely to them. The patient can even become childish or unreasonable.

The second phase is the TURNING POINT, when the infection comes under control or bleeding stops, and tearing down of the tissues ceases. The fever subsides or the temperature comes to normalcy. The patient begins to ask for some food, makes query about the surroundings and his/her condition. The negative attitude moves towards positive, less discouraged, becomes happier and begins to talk.

The third stage is the MUSCLE BUILDING phase, when the patient regains strength, attitude continues to be positive. The patient begins to eat better and often complains about the food, asks questions about home and outside interests. S/he starts asking the doctors to discharge him/her if in hospital. Most patients we meet in hospitals are said to be in this third phase.

The fourth stage of healing is the FAT BUILDING phase. The reserved fat that was utilised during the infection needs to be built again. Here the patient eats well, increases weight, sexual drive returns, shows greater interest in visitors to talk to, wants to stay out of bed and returns to normal work.

With such a basic information about the dynamics of sickness a pastoral helper may concentrate in some of the areas of the patient's concern. It is also true that a pastoral helper should always remember the family members of the sick person who are more affected than the sick person.

20:3 Things to Remember in Helping the Sick

1. *Suffering and Sickness* in the face of a Loving God: (see also Suffering below). This question will come to the patient, especially if the patient is a new member of the faith. It is important for a pastoral helper to convey the truth that our life in Christ does not mean we are outside human finitude. It is important to convey to the patient that God suffers with and cries with those who bear human suffering, the human way which God Himself had walked with Christ. A pastoral helper may use religious resources like prayer and scriptures in our human attempt to seek the will

of God, not forgetting that the option always is God's. The pastor, from his/her faith experience should approach the suffering human in a realistic manner, not with superficial promises.

2. *Anxiety and Fear:* Though a limited amount of such experiences may help persons prepare for action, its presence beyond the required amount can impair human functioning. Normally, the sick person is stricken with various fears and anxiety including the fear of death. It is time when they need assurance that their sickness is not fatal, or that their family members at home are well kept. The sick persons will have the fear of economic loss, time waste and mounting of expenses as a result of the sickness (including hospital bills, if hospitalised). Above all, there is also the fear of the unknown, especially, if the person is a bread winner in the family, or if, the sick person is hospitalised for the first time.

3. *Dependence*: The patient may become *dependent,* acting even childish and being disturbed by little things (inappropriate response to stimulus). One may become self-centred, experience self-pity and guilt feeling, though these would not have been the experience of the person in normal life. A pastoral helper should keep these possibilities in mind, lest s/he himself becomes irritated by the patient taking the patient as rude or unfriendly.

4. *Loneliness* is a natural experience of a sick person whether at home or in the hospital. Some patients may demand that some friends or members of the family should remain always near them. This perhaps is one reason why 'visiting the sick' becomes an obligation for those who are well. Human company is more valued than material gifts. For, humans are social beings and an isolation from the human company is a psychological torture. The company, comfort and cheer rendered to the sick by the community can contribute to the patient's better response to the medication. These days, more discoveries are made about better care of even those whose sickness are considered terminal. The *Hospice Movement and the Palliative Care* concepts of today have emerged to care for the suffering human unto the last. *Hospice is* derived from a medieval word 'for a place of shelter for travelers on a difficult journey'. Dr. Cicely Saunders, a lady physician of Britain, who saw the unsatisfactory way of treating the terminal patients in hospitals, developed this *HOSPICE* method for modern care for the dying. Cicely Saunders found the extended treatment and tests conducted to the dying patient unnecessary. Therefore, the patient is taken home and given treatment and support along with the members of the family. The caring work continues till the recovery period of the bereaved

members. Hospice care attempts to focus "control and relieve the emotional, physical and spiritual suffering of the terminally ill."[1]

5. The *Freedom*[2] of the person is curbed as the patient will have to submit to the regulations of treatment. In a sense, the sick person has to keep several laws imposed on him by the care takers (doctors, nurses and other care takers). The daily wage earner or the farmer who lives from hand to mouth will find it very difficult to remain chained by such laws. Quite often the farmers will say 'Who will go to my field if I remain in bed'. They will also refuse to be hospitalised even in cases of extreme necessity. Food restriction is one that they cannot comply with and they often eat or drink behind the helpers back. Instructions like, remain in bed, do not talk or smoke, etc., will disturb the patient very much. Such regulations, though meant for their good, may cause the patients' bitterness. It should therefore, be a task of the pastoral helper to motivate the patients to exercise restrain in so far as these do not mean reduction of freedom for a long time.

6. Avoid the idea that you should always talk to the patient or, even that you should be always helpful to the patient in some ways. Preparing to go visit some patient may make you think what you should say or do something to solve the problem. Your physical presence to the sick is more important though you may sometimes bring solutions. Do not expect that the patient should respond to series of questions you may put on him/her either. However, let the patient talk more than you do if the patient is in a position to talk. This is a very important principle of caring. You may even meet the patient without a word till an appropriate time to talk comes. The three friends of Job did so (Job. 2:13) for a purpose. When you have to talk, avoid sermonising or moralising knowing it is not a time for moral or logical debate.

7. *The family members* of the sick person are often more worried than the sick. They are often found shuttling between home and hospital, and waiting in great anxiety outside operation rooms. A pastor's informal conversation with them in their homes, hospital waiting rooms and prayer with them will ease much tension. A pastor's ministry to the sick includes ministry to the family members of the sick as well.

20:4 Useful Tips in Visiting the Sick in the Hospital[3] (Etiquette of the Sickroom)

1. *Co-operation:* You as a pastor, are one of the members of the healing team in as much as the hospital chaplaincy has become a vital ally of the

medical team in most hospitals. You are perhaps known to everybody including the hospital. Remember to co-operate with and do anything only in conjunction with the doctor in-charge. Hospitals with chaplains will also be a contact point in approaching the hospital. Get proper information from the relevant person concerning the patient, visiting hours and other regulations. Contact also the family members of the sick if they are available, to get some information about the sick.

2. *Prepare yourself* spiritually and emotionally so that your presence there may communicate peace and comfort, not only to the sick but also to other people around there. Be sincere, genuine in approaching the sick, prepare to say the appropriate word at the right time. Even if it had been a difficult day for you at home do not communicate these motions to the patient, or, if it had been a sad experience in the previous room. This can be avoided by taking a minute or so in between the visits.

3. *Signs and notices* in the ward and the hospital in general are meant to be observed. When the door is found closed do not enter forcibly to avoid embarrassing the patient or disrupting the treatment. Sign boards like 'No Visitors' should be respected. Other regulations relating to *fire safety or cleanliness* should be respected. When a patient is asleep do not disturb the patient. Patients are often induced to sleep for a purpose.

4. Keep in mind the *Mechanical things* like where you stand or sit to talk to the patient. Do not sit where the patient has to turn to look at you. Be in an easy view of the patient. Do not sit on the patient's bed unless s/he is very close to you or unless you are permitted to do so.

5. *Excuse yourself* when the doctor or other visitors are present unless you are invited to be present. At any case do not overstay in a patient's room to tire him/her. Do not initiate to shake the patient's hand unless the patient offers it first.

6. *Do not communicate negative emotional feelings* as a result of odor, sight or the conditions of the patient. Do not whisper in presence of the patient with other visitors. Neither tell something thinking the patient will not hear.

7. Do not discuss other people's illness or your own illness. Do not discuss about the way the doctors treat patients, nor one doctor's expertise excelling the other. Neither prescribe certain other treatments other than what is done in the hospital concerned. Some visitors have the tendency to criticize the facilities of the hospital or the kind of treatment given in the presence of the patient, suggesting even injection or otherwise. Attempt

to build up confidence of the patient in the doctors and those who care for him/her.

8. Assure the patient of your prayers and visit as you leave the room. Keep in touch with the patient through phone or relatives to know the patients condition even though you cannot visit again.

20:5 Suffering

The question of suffering in the context of an Almighty and ever loving God has been an issue since the time of Job. We continue to ask God why He cannot spare His children from the cruel realities of human life - that is, why does the icy hand of death remain if God can conquer death! Recently I was reading an account of a suffering man, as to how he sees suffering in the midst of nursing his invalid child. He recounted the Hindu idea of suffering as a *lila* of God or the Karma of the sufferer, and that the purpose of suffering is to perfect our devotion to Him. His survey of the Quranic idea of suffering concluded in the same manner - to instruct the person all the better, and that it is Allah's will which cannot be questioned. He summarised the teaching of the Quran as well as the Bible on suffering, as, "But he puts suffering and set-backs in your way to test your faith in Him."[4]

Then the author concluded the question still unanswered - Why a compassionate and all powerful God allows suffering of His children on earth. Then he confessed, "But I am an ardent idolator; I bow to pictures and idols, I visit temples and Buddhist shrines and Sufi dargahs - specially Hindu temples."[5]

He could not reconcile suffering to an Almighty and compassionate God but he continues to seek God. This is the mystery of life.

The church has also interpreted this mystery of suffering in many different ways - that suffering and evil come from outside God's knowledge, or that suffering comes as a result of human sin, or even that suffering comes to test or perfect our faith in God. The word *"Pain"* itself is said to have come from a Greek word *Poine,* meaning 'penalty'. This idea of pain and suffering remains in many Christians even today as it was in the time of Jesus (Jn. 5:14, 9:1). On the other hand, many Christians continue to question God in their suffering. Some pastors claim that if they pray in genuine faith, pain and sickness will go instantly.

To be helpful to a suffering world pastors should have their own understanding of the mystery of suffering and death. It is the conviction of the church that suffering will continue even on the saints so long as they are in flesh and blood, but that Christ Jesus has given a new meaning in our suffering and death. Christians continue to trust God even in the midst of death (of also Ps. 23:4). In Psalm 23:4, the psalmist touches few key ideas of what death means to the believers. It is a *walk through*, it is a *shadow* and that *God is with him* as he passed through death. It is a walk through to a further destination it is only like a shadow that death comes to us beyond that shadow is life again - a life of bliss. This is in line with what we mentioned above in relation to a healed person, that we die as healed persons. If God would take away pain and death literally from this life it would jeopardize the idea of the incarnation of Jesus Christ.

The idea of suffering in the book of Isaiah and Jeremiah was that the suffering servant bears the pain that others in turn will be healed, as quoted above. The suffering is to open ways for those who would suffer.

This is what Christ did. He conquered suffering and death by going through them. We are invited to follow what Christ has done for us. However, it remains true that in Christian understanding the Cross is culminated in the Crown of history as exemplified by the resurrection of Christ. It is therefore, necessary for a Pastoral Carer to know that they cannot give unrealistic promises to the sufferers e.g. to tell the patient that God will miraculously wipe out human pain and suffering. The idea that once in Christ all human hardship-physical, mental and spiritual process are transcended automatically, is unrealistic.

20:6   Death and Bereavement

Dying: The mention of *DEATH* itself is a shocking stimulus. We all think of the death of others not of ourselves. We hear or read of people's tragic deaths or peaceful passing away. We seldom think of our own death, especially if we are young. The cruel fact is that death respects neither people, their age, sex creed nor status. For, as mentioned above, our faith in Christ need not necessarily change the law of physics or biology. God only helps us to bear these realities of life in courage and meaning. Sickness, pain, loss and death are inevitable part of life.

The eternal life that we have from Christ cannot be destroyed by death. The flesh will die and decay but the life which Christ has healed will continue to live beyond the physical death. This is what Jesus referred to when he said, "...though he die, yet shall he live" (Jn. 11:25). It is more meaningful to live out this mortal life in victory than a miraculous escape from it to eternal pain. Christians believe death is in fact an event of transition that opens to a much glorious meaning of life.

We have to be precise. What we can do is to understand the dying person, the dynamics of the dying process so that we can help them die meaningfully. One classic book to which any one talking on death refers is, *Death and Dying*[6] by E. Kübler Ross, the product of her massive research with hundreds of dying persons. P.J. Prashantham,[7] based on this book has underlined the stages of dying as follows, I quote this book because it is readily available with us besides its easy reading. The dying person goes through these dynamics:

Denial: The initial reaction of the person refusing to believe that s/he is dying. This is what we have said above, that we think of others death only.

Anger: When a person takes death as reality one reacts in resentment against the care-takers, doctors and friends. "Why me of thousands?" The helper should know the importance of catharsis of this feeling.

Fears: Fears and anxiety fills the dying person. There is a fear of loneliness and pain, especially that she/he may not be able to cope well with. Therefore, being with the sick person is of great comfort to the person.

One may become regressed to child-like behaviour in discouragement. A sense of meaninglessness of life may appear questioning oneself "Who am I ?"

Fear of loss of family, friends and even one's body itself.. Above all these will be the fear of the process of death itself. Some may fear even the judgement that is believed to follow death. With all these the person may become depressed even refusing to have visitors.

Bargaining: Some persons may even negotiate with doctors or God with a promise to do good if s/he is saved from death. S. Hiltner adds that the promises made are often forgotten when made well again.[8]

Acceptance: Finally the dying person comes to a point where he realizes that death has become inevitable. At this point one may even write a will and make settlements with the living.

Important Pastoral approaches in this situation may include:
Reconciling, Guiding and Sustaining ministries as Hiltner well pointed out to be the tasks of Pastoral Care.

Reconciling will include forgiveness, confessions and re-union of the dying and the living, especially with whom the dying feels need settlement. More importantly, the person's reconciliation with God. Under guiding care may include leading both the living and the dying to see relation of this event to their faith. Christian understanding of suffering and death, God and after life will also be presented. Sustaining ministry is the most important of all. This is necessary even when healing is impossible.

The presence of the pastoral carer or other church workers itself is a comfort to the people around there. Where applicable, the pastoral carer can use word and sacraments in this caring situation.

20:7 The Bereaved

More like the dynamics of the dying person the bereaved person goes through stages of grief. The first experience on hearing the news of the death is,

i)   *Shock*: Overwhelmed by the sad news the person may remain stunned or dazed. This is a state of psychic numbness where the person cannot feel anything.

ii) *Denial*: The person refuses to believe, at least initially that the love one is dead. This state, if prolonged, is said to be detrimental to the grief process. The counselor helps the person to accept the fact of the loss and to work through the stages of grief.

iii) *General Emotional Reaction:* Dr. Carrington has divided the emotional reaction to two types.[9]

General and specific reactions - In general, the need of catharsis or release of pent-up emotion should take place without delay (see Catharsis above). The emotional pain should not "freeze-up." Oversympathy, comforts and generalisation of the experience will prevent the catharsis. As sobbing it out becomes a necessity advise to sleep or serving sedatives will also hinder the process.

The responses of the helpers should facilitate the catharsis. For this purpose the person may be encouraged to talk of the deceased.

iv) *Among the specific emotional reactions are:* a) Depression - The intense experience of grief makes this inevitable. This may remain until the pain is expressed. There is no use cheering up the person except to help ventilate it by the therapeutic relationship. This is often accompanied by experience of loneliness in which the presence of the pastoral helper or the friends becomes helpful.

v) *A Sense of Guilt*: This is another important emotional reaction. Whatever amount of help rendered to the deceased the bereaved may feel she/he could have done more. Sometimes the person may feel the loved one died as a result of this negligence or failure to act timely.

There is no need of correcting or confronting on the part of the helper. Instead, responses like, "You feel you could have done more than what you did" will be helpful.

vi) *Hostility*: This reaction is also common especially towards the doctors, neighbours or those involved in the cause of the death, eg. accidents. In such expressions the counselor need not seek intellectual argument. Rather, an understanding listening is helpful. This does not mean the counselor should encourage hostile feeling either.

vii) *Idealisation and Remembering*: Certain objects like the deceased's property, events like birthdays, behaviour and mannerism will keep reminding the bereaved of the deceased. Sometimes the deceased person is idealised and praised, even with exaggeration, e.g. "No other man could be so good as he was" etc. even though in life it was felt differently.

viii) *Re-organisation and acceptance*: This comes as the last stage if the grief process was followed normally. Here the living person or persons re-organises the structure of activities, e.g. Who will now be the bread earning member of the family etc.

In the stage of acceptance the bereaved takes the situation as a reality and prepares to live without the deceased.

On the part of the Counselor, training will inform him of these dynamics and be better prepared to understand and help the bereaved.

20:8 Suicides

It is a self-murder, a deliberate act of self-injury resulting in death. Sometimes, actions and behaviour that can in the long run destroy one's life are also described as suicidal or slow-suicide, e.g. smoking, drinking, drug use or even over indulgence in eating. Acts of self-injury in which there is little or no intention that death should result are called 'Para-Suicide'.

Causes of suicide are various, from temperamental disposition of the person to existential crises, from a friendly or familial trifle to an unbearable pain or loss. To Sigmund Freud, the death instinct (Thanatos) in human sometimes turn inward leading to suicide. Geographical or seasonal factors also influence suicide, for instance, certain countries or part of the seasons seem to top in suicide rate. It is reported that the months of April, May, and September score high in suicide rate, whereas the months of March, June and August are said to score low. Depressions have 500 times more possibilities than other causes of suicide.

Incidence and Statistic

The Bible records suicide cases of Abimelech (Judges 9:54), Samson (Judges 16:28-31), Saul (1 Sam 31:1-6) Ahithophel (2 Sam 17:23) Zimri (1 Kings 16:18-19) and Judas (Mt. 27:3-5). The early church considered it self - sacrifice and martyrdom. However, the church, from St. Augustine's (4th cent. A.D.) began to see it as sinful. Saint Thomas Aquinas (1225-1274) also reaffirmed it as sin. The Church today continues to disapprove this act. Even the question of Euthanesia is debatable today.

The suicide cases are always under-reported for many reasons. However, an average of 10,000 people are reported to commit suicide everyday. The yearly estimate in the US is 25,000, Hungary 40 per lakh, India about 50,000 a year. Sri Lanka was reported highest in Asia, that is 45 per thousand.[10]

In 1992 Hungary was reported highest in the world (40 per lakh a year) but in 1992, Pondichery was reported highest (60 per lakh a year).[11] Kerala is sometimes reported highest in suicide rate in the country, 27 per lakh, but the same report says Ichabatgram Village (W. Bengal) has an incredible 200 suicides per lakh.[12]

At any case, the highest suicide rate in the world seems to be in India. In India the age group 15-40 is said to be the most prone to suicide and 25 years the peak.

Suicide tendency is a general human behaviour from the sweeper to the king. For every success of suicide there are ten attempts that failed. A Princess was reported having attempted suicide in 1986.[13]

Once in the class, a teacher asked all of us if we had ever meditated suicide. None of us said yes but the teacher said that was not true. Suicide attempts are often described as 'cry for help' because it is reported that 75% of them inform others of their intent, overtly or covertly. The problem lies in the people who hear such signals but do not take the matter seriously, Therefore, it is important that the neighbours, especially the care takers take any such signals as serious. Those who had attempted before have higher tendency than others.

One must take serious note of direct expressions like 'I want to kill myself" or indirect like, "I wish I do not get up from sleep" or "Life is boring, no use living". All these signals are "distress signals" meaning, "Please help me get out of this situation. I cannot handle it. Otherwise I will be forced to end my life."

20:9 Intervention

a) Provide accepting and supportive help. Seek the family's support and help.

b) In high risk situations, professional care should be sought. These days there are counselors, psychiatrists and community care centres and half-way homes. Some of these helping agents have phone facilities.

c) Determine the suicide risk (evaluate the potential through information)

Most of the people who commit suicide have proper plans as to the mode, time and place. Some even rehearse it. In the west pills and gun may be the most used. In India, hanging is the common mode. Direct question may be asked as to how the person is going to kill himself.

d) Listening is a vital approach, here as in other helping acts. For the suicidal communicate their problems and respond well to sympathetic listeners.

e) Clarify whether the fear or cause is imagination or irrational. Talk also of the consequences.

f) Make a contract to wait, "Will you agree to wait till we try if we can help?" or "Will you agree to live?"

g) Be in touch, making frequent visits.

h) The pastoral helper may use religious resources. Besides prayers and scriptural admonishing to ensure hope in Christ. The pastor may also help the person resolve guilt and meaninglessness in life, especially the person's relation with God. Even words like, "Jesus had died for you to live, why do you want to die?"

20:10 Care and Mission with Persons with Disabilities (PWD)

God is the Creator of the persons with abilities and also the persons with disabilities. Humans understand God as of beauty, strength, speed, perfection, the triumphant, and Almighty. On the other hand God portrays himself at times as disfigured, weak, defeated, rejected, stigmatised, and homeless. Humans are created in God's image to bear these varied forms and characteristics of God. In some cultures God is reported to have appeared to individual's incognito, in the form of a beggar, hungry, weak, and shivering manner.

Some Common Types of disabilities:
  i.   Visual

  ii. Hearing and speech

  iii. Physical

  iv. Developmental

Physical disabilities include: Cerebral Palsy. Spina, Bifida, Polio, Fits-Epilepsy, Muscular Dystrophy, Cystic Fibrosis, and Juvenile Arthritis.

Developmental Problems include: Mental /Emotional/Behavioral.[14]

The persons with disability, often abbreviated PWD, are said to form a tenth of every country's population. They are treated as persons who are unfortunate, cursed, useless, and thus objects of ridicule and charity. Their divine right as bearing the image of God and their social right as equal citizens are often overlooked. Their abilities are often underestimated and chances not given to exercise and contribute in the society. Until recently the Church herself regarded the PWD as objects of the abled peoples' piety and not considered as part of the people of God forming the Church. There is an increasing understanding within the church to change this attitude. In fact the WCC has taken up a big stride in this regard, even constituting the Ecumenical Disability Advocates Network (EDAN) that keeps meeting in different parts of the World to assess situations and propose ministerial implications. The United Nations has also taken up this concern seriously and created Commissions, resolved rights of the PWD requiring ratifications by the countries of the world. India ratified the UN proposal and created a law concerning the rights of the persons with disabilities in 1995.

God has made few people with good sense and right thinking to realize lately how the PWD are also very much a part of the human communities with political and divine rights and privileges. Nation legislates; Churches form ministerial concerns and missional targets to reclaim the lost population, the PWD, from the human family. Many theological curriculums are now filled with these concerns.

The pastoral caregivers may do well to remember the PWD want to be treated like every else. Treat PWD therefore with respect and dignity. The PWD have their obligation like any other persons though theirs may be harder to meet than those abled persons. Be considerate and do not limit your discussion with their disabilities only. Discuss areas including work, sport, events, interests and hobbies. Do not appear hurry, match with their speed and space. Consider the PWD as a whole person always and so do not hesitate to say to a visually impaired person, "see you later' or 'do you like this shoes' to an amputee. Maintain a good eye contact, talk directly to the person, not the companion. Address the PWD by the first name as you do to everyone else present there. Do not assume the PWD is sick or that they are always helpless. Allow him /her to do things s/he can, for example, pick up the crutch or boarding a bus unless physical danger is likely. Make public places accessible to the PWD and respect the place designated for the PWD. Do not be scared of the PWD and lend a hand when required finally, understand the PWD, volunteer to help and support the PWD, spiritually, socially and legally. Remember, physical and mental disabilities are not handicaps, but negative attitudes are.

Some basic literature on the subject include:

1. *Henry J.Nouwen ,*   Adam: God's beloved

2. *WCC,*   A Church of all and for all: An interim Theological Statement

3. *Wati L., edited,*   Disability Discourse for theological Institutions

4. "   Disabled God amidst broken people

5. "   Persons with Disabilities in society

6. *Insa Klasing,*   India Disability and Social Exclusion in Rural

7. *Nancy, E.,*   Disabled God

8.	*Joe and Kutty,*	Persons with Disability in Society
9.	*Colston, L.G.,*	Pastoral Care with Handicapped Persons
10.	*Kabue & Arne*	Interpreting Disability,
11.	*Abrams, J.,*	Judaism and Disability
12.	*Cariappa Meena*	How to help your Disabled Child, Delhi
13.	*Coulter, David, et.al eds.*	Journal of Religions, Disability and Health, Quarterly Journal, New York
14.	*Linton, Simi,*	Claiming Disability: Knowledge and Identity, New York
15.	*Shapiro, Joseph*	No Pity: People with Disabilities Forging a New Civil Right Movement, New York.

ENDNOTES

1. From the author's memory of Dr. Dogdson's teaching.

2. See also V.T. Kurien's *Intro to Pastoral Counseling*, CLS, 1970.

3. Thomas F. Kemp, *An Outline of Pastoral Counseling.*

4. Arun Shourie, *Missionaries in India*, ASA, N. Delhi, 1994, pp.1-2.

5. *Ibid.*

6. Elizabeth K. Ross, *On Death and Dying*, 1969.

7. B.J. Prashantham, *Indian Case Studies for a Therapeutic Counseling*, CCC, Vellore, 1975, p.101f.

8. S. Hiltner, *Theological Dynamics*, Abingdon, 1972.

9. Mitton (ed.) *First Aid in Counseling*, T&T Clark, London, 1968.

10. North-East Times, Guwahati, Sept. 1, 1992.

11. The Eastern Clarion, Jorhat, June 30, 1992.

12. India Today, Sept. 15-19.

13. Clarion, June 6, 1992.

14. OPENDOORS: a Guide For Persons with disabilities, their families, and Interested Persons. Published by the Organisation of American States & NCPWD.

CHAPTER 21

Understanding Human Personalities

21:1 Some Personality Marks

21:1:1 *An Egoist*: This person's attitude to life is simple, direct and above board - every decision s/he makes is based on the answer to one question: "What's in it for me?" If his/her selfishness, greed and ruthless desire for self advancement hurt other people, that's too bad. But her/his motto is "Me first."

21:1:2 *An Egotist*: S/he is at the height of conceit: always busy telling others about his/her success and says. 'Let me give you my opinion - I know, because I am an expert at practically everything.' S/he is boastful to the point of being obnoxious - S/he has only one string to his/her conversational violin, that is, himself/herself, and s/he plays on it a number of monotonous variations about what s/he thinks, what s/he has done, how good s/he is, how s/he would solve the problems of the world, etc.

21:1:3 *An Altruist*: His/her secret of true happiness is the welfare of others. Never mind his/her own interest but wants to see how the next fellow is getting along.

21:1:4 *An Introvert*: Like a biochemist studying a colony of bacteria under the microscope, s/he minutely examines every thought, feeling and action. Probing futile question like "What do other people think of me?", "How do I look?" and "May be I shouldn't have said that." These thoughts are his/her constant nagging companions, for he/she is unable to realize that other people do not think of him/her as much as s/he thinks. She may seem unsocial but his/her greatest desire is to be accepted and liked. S/he may be shy and quiet, often moody and happy, and prefers solitude or at most the company of one person to a crowd. S/he has an aptitude for creative work and is uncomfortable engaging in activities that require cooperation with other people.

21:1:5 *An Extrovert*: S/he is a wonderful salesperson because s/he can always get interested, sincerely, vitally interested in other people's problems. S/he is the life of the party, because s/he never worries about the effect of his/her actions, never inhibits himself/herself with doubts about dignity or propriety. S/he is usually happy, generally full of high spirits, and s/he loves to be with people and lots of people. His/her thoughts, interests and the whole personality are turned outward.

21:1:6 *An Ambivert*: His/her personality is both introvert and extrovert like most of us. A conscious balancing of these two "Verts" should make a pleasant personality.[1]

21:2 Human Temperaments

Hippocratic personality type given by Hippocrates based on humours (or fluid of the body). His followers believed that health was governed by the balance of 4 body fluids, or humors: Phlegm, blood, black bile, & yellow bile.

The knowledge of temperament is of special importance for our knowledge of a person. By temperament we mean the basic mood of a person's soul, characterising his/her reaction - sensitivity according to mood, strength, depth and length of time.

In accordance with the combination of strong and weak reaction sensitivity and reaction time we obtain four temperaments.

1. The choleric temperament, with reaction sensitivity and long reaction-duration (often angry, easily made angry)

2. The sanguine temperament, with strong reaction-sensitivity and short duration. (hopeful, optimistic)

3. The melancholic temperament with weak reaction-sensitivity, but long reaction - duration (sad, low, spirit)

4. The phlegmatic temperament, with weak reaction-sensitivity, but short (weak) reaction duration. (slow to act, feel or show emotion or interest).

21:3 The Choleric Temperament

The choleric is characterised by strong reaction - sensitivity. The reaction-duration is extensive too. He/she is the type of the strong personality and strong willed leader and fighter.

The choleric disposition of a person is seen in the physical habitus He/she has a powerful, set physique, broad shoulders, strong muscles and strong nerves. His/her facial expression is serious, his look is sharp, and penetrating. Sometimes passionate. The mouth is thin lipped and the hips are firmly closed together. His/her gait is firm and self-assured, his voice is strong and has a pleasant sound. The choleric of not less than average intelligence, has as a rule, clear common sense. He penetrates into the depths.

And s/he envisages a situation in its totality. At the same time he disregards trivial things or aspects, including the personal feeling of others. Shows no understanding for the feelings and moods of other people and so tends to become inconsiderate and offensive. His will is energetic. He/she is ready for a heroic display of strength, for fighting, for sacrifice, for everything sublime and ideal. His/her understanding virtue is magnanimity.

He is always optimistic. He always relies and under all circumstances on the strength and capabilities of his ego. His/her maxim is: "Conquer or die, bend or break, by hook or by crook'. S/he moves within extremes. What s/he wants is all or nothing. Everything centres around his/her beloved ego. She does not like to acknowledge the achievements and success of others. His/her neighbour, and indeed, the entire creation. His conceit is the source of his hypersensitivity, his self righteousness his arrogance, his negativism, his unyielding spirit, his social attitude, and often, of her/his indisciplined rage which overpowers him at times with lightning speed.

However, if the choleric sets out to improve himself then his temperament becomes a strong support in his striving after sanctity, and he/she will utilize all his ambitions, all his urge for self esteem, to become pleasing to God and to achieve great things for the kingdom of Christ. The choleric has great aptitude for prayer. The religious choleric is grateful if he is told of his faults. The gifted choleric achieves great things in his professional work. His natural disposition urges him on to unceasing world. He cannot allow himself a tune of rest, when some work is urgent.

His attitude is independent, bold and fearless. Everything depends on whether the choleric develops his positive gifts and endeavours to conquer, the darker side of his character. He needs the clear goal; the service of God for the love of God.

The choleric tempered priest must also unceasingly aspire after true humility of heart and he must realize that he is, inspite of his gifts and talents, a useless servant before God. But inspite of all his endeavours the choleric priest will be more respected than loved by his faithful. This should be for him a persistent incentive to strive after love, and it should also be a never ceasing source of humility.

21:4   The Sanguine Temperament. (sure, optimistic)

The sanguine temperament is characterised by its liveliness and inconsistency.

The sanguine person can also be recognised by his/her external appearance, his nervous system is lively, and easily excited. S/He is, as a rule, of slim figure, pleasant. And his/her body is beautifully built. His look is cheerful, but unstable, his gait is fast, but somewhat uncertain.

The sanguine has a pronounced appreciation of outward appearance. His intellect is swift and lively, but he finds it difficult to concentrate on a specific subject matter and to direct his will power towards a firmly determined goal. He does not possess 'staying power.'

His emotional life is tender and warm. He is easily ruled by moods. A serene, superficial, and often even frivolous philosophy corresponds to his nature. S/he cannot discover tragedy anywhere. Laughing and weeping quickly follow each other. He is the born partner and companion who finds it easy to get on with people; hence he is liked by all and popular everywhere.

The sanguine meets many obstacles in his striving after sanctity. This follows from his temperament. His superficial, frivolous, easygoing disposition is responsible for his slow progress in matters of any depth. Anything that means effort, strain, sacrifice, renunciation, mortification he finds boring. His/her main interest is sensual satisfaction (not necessarily sexual). S/he is very fond of himself, he is very open to praise and flattery, and S/he is also easily depressed by blame and reproach.

He wants to take part in everything. Curious and talkative and even 'gossipy', S/he confides in anyone. He finds it very hard to keep a secret. He finds inner concentration quiet withdrawal into prayer and mortification very difficult. S/he is more inclined to auto-erotic exhibitionism and to jealousy. S/he many easily surrender to frivolous, ill considered, careless and carefree lust and hedonistic intoxication. He is strongly inclined to flirtations and superficial love affairs. The sanguine temperament has also its advantages for the religious aspiration of the soul. He simply cannot be wicked for any length of time. He cannot bear a grudge against a person. This disposition also shows itself in his relationship to God. Once he has established a sound relationship with God, he will not part company with him for any length of time. His feelings urge him to reform. Of course, also this is a passing, short-lived mood. His contrition does not go very deep, indeed, often enough it remains very much at the surface. Yet, he is open to criticism, and he does not mind being told the truth, just as he himself knows how to reprimand others without hurting them. His rage is over as quickly as it arises. He knows how to behave, he easily assimilates.

In his self education he must set himself clear maxims by which he will bind himself. He must persistently work to strengthen his character. He should train and strengthen his will, and he should force his intellect to take an interest in serious matters.

The priest with sanguine temperament will find it particularly easy to find his/her way into the hearts of the young and to be successful in this kind of work, for the temperament of children and of many adolescents is preponderantly sanguine.

But he/she must see to it that his mirth does not deteriorate into a kind of silliness, so that people in vain for any depth of soul in him/her: in that case, he/she would not be taken seriously and would not be respected as a person worthy of confidence and trust. The sanguine priest needs self-discipline. If he fails here, he/she will miss the greatest achievements of his/her priestly talk, namely, to guide souls to God.

21:5   The Melancholic Temperament

The characteristics of the melancholic are explained by the association of a feeble reaction-sensitivity with a strong intensity of reaction (once he does react). Indeed, the melancholic is so intense in his/her reaction's that he/she can neither overcome nor forget certain deep impressions. These facts alone explain that the melancholic temperament of them all are the most difficult to understand.

The melancholic is characterised by a drawn and often weak appearance. His/her nervous system is hypersensitive and irritable. His/

her gaze is quiet and turned inwards, as it were, his/her gait is slow and measured. He/she gives the impression of being preoccupied. His/her feature often express something like suffering or worry. He/she is a man of contradictions, frequently an enigma to himself/herself during melancholiacs, we notice a great difference between those who are driven along by their temperament, and those who try to master it.

The emotional life of the melancholic is rich and very tender. Outer influence can shake him/her to the core. The melancholic is taciturn, always occupied with his/her inner self. He/she likes to avoid social contacts and the busy world, in order to build up in seclusion a world of his/her own. So it comes about that s/he often appears absent-minded in the midst of a serene and interesting conversation, yet he/she is infact always active and always busy. But he/she lives almost invariably in two worlds/and preferable in his/her own world rather than in the world that surrounds him/her.

In all this, he/she often feels lonely and forsaken; no one (he/she thinks) understands or loves him/her. He/she believes that the people do not want to have anything to do with him/her, that no one has sincere affection for him/her. The melancholic displays a certain over anxiety. He/she is overconscientious, he/she is reliable. He/she has great understanding for the sufferings and afflictions of other people. He/she has a strong sense for beauty.

Again and again, he notices his clumsiness, his/her shy nature, helplessness and lack of self-confidence in his/her dealings with other people. He/she notices repeatedly how other people laugh at him/her and his behaviour. This deprives him/her of the last vestiges of trust in other people. He/she becomes suspicious and misanthropic. Likewise, in striving for sensitivity, he cannot finally and decisively make up his/her mind. He/she procrastinates, he defers decisions, even those that are of the utmost importance to himself/herself and to his/her life. Failure discourages him/her completely.

In the melancholic, pride also plays an important role. This pride shows itself as fear of failure and ridicule, due to his/her hypersensitive reaction to feelings of shame. He/she trusts people only with great difficulty. But if he/she has found a person to whom he does open up, then he watches jealously lest his/her confidence maybe betrayed. He/she finds it difficult to see the good properties in himself as well as others. His/her failures, his/her ever renewed lapse into sin, make him/her so deeply unhappy that he/she risks turning away from God altogether and may develop a certain depression and resentment, and even open hatred against God. The melancholic has a natural gift for piety. He/she feels a great longing for ultimate values, for lasting happiness, for refuge in God, for life eternal.

21:6   The Phlegmatic Temperament (not easily agitated)

The phlegmatic temperament is precisely the opposite to the choleric temperament. It is characterised by weak reaction-sensitivity associated with weak reaction-intensity and reaction-duration.

The phlegmatic is often obese. He/she is clumsy, slow and immovable. His/her nervous system is slothful. His/her look is without fire and energy, his/her gait carefree and slow. He/she likes to sleep much and eat much; he loves his/her peace.

In spiritual respects the phlegmatic is indolent and inactive. Hardly anything can get him/her out of his repose, unless someone tries intentionally to disturb his/her tranquil mood. This longing for repose is his/her domineering characteristic. The result of this is weakness, laxity, lack of energy. His/her intellect is not disposed to deep thinking. His/her emotions are scarcely developed. He/she likes a quiet, undisturbed life of routine.

The greater disadvantage to the phlegmatic in all his/her activities - and this includes above all his/her striving after perfection - is his/her dull, unimpassioned disposition, his indolence and inertia. Nothing can move or shake him/her. He/she lacks everything that makes a strong personality.

Inspite of all these weakness, his temperament also has its advantages. The phlegmatic does not undertake anything with undue haste. He/she hates every excited, hurried performance. Once he/she undertakes anything, he sees it through. He/she does not make any claims in any respect. He/she is peaceful and social and is on good terms with everyone, although he is not a community type..."

Summing up, the phlegmatic lacks inner drive and energy. What he/she needs is more initiative more sense of duty, more liveliness, more joy, more courage for life. If he/she can gain these, he/she will fill his/her place in life, though he/she will not fight the great battles of life. He/she will move often than not just be drawn along behind by those who storm ahead. But he/she certainly can be of assistance to these conquerors, simply because his/her considered ways will act as a salutary brake on more stormy characters.[2]

21:7   The Four Selves of a Person

The well-known *JOHARI WINDOW* presents the basic understanding of both intrapersonal and inter-personal communication. Joseph Luft and Harry Ingham developed this model of the human self (hence the model is named after the inventors' names), to say that every human person has four windows of the self. The descriptions of this model and four basic life positions that follows is best done by J.A. Devito which the present writer quotes here with acknowledgment.

Known to Self Not Known to Self

	Known to Self	Not Known to Self
Known to Others	Open Self	Blind Self
Not Known to Others	Hidden Self	Unknown Self

21:8   The Open Self (the Section Known to oneself and to Others)

The open self represents all the information, behaviors, attitudes, feelings, desires, motivations and ideas that are known to the self and also known to others. The type of information included here might vary from one's name, skin color, and sex to one's age, political and religious affiliations, and batting average. Each individual's open self varies in size, depending on the situation and the individuals the person is dealing with. Some people for example, make us feel comfortable and support us; to them, we open ourselves.

"The smaller the first quadrant," says Joseph Luft, "the poorer the communication." Communication depends on the degree to which we open ourselves to others and to ourselves. If we do not allow others to know us, that is, if we keep the open self small, communication between them and us becomes difficult, if not impossible. We can communicate meaningfully only to the extent that we know each other and know ourselves. To improve communication, we have to work first on enlarging the open self.

Note that a change in the open area–or in any of the quadrants–brings about a change in the other quadrants. Visualize the entire model as of constant size but each section as variable, sometimes small, sometimes large. As one section becomes smaller, one or more of the others must become larger. Similarly, as one section becomes larger, one or more of the others must become smaller. For example, if we enlarge the open self, this shrinks the hidden self. Further, this revelation or disclosure in turn leads others to decrease the size of our blind selves by revealing to us what they know and we do not know.

The Johari model emphasizes that the several aspects or dimensions of the self are not separate and distinct pieces but are parts of a whole that interact with each other: each part is intimately dependent on each other part. Like our model of interpersonal communication, this model of the self is a transactional one.

In Figure 2. two models of the self are presented to illustrate the different sizes of the four selves, depending on the particular interpersonal situation. In Figure 2 (left) let us assume that we are with a friend to whom we have opened up a great deal. Consequently, our open self is large and our hidden self is small. In Figure 2 (right) let us assume that we are still a bit uncomfortable. Thus our open self is relatively small and our hidden self is large. These models are, of course, hypothetical illustrations designed to explain how the different selves may change from one situation to another. We have no measuring instrument which would allow us to measure accurately the relative sizes of these four selves.

21:9   The Blind Self (Blind to Self but known to others)

The blind self represents all the things about ourselves that others know but of which we are ignorant. This may vary from the relatively insignificant habit of saying "you know" or rubbing your nose when you get angry or having a peculiar body odor to something as significant as defense mechanisms or fight strategies or repressed past experiences.

Some people have a very large blind self and seem to be totally oblivious to their own faults and sometimes (though not as often) their own virtues. Others seem overtly concerned with having a small blind self and join every encounter group. Some are even convinced that they know everything there is to know about themselves, that they have reduced the blind self to zero. Most of us lie between these extremes.

FIGURE 2: Two Models of the Four Selves

Open Self	Blind Self
Hidden	Unknown Self

Open Self	Blind Self
Hidden Self	Unknown Self

Interpersonal communication depends in great part on both parties' sharing the same basic information about each other. To the extent that blind areas exist, communication will be made difficult. Yet blind areas always exist for each of us. We may be able to shrink our blind areas, but we can never totally eliminate them.

Although communication and interpersonal relations are generally enhanced as the blind areas becomes smaller, do not assume that people should therefore be forced to see themselves as we see them. Forcing people to see what we see may cause serious trauma. Such a revelation might cause a breakdown in defenses: it might force people to see their own masochism or jealousy or prejudice when they are not psychologically ready to deal with such information. Such revelations are best dealt with in the company of trained personnel.

21:10 The Hidden Self (Not known to others but known to self)

The hidden self contains all that you know of yourself and of others but that you keep to yourself. This area includes all your successfully kept secrets about yourself and others. In any interaction, this area includes all that is relevant or irrelevant to the conversation but that you do not want to reveal.

At the extremes we have the overdisclosers and the underdisclosers. The overdisclosers tell all. They keep nothing hidden about themselves or others. They tell you their family history their sexual problems their marital difficulties, their failures and successes and just about everything else. For them this area is very small, and *had they sufficient time and others sufficient patience, it would be reduced to near zero.* The problem with these overdisclosers is that they do not discriminate. They do not distinguish between those to whom such information should be disclosed and those to whom it should not be disclosed. Nor do they distinguish among the various types of information that should or should not be disclosed.

The underdisclosers tell nothing. They talk about you but not about themselves. Depending on one's relationship with these underdisclosers, we might feel that they are afraid to tell anyone anything for fear of being laughed at or rejected. Or we may feel rejected for their refusal to trust us. Never to reveal anything about yourself comments on what you think of the people with whom you are interacting. On one level, at least, it says, "I don't trust you enough to reveal myself to you."

The vast majority of us are somewhere between these two extremes. We keep certain things hidden and we disclose certain things. We disclose to some people and not to others. We are, in effect, selective disclosers.

21:11 The Unknown Self (Not known to self or others)

The unknown self represents truths that exist but that neither we nor others know about. One could legitimately argue that if neither we nor anyone else knows what is in this area, we will not know that it exists at all. Actually, we do not know it exists; rather, we infer it exists.

We infer its existence from a number of sources. Sometimes this area is revealed to us through temporary changes brought about by drug experiences or through special experimental conditions such as hypnosis or sensory deprivation. Sometimes this area is revealed by various *projective tests or dreams.* There seems to be sufficient instances of such revelations to justify our including this unknown areas as part of the self.

Although we cannot easily manipulate this area, recognize that it does exist and that there are things about ourselves and about others that we simply do not know and may never know.

ENDNOTES

1. Norman Lewis, *Word Power Made Easy,* Pocket Book, N. York, 1972.

2. Willibald Demal, *Pastoral Psychology in Practice, Mercier Press,* Bridgestreet, Cork, 1955.

CHAPTER 22

Understanding and Helping the Youth

22:1 Understanding and Empowering Children

The ruler of today was at one time a human embryo. The quality of life lived today is shaped even before the embryo is born. In some cultures the age of the person is said to count beginning from the day of conception in the womb. God announced that he called his prophets even while they were in their mother' womb. Care for a person's soul, therefore, begins from the fetus if the person is to born hale and well. When the person is borne, another stage of grooming of that soul begins for shaping a health personality. Every Caretaker of children is aware of the Freudian "Formative years' (0-5,7) years of a person, which is crucial and the way the caretaker use and abuse that period of the child result in rise and fall of the person. A person is said to learn the greater part of what s/he should know about life and the world around during this formative years'. Even some of the physical development retarded by malnutrition at this stage cannot be recovered during the rest of the person's life. Childhood is therefore a time when the world around can contribute in shaping the person healthy, happy, and courageous to face the world. If the child of today is the parent of tomorrow how important it is to make that child a fully living person.

Beside the physical and intellectual development, the child at this stage develops the 'trust –psyche' or the 'mistrust- psyche', depending on how the mother or the world around treats the child from the time of birth. The mother or any surrogate care taker of the baby is said to communicate trust or mistrust to he baby by the way the baby's needs are met, caressed or stroked positively, or otherwise negatively impacted to develop mistrust of the world in which the baby is born.[1] In the child's life s/he either trusts or mistrusts the world and others depending on what it was experience in its first relationship. Only a rightly parented or healthily socialised child can experience life in its fullness. The present writer has inquired the subject using some of the following factors, like culture, faith tradition, science of human behavior, the legal system, and experience.

22:2. Children in Culture: In the culture of the mainland India the male child is said to do through several rituals *(samsaras)* to become fully human.[2]

1) *Namakarana* (0-1 month), the early infancy at which the mother ceremoniously places the baby at the father's lap for naming the child.

2) *Nishakarmana* (1-4 months), at which the baby is taken out look at the moon, which is to ritually introduce the child to the world and the cosmos.

3) *Annaprasana* (4-9months), at which the child is given solid food for the first time. This is the stage of weaning, the process of individuation and separation from the mother.

4) *Chudakarana* (three years) At three years the child is tonsured marking the child's psychological birth. The child is also taken to a temple of mother goddess and the baby's hair is offered to the mother goddess. The child is then clothed in white dress marking its separation from the mother to enter the community. After this tonsure only the child enters the stage of socialisation.

5) *Vidyarambha* (2-7 years) The child begins to read and write.

6) *Upanayana* (7-12 years) this is the child's social birth into the wider community. By now the child is aware of what is allowed and what is forbidden. The child, for the last time, shares food with the mother. Then, leaving the world of childhood the child enters the social birth.

Having underlined this childhood *Samsaras*, the cultural process that makes the boy child complete the childhood satisfactorily, Sudhir Kakar adds:

> "The Indian daughter is not severed from the company of her mother and other women in the household, although like brothers, she is given new, 'grown up household tasks and responsibilities... thus in folktales, however many sons a couple may have, there is often one daughter in their midst who is the parents favorite"[3]

In the present writer's tribal culture there are pre-natal and post-natal care for the person in the making. When the mother carries she is not exposed to any situation that may cause her stress or trauma lest the fetus is affected. The pregnant woman is not allowed to see dead body, which may shock her or cause her fear. She is not allowed to go to the jungle lest she meets tigers or bears that might frighten her. Tribals believe in magic and so the pregnant women is not allowed to eat fruit or vegetables that are irregular in shape, or animals and birds that are tabooed by the society. When the child is born the male child is named on the 6th day and the female child on the 5th day. On that day the child is lifted and places a while on the backs of the baby carriers, telling sex appropriate words or saying that may encourage the baby to grow up. After the naming ceremony the male child goes through series of rituals involving offering drinks and meat to senior members who are due to receive such tips and pray for the fortune of the child. Every ritual event grades the child letting him know that he is achieving and moving forward to adulthood. By the 15th year approximately, these ceremonies are completed and the boy in dignity enters the world of adults. The present writer grew up in a station outside the village where these ceremonies are not done. When he frequented his village he was often called a lay boy, meaning one who did not celebrate his boyhood and entertained the elders (*Boyhood samsakaras*).

The girls of the tribal families grew up without much of those developmental rituals but they were nevertheless well accepted in the family. Hard work, ingenuity in feminine arts and modesty in character are expected of the girls in the family. The parents are constantly reminded by the tradition that girls are like vegetables to be given anyway to the neighbor in marriage. Fullness of life among the tribal children are marred only by poverty, broken homes that caused hardship and the home situation which are not conducive for healthy growth. In such situations children are liable to hard labor, malnutrition, deprivation of fun and leisure. In such a situation the childhood becomes a;; work but no play, in a psychological terms. Till very recently tribal children are entirely in the mercy of the parents and adults and adults around them. There were no NGOs or Child's Right Societies who may help the children overcome the preventable misfortunes and disadvantages to grow healthier and live life to its fullest.

22:3 The Child and the Faith Tradition

In the Judeo-Christian tradition the child is a heritage from God and so gift to the human families (Ps. 127:3-5). Children came to the family for developing their childhood with the help of the parents and parents to take the divine responsibility to train them and bring up in the discipline of the Lord. The parents have the divine mandate to teach their children the word of God (Dt. 6: 6-7, Prov .1:8-9). Parents are advised to teach their children at the right time (Prov. 22:6), and not provoke them to anger and discouragement (Eph.6:4.Col .3:21). This procedure of upbringing was supposed to bring the children into fullness and happiness.

To Jesus, children are the model citizens in the new kingdom he was establishing. If the adult and the wise would enter his kingdom they should come to the gate and shed their critical faculty at the gate and enter the new kingdom of Jesus in simplicity and trust like a child (Mt. 19:13-15). Jesus accepted the praises of children as genuine and acceptable (Mt.21:15-16, cf.Ps8:2). Christian parents have the divine mandate to care, nurture, teach, and model children presentable to God. For, fully developed Christian child should be development of the body, the soul, the intellect, the social, and the spiritual (1Sam. 2:26,Lk.2:52).

22:4   The Child and Psychology

It is not enough for parents and the adult world to draw insight from culture and faith tradition alone to bring up children in their fullness of life. Church ministers often sideline the insight from human science and draw heavily from the scriptures to find guidance. But psychological insights have much to reveal and compliment the scriptures of human nature. In brief presentation like we can only highlight the basic truths that may help us help children grow to fullness of life. The above-mentioned 'formative years' of any person's life is a crucial period.

> A Jesuit priest is said to claim, *'give me power tutor the first seven years of any man's life, and he will not escape my influence although he live a thousand years'* [4]

The way parents and the adult world use or abuse this period causes the person to lose and win in life. For, it is said the child learns this period almost everything he/she has to learn the rest of the life. Freud would have the parents know the child's experience of acceptance, rejection, trauma, frustration, deprivation and repression, during this period and the parents deal with these factors wisely. In the child's psycho-sexual development their experience of Oedipus and Electra complex at this stage is to be noted seriously for a healthy development of their sexuality.

Eric Berne and the Transactional analysts would have the parents note factors that develop the *life positions*[5] early in their childhood. Transactional analysts believe everyone is born valuable and with capability. It is the parents and the adult world around the child who may shape the child either to healthy, happy and fully living personality or spoil the child to negativity and fatalism. Parents use of *strokes,* especially the positive strokes, are very vital factor in shaping a healthy personality. Human life begins with positive stroke in the form of the mother's milk, then continues through caressing, verbal encouragements and gestures of acceptance. The child is said to know those strokes, positive or negative even before it can speak.

What Eric Berne speaks of the *free child*[6] which is one of the ego states of a person of any age is comparable to a child who is living in fullness, For, the free child is spontaneous and joyful, fun loving and living life in full. But the adapted child is always conscious of the sanctions of the adult world and at times acts superficially just to please the adult world. A fully living child is not constricted by obligations moral demands and outside control with much do's and don'ts. The child is not to be overburdened by work beyond its capability. The present writer once took his 5 years old daughter to a school to admit her in Standard-1 but the Headmistress told him to keep her in KG-2, saying, 'let her enjoy her childhood, do not overburden her now'. The parents realised that keeping the daughter in Standard -1 at that age would have tied her down to the heavy assignments and routine work, thus robbing her of her real childhood at her age. It is true many parents expect their children to achieve beyond the children's capability. At times parents are said to pressure their children to achieve even those standards parents themselves could not achieve when young.

Considering the children's life from the psychological point of view one cannot but refer to the well-known development psychological point of view one cannot but refer to the well-known developmental psychologist, Erik Erikson.[7] It will suffice to mention the basic tenet of his theory for our guidance:

If the baby is helped to develop the **basic trust** through the affectionate relation with its mother or the world around, the child can live confidently and face the world in trust relationships. If at this early period the baby is neglected or rejected a **mistrust** of the mother and the rest of the relationship will be developed. With this early impression of mistrust the baby will grow to live mistrusting itself and the rest of the world. This person cannot live life in fullness because s/he does not enjoy living. Here the attitude of *I am not OK,* is formed.

This child will live in fear, suspicion, feeling of rejection and uncertainty. On the other hand the baby with the *trust psyche* will trust self and others and aspire to actualize in life. That is to live life in its fullness without constriction by fear and suspicion.

The next stage in the gaining of **autonomy** by the growing child, by trial and error process the child must learn how to do things itself without depending on the adults. When parents overprotect and over control the child they communicate to the child that s/he cannot do anything without the parents help. This is unhealthy way of parenting because the child becomes dependent. The child must explore, fall and rise to learn the art of living. Over imposition of parental values and authority suppresses the child from spontaneous living. The child should also establish its **identity** as a unique individual. The last of the eight stage of growth by Erikson is very interesting. Erikson says that those who live each of this stage of growth successfully they reach the last stage-integration, whereupon the person is satisfied that life was worth living and that s/he lived it well. This person will not fear death but accept it as a stage in growth. On the other hand the person who live these stage of life haphazardly and deceiving oneself, that person will reach the last stage-**despair.** This person will be scared to face death. In other words, Erikson would say that one who lives each of the stages successfully is a fully living person.

22:5   The Right of the Child

The right of the child in a given cultural including the law of the land are meant to promote fullness to life to the children. Perhaps all cultures have provisions for protecting children's rights. In tribal culture, especially in the present writer's culture there are commonly accepted rights and privileges of the child, namely, the right to be given the best part of the food, the right to be fed first, right to be protected at any cost, even prior to the comfort and safety of the adults, right to be excused at fault and right to be loved by all at all circumstances.

The law of the land has many clauses to protect the rights of the children. The law has its concessions toward children, the separate juvenile court being an example.

The machineries of national and international legislations protect children's rights. The International Year of the Child is observed to make the cause of the children known worldwide. The International Committee on the Right of the Child, National Policy and Charter for Children (India 2001) and National Commission for children, beside many NGOs, to cite a few. Such forums aim to foster *survival, protection,* and *development* of the child. Joshi[8] defines each of these provisions, thus:

Survival is a right now denied to more than fifteen million children under the age limit of five, who die every day on account of a cause that are easily preventable. The term **Protection** also connotes the child's rights to a name and nationality. Every child has the right to be shielded from abuse –physical, mental, or sexual and from involvement in warfare. **Development** implies the child's right to adequate nutrition, primary health care and basic education. These rights are to guarantee children fullness of life in their childhood through better learning, and enough play. And more importantly, love and affection in abundance is a must.

22:6   Implication for Care

Caring for children will require considering the factors highlighted above, such as cultural sanction resources from faith traditions behavioral issues, and life experience. Must like the advice in the book of Proverbs the cultural insight for Children's welfare are concrete and practical. Many celebrities in India avow their parents' admonitions and encouragement, which are rooted in the tradition and culture of India. As children are more exposed to what may be called *"evolving culture* 'today, the parents and teachers need examine such new cultures to see that are not detrimental to life in fullness understood from our context. For, the components of life in fullness may not be the same across cultures. Christians often talk of the Gospel values as the litmus test of any cultural values. This should be so as long as we approach from the ministerial or pastoral launch pad.

The behavioral science is often sidelined by the Church ministers. There are such ministry who claim that the Bible is the guide to all human needs and actions and so there is no need of valuing the insights from other disciplines of the world, whether it is of science, medicine or psychology. That way Christian minister throw out that non-biblical insight in strengthening even the biblical teaching where applicable. Does it not help us to understand Paul's inner struggle in the light of the theory of the unconscious mind (Rom.7:7)? Does it not help us to understand passages like Psalm 32:3 ff better in the light of the function of catharsis in human emotion? How much better to read Proverbs 22:6 in context of the Freudian theory of the formative years? Or Proverbs 22:6 in context of the Fredian theory of the formative years? Or of Paul's advise to parents in Eph.6:4, Col.3:21, in context of repression of strong emotion?

The ministers need to acknowledge that the advent of the behavioral science has revolutionised our understanding of human nature and thus advanced life to live in fullness. Children today are more burdened with the rapidly changing values, their developmental crisis, their higher motivations countered by want of resources to pursue, their innocent faith in the exaggerated media, their need of preparation to enter this competitive world – all these require professional help for children to face the day. Therefore, higher training of the help for children to face the day. Therefore, higher training of the helping profession using insights from many sources is called for.

One frequently prescribed method of ministry to the children today is the **Play Therapy** [9] as a very comprehensive approach. Play therapy not only solves their problems but also instills creativity and socialisation. Children begin to learn how to solve their problem themselves. The helping person and the family are often involved in play therapy. Initially the child may be alone while the helpers keep a watch and later the others may also join in. As play is a natural expression for children it becomes effective. Children rarely deal in logical or abstract thoughts but they major in concrete and practical activities. Parents are advised to let the children play at home with their own toys and parents themselves joining in the play.

Most importantly, the pastoral care taker to children should also see that the children become aware of the presence of the unseen Spirit – God. To understand this unseen God the parents and caretaker have to demonstrate God in their own life examples. Each of the Eriksonian stages of development referred to above can be seen from the spiritual perspective too. If the mother can instill the basic trust to the baby and if that trust psyche is used later to affiliate with God in trust relationship, the mother is rightly called the first evangelist to the soul. This can be future studies in light of James Fowler's Stage of Faith Development. [10] This love relationship at home is drawn from the love of God who first loved us and in whose names all families are named. Children should therefore be taught what it means by loving God, loving neighbor as self. Dignity of life is given in its fullness by God alone. God the Creator guards the sanctity of life and dignity of His image in humans of all ages including the children. Therefore, respect for this God-given life should be taught to the children.

The nature of children's growth can take the pattern of Jesus' growth as a child: growth in wisdom (psychological), in stature (physical), in favor with God (spiritual) and with human (social). Howard J.Clinebell, the internationally acclaimed pastoral teacher, trainer and counselor speaks of six dimensional human growths[11] The six dimension are: growth enlivening one's mind; growth vitalising one's body; growth renewing our relationships; growth relating to the biosphere; growth in relating to organisations and institution, and finally, spiritual growth, Clinebell points out that, of these six dimensions of growth spiritual growth is the center around which all other dimensions revolve.

In Clinebell's own words

> Spiritual growth is the key to all human growth. Because human beings are inherently transpersonal and transcendent, there is no way to "fulfill" oneself except in relation to the larger spiritual reality. By experience an intimate growing relationship with this reality, we connect with the Sources of all growth and creativity. Spiritual growth work aims at liberating "vertical dimension" of our lives. It seeks to liberate our belief system, our values, and our relationship with God so that our lives will become more open to these deep well-springs of growth."[12]

We can talk of life fullness only in relation to the One who gives that life in abundance, the ground of our beings. Therefore, spiritual development of the children becomes essential part of their growth. The ministers will do well to organize seminars and consultation for educating the parents to facilitate luxuriant growth of the children with whatever resources available in the given families. Family education seminars and retreat are important to enable the parents to foster methods that children grow in fullness. The parents are the immediate guardians of the child and the parents should see that their over ambitions and undue expectation from the child does not rob the fullness of childhood. If all parents are oriented on what *J.Piaget* talks of the stages of cognitive development, what E.Erikson talks of the stages of psycho-social development, *L.Kohlberg* of moral development, *S.Freud* of psycho-sexual development, *J.Fowller* of faith development, then they will be better equipped to understand their children and not lay undue burdens to rob their childhood. The French philosopher and educationist, *Jean Jacques Rousseau,*

Regretted in his old age why he mistakenly put all his infants in founding homes that spoiled their childhood for want of parental affection at home. His famous book, *Emile* (Written in 1762) was written to correct the parental of his time. Emile, was Rousseau's imaginary child who he wanted to live as animals, just as a child of nature, to let the child have a chance to be a vegetable and animal first of all, not to try to make a social being out of him/her until s/he ready to be one.[13] Not many parents may go to the extreme Rousseau took but he had a lesson for parents in that the latter often socialised the kids prematurely and impose adult values on the child instead of allowing the child to enjoy his/her childhood in fullness. Even as Christian ministers are oriented with the developmental psychology of the child the teachers and the caretaker should also be informed in this matter. The curriculum of the schools should also have this basic truth about the shaping of the human person in childhood.

Let this section be concluded with a poem on The Child's Appeal by Mamie Gene Cole:

I am the child.

    All the world waits for my comings.

    All the earth watches with interest to see what I shall become.

    Civilisations hangs in the balance,

    For what I am, the world of tomorrow will be

I am the child.

    I have come into your world, about which I know nothing.

    Why I came I know not;

    How I came I know not.

    I am curious; I am interested

I am the Child.

    You hold in your hand my destiny.

    You determine, largely, whether I shall succeed or fail.

    Give me, I pray you, those things that make for happiness.

    Train me, I beg you that I may be blessing to the world.[14]

Youth is sometimes considered not a matter of age but a state of mind. However, technically a youth is a person living between childhood and adulthood. It is also considered in three stages early adolescence (10-14) middle adolescence (11-24) and later adolescence (25-30).

In any country, youth is considered a powerful force. This force can be misdirected by wrongly motivated leaders or it can be properly guided to fight evils of the society. In India it is reported that youth population is 40% and above of the total population.

Youth is a period of transition - from dependence to independence, from parental protection and care to a world of autonomy, from idealism to reality encounters in practical life etc. They face various developmental crises, physical changes, emotional and psychological changes and crises of identity in the society. As physical changes take place they can be sometimes depressed, impulsive, and irrational. They are sometimes misunderstood by the society as "terrible teens", "trouble maker" or even "ungodly" or "anti-social". Sometimes they in turn brand the parents as "oldies", "policemen" they feel they are always misunderstood and pre-judged.

An educationist, Reuel Howe, cautions us - "We should not conclude that life with young people consists of problems only. For, the truth is, adolescents are exciting, companionable, mysterious, lovable and loving, and they move through their days with all their speed, thrill and ups and downs."

Youth problem can be multiple. We cannot deal with all of the problems youth face as they grow to maturity. Let us see two models of youth that may help us to understand youth. We cannot avoid referring to these classic studies when we talk of youth.

22:7   Erik Erikson

As a developmental Psychologist Erikson based his study of human growth on a psychosocial development. His eight stages of growth is a renowned model in the study of persons. Erikson holds that development is a two fold process in which the psychological development of individuals (that is, their personalities and views of themselves) grow along with the social relations they establish as they grow day by day through life. He says, a person goes through eight stages, each stage the individual faces new situations and encounters new problems (psychosocial crises).

That is, either they *emerge from the new experience with greater maturity and richer personalities or, they may fail to cope successfully with the problems resulting in the arrest of development. Our knowledge of these dynamics of growth will greatly enhance our help to let them grow to happy and responsible citizens.*[1]

CHART:

	Stage	Crisis	Favourable outcome	Unfavourable outcome
Childhood				
infancy	*First year of life	Trust versus mistrust future events.	Faith in the environment.	Suspicion, fear of future events.
early childhood	*Second year	Autonomy versus doubt.	A sense of self-control and ade-quacy.	Feelings of shame and self-doubt.
play age	*Third through fifth years	Initiative versus guilt.	Ability to be a 'self-starter', to initiate one's	A sense of guilt and inadequancy to be one's own.
school age	*Sixth year to puberty	Industry versus inferiority	Ability to learn how things work, to understand and organize.	A sense of inferi-ority at underst-anding and orga-nising.
Transition Years				
	*Adolescence	Identity versus confusion	Seeing oneself as a unique and integrated person..	Confusion over who and what one really is.
Adulthood				
	*Early adulthood	Intimacy versus isolation	Ability to make commitments to others, to love.	Inability to form affectionate rela-tionships.
	*Middle age	Generativity versus self-absorption	Concern for family and so-ciety in general.	Concern only for self-one's own well-being and prosperity.
	*Aging years	Integrity versus despair	A sense of inte-grity and fulfill-ment; willingness to face death.	Dissatisfaction with life; despair over prospect of death.

22:8 Moral Development

The second model of development is that of Lawrence Kohlber's stages of moral development. The moral behaviour of early years are mostly based on a desire to obtain approval and avoid criticism. When they reach adolescence, the standards take a new form, dictated not by mere self-interest but by principles. The following is Kohlberg's model of moral development:[2]

Preconventional Level Seven year old Children are oriented to the conse-quences of their behaviour :

Stage1: Defer to the power of adult and obey rules to avoid troubles and punishment. Here the behaviour is based on self interest, to avoid punishment and get reward.
Stage 2: Seek to satisfy their own needs by behaving in a manner that will gain rewards and the return of favours.

Conventional Level :

Stage 3: Want to be "good" in order to please and help others and thus receive approval. Behaviour seeking people's approval.
Stage 4: Want to "do their duty" by respecting authority (parent, teacher, God) and maintraining the social order for its own sake.

Postconventional Level :

Stage 5: Think in terms of the rights of others; the general welfare of the community; and a duty to conform to the laws and standards established by the will of the majority. Behave in ways they believe would be respected by an impartial observer. Become concerned with abstract moral values and dictates of their own conscience.
Stage 6: Consider not only the actual laws and rules of society but also their own selfchosen standards of justice and respect for human dignity. Behave in a way that will avoid condemnation by their own conscience.

22:9 Areas of Youth Problems

Elizabeth Hurlock has underlined some of the problems of the growing youth as follows:[3]

1. Problems Relating to Home: Relationship with family members, discipline.

2. Relating to School: Grades, relationships with teachers and friends, extra-curricular activities.

3. Relating to Physical Condition: Health, exercise.

4. Relating to Appearance: Weight, attractiveness of features, sex appropriateness.

5. Relating to Emotions: Temper outburst, moodiness.

6. Relating to Social Adjustment: Acceptance by peers, leadership roles.

7. Relating to Vocation: Choice, training.

8. Relating to Values: Morals, drugs, sex.

9. Relating to Modernity: Novelty, Science, Etiquette (Not Hurlock's)

Besides the above which are more of personal problems, there are also some common problems, concerns caused by the identity confusion of the growing youth: *Achieving greater independence, being misunderstood or misjudged by others,* and *having more rights and privileges and fewer* responsibilities imposed by the parents. Special difficulties arise from problems *like achieving economic independence, assuming the approved sex* role, and *preparing for family life*. These problem are intensified if the developmental task (See above, Erikson's) of childhood has not been mastered.

22:10 Developing a helping Relationship with Youth

1. *The importance of Trust and Acceptance*: We have seen from Erikson's stages of human development that trust is a key factor in a person's relationship with the world around. This trust is first developed by the mother (or others in lieu of the mother). This trust becomes a great need in certain individuals (e.g., the I AM NOT OK people). By nature, youth will react to authority and power but they can be appealed by a trusting relationship where confidentiality is respected. In such relationship they can express freely to the helper. This requires the helper's attitude of love and *acceptance* that makes the youth feel confident and worth. Many youth problems are caused by the rejection of the parents or the society.

The concept of acceptance is a vital factor in counseling. Acceptance of the person irrespective of creed, status, sex or behaviour is the pre-condition of any therapeutic relationship. In fact some of the destructive behaviours of youth are due to their search for recognition and acceptance by the group (smoking, drinking, drug use, crimes or moral laxity etc.). Many pastors are found to be *moralistic, authoritarian* and *judgemental*. Such an attitude will simply create a chasm between the youth and the care takers. Acceptance does not mean condoning of evil. In an accepting relationship moral and intellectual questions are bracketed, at least for a time, to concentrate in the wounded person (cf. the Good Samaritan). However heinous the behaviour may be the person is a creation of God who for a moment is entangled in trouble, and thus in need of other human beings. This attitude is much like Jesus' attitude of disapproving the sinful behaviour but loving and accepting the person. Pastoral counselors find this ground as their need of accepting the erring person. For, "while we were yet sinners, Jesus died for us." Recently, an American Narcotic expert spoke in a seminar in India saying, all care takers of the addict must remember the 3A's: Attention-Acceptance-Affection. It is true that many a times the society is indifferent to the needs and problems of youth, often branding them with negative labels. If we pay attention to their needs they can be appealed. So also, without a genuine affection for them we cannot enter into a helpful relationship. Carl Rogers, emphasizes genuineness as one inevitable quality of a helper. This is more so in helping youth. (See also p. 186)

2. *Listening and Catharis*: The society is often negative and prejudiced against youth. Prejudice implies 'judging before', even before listening to the story. For this section, see above, 'Listening' and Catharsis.

3. *Confession*: Many a times young people realize the way they had failed to live up to their own expectations (also parental and societal expectations) this causes guilt feelings and the need of confession thereof.

The helper's sympathetic listening and reflecting of feelings will help them hear their own feelings and expressions and thus prepare them to deal with them. Confidential respect on the part of the helper will be very important in such situations. Besides, the pastoral helper's reassurance of God's love and forgiveness will encourage the youth to change. The person may also be asked to join church groups and actively involve in common life of the church.

4. *The Helpers Attitude*: As young people sometimes tend to be negative and cynical the helper should have a positive attitude and help the person to think positively (the power of positive thinking). The helper should have the attitude of sympathy, understanding and communicate a caring attitude even when the person is found guilty. Compassion to human situations like that of Christ's is a standard attitude for any caring situation. I AM OK, YOU ARE NOT OK attitude (that is, 'holier than thou' attitude) is not helpful. The helper's humble attitude as that of Christ's is expected. Wayne E. Oates, a veteran pastoral

counselor, suggests that the helping person should be a 'brother-man' (or sister-woman) to the person in need. This is also to mean, the helper is a *wounded healer* too, as seen above.

The above points are few among other skills of helpers which may be considered constant in all helping situations. In all these, the helper's insights from the scriptures, cultural heritage and the science of human behaviour are the sources of information.

22:11 Human Ageing

Ageing is the gradual decay of the human organic system, becoming more marked toward the end of life, ending in the breakdown of the system and finally, in death. These changes are not pathological but biological. Thus ageing is not a source of regret or loss. It is a sign of progress and fulfillment of life. As the person gets older the society and the government increase their respect and call them *"senior citizen'*.

Some of the common manifestations of old age are: body slow down, hearing weakened, limbs swell and tremor, loss of energy, feeling unwanted, loss of purpose in life, loss of one's own destiny, feeling abandoned, not touched or loved, depressed, falls, decreased mobility, incontinence, fear and loneliness increased and there is a new realisation of the nearness of death. These are the dominant symptoms of geriatrics. Above all, loneliness is the pain of a felt inability to satisfy the basic human need for intimate relation with other persons. It is an unpleasant, subjective experience. Adam, was lonely and God gave Adam a companion. Human existence is relational as they are social beings.

The Bible tells us of Methuselah, exceptionally living for 969 years. However, many of the patriarchs lived well pass 100 years. The Bible affirms that wisdom increased by age (Job 12:12), it also shows the older people' experience of rejection and frustrations) Ps 71:18). Ecclesiastes 12 pictures the old age in pessimistic manner but realistic, anyway.

All is not, however, a modern 'vanity' of 'vanities'. Every person including those who are old can find meaning in life when one finds God and keeps God's commandments (Eccl.12:13). While young people have strength the elderly should be respected for their wisdom and experience (Lev.19:32; Prov. 16;13,20:29). In turn the elderly are to be temperate, dignified , sensible, sound in faith, loving and willing to persevere, teaching what is good and not malicious gossip or excessive drinkers (Titus 2:2-3). This is a picture of hope and in no way should this be more apparent than in the community of believers. Christian are commanded to honor their parents, that it may go well with them and that they may enjoy long life on earth (Eph.6:3). The Bible is realistic and its portrayal of old age positive in its attitude toward the value of old age, and specific in its command toward how we should treat old people. They are to be respected, cared for and loved as human beings (G.R.Collins, Christian counseling)

According to a developmental psychologist, Erik Erikson, old age is the eighth stage of a person's life cycle. This stage is either the stage of **integrity** or despair. Integrity in simple meaning is, "a sense of coherence and wholeness resulted from the positive living out of the earlier stages. Such a person, "has taken care of things and people and has adapted oneself to the triumphs and disappointed of being, by necessity, the originator of others and generator of things and ideas". He/she has inherited the fruit of the previous stages. Such a gradually mature person has the matured fruit- that is integrity. The opposite experience is **despair** that reveals an often unconscious fear of death. The person experiencing despair will feel time was so short, too short for the attempt to start another life and to try out alternative roads to integrity (Identity and Life Cycle p. 104). The pastoral concern for the aged will imply recognising the later life as a part of the abundant life rather than ill fate or pathological. We should also recognize the image of God in the old, the weak and broken. The older people are still humans with their right to be loved, cared by the rest of the family of God. This will imply that, when possible, the family should keep the old in their homes and extend affection and care. Homes for the aged are fine when familial care is not possible, but such homes are not the best when the other members of the family live in their homes and the older one left to the care of the institutions. Whether at home or in other institutions love for the aged should continue.

Caring for the aged will also require recognition of their experience (psychological or physical), the common phenomena of ageing and responding to such special needs in a caring manner. The Church as a caring community should reinforce the cultural ethics that regulates people to be kind and sympathetic to the old people. Today, even the terminally ill caring them with the family affection and making them die in dignity and love. So should the attitude of the society be towards the aged person.

ENDNOTES

1. Erik H. Erikson, *in his Identity and the Life Cycled: selected papers (New York, International Univ.Press, 1978)* pp. 55-100. See also his childhood and society (NY, W.W.Norton, 1950/1963).

2. Sudhir Kakar , a renown Indian psychoanalyst, has written two books on childhood in India, namely, *Indian Childhood (Delhi, Oxford University Press, 1979)*, and *The Inner World* (OUP Delhi,1978).

3. Sudhir Kakar, *Indian Childhood: Cultural Ideals and Social Reality (Delhi, Oxford University Press,1979)* p.39.

4. W.L. Carrington, *Psychology, Religions and Human Need: A Guide for Ministers, Doctors, Teacher & Social Workers* (London, Ephworth, 1957, 1961), p.22.

5. See Thomas Harris, *I am OK, you are Ok* (Harper& Row, 1969).

6. Eric Berne, Transactional analysis in Psychotherapy, (Ballantine Books, NY 1961). Followed by many other books on this theory, viz., Games People play, What *do you say after you say Hello...* etc.

7. Erik H.Erikson, *Identity and life Cycle...*

8. Uma. Joshi, 'The Rights of the Child' in *Sentine 1*, Oct, 28, 2001.

9. V.Axline, *Play Therapy: The Inner Dynamics of Childhood,* (New York, Ballantine Books, 1974).

10. J.W.Fowler, *Stages of Faith Development,* 1981. See also.
J.W. Fowler, *Faith Development and Pastoral Care,* 1987.

11. H.J.Clinebell, *Growth Counseling: Hope-centered Methods of Actualising Human Wholeness* (Nashville, Abingdon, 1979/1988).

12. H.J Clinebell, *Growth Counseling,* p.101.

13. Donald Butler, *Religious Education,* p.72.

14. From Charles Wallis, *Worship Resources for the Christian Year* (New York, Harper Row, 1954) p.297.

15. Kakan and Havemann, *Psychology,* Hardcourt Press, Jouvanorich, Inc. N. York, London: Toronto, 1968, 1980, pp.501 & 505.

    For more details, see Clinebell, Basic Types..., *op.cit.*

16. Kakan Havemann, *op.cit.,* p.501.

17. Elizabeth Hurlock, *Adolescent Development,* MacGraw Hill, Tokyo, London, Delhi, 1973, 1955, p.8.

CHAPTER 23

Sex and Marriage

The talk on human sexual behaviour range from extremes of asceticism to license. The Church takes a position in between. The church takes sex as a good creation of God. Its abuse to promiscuity and selfish gratification is not approved by the Church. The married couple experiences mutual affection and satisfaction in the spirit of 'companionship'. The Church holds that sexual relationship should be confined to married couples, and that marriage should be monogamous and for life time.

In the Old Testament, we find the newly married man excused from a military service for one year to be with his wife and cheer her (Deut. 24:5). Infidelity was not tolerated. No adultery permitted. Both the sexes involved had to be killed (Ex. 20:14, Lev. 20:10). There were cases of polygamy in the O.Testament, like, Abraham, Jacob, Lamech, David, Solomon, etc. for some reasons, like their insignificant number in the midst of great nations. Intercourse with the same sex or with animals were prohibited. The men of Sodom who tried to violate that law and abuse the male guests of Lot was 'sodomy' from the city sodom (Lev. 18:23, Ex. 22:19). *Onanism,* (coitus interruptus) is another term used today related to human sexual behaviour (withdrawal) from Onan, who refused to raise children for his deceased brother as the law of Levirate required Gen. 38:9.

The Greco-Roman world has also left a profile in today's understanding of sexuality. Roland Bainton, has quoted Epictetus as saying, "He who looking at a woman says, "Lucky is her husband" has already committed adultery with her in his heart.[1] Family planning seems to have existed as early as 100 B.C., for, the drugs relating to abortion and 'atokeion', and drugs relating to contraception seem to have been used early. The stoics considered life as formed at the moment of birth itself. Platonic tradition would place the time of concepting for the presence of the soul. Aristotle believed the soul is formed at the 40th day from the conception for male and at the 90th day for female. Bainton, opines that the church at one time took this position when the translators of the Septuagint added phrases not found in the original, like, "life for life for a miscarriage in case the embryo was formed already, or differently if the embryo is yet unfound'. This matter is found in Ex. 21, 22, 23). This was to mean that when the foetus resembled human, the miscarriage was retributed by life.

In the N. Testament, we find the Kingdom of God and its cause primary and everything else secondary in the life of the believers. This is especially so because of their expectation of the imminent return of the Lord. Marriage and family life was not important when they were in conflict with the call of the Kingdom. Lk. 14:26, speaks of forsaking parents or siblings for Mt. 19:12, refers to one who became eunuch for the sake of the Kingdom of God. We find Jesus also teaching like that of Epictetus' in regard to looking at a woman with lust (Mt. 5:28). But Jesus seems to have reaffirmed the Mosaic law regarding marriage and divorce (Mt. 19 or Mk. 10). Divorce was allowed only in the case of adultery. Pauline opinion on the topic is also in context of the imminent return of the Lord. Marriage was to be optional, depending on the degree of one's urge for sex (2 Cor. 7, 1 Thess. 5:3-6), but virginity was preferred. However Eph. 5:32 and Heb. 13:4 are texts honouring marriage as sacred. Human marriage is also compared with the spiritual marriage of the church with her groom Jesus Christ. Although the situation in which he lived made Paul write implying womens' subjugation, his attitude towards women was that of equality in the sight of God (Gal. 3:28). In Pauline equation, the woman was taken out of man but man is born of woman. So, Paul would emphasizes on mutuality and equality of the sexes.

An outstanding religious educationist, Reuel Howe, declares that we should use things but love humans. We should not value the person's ability more than the person's being. One can reduce his/her neighbours to things by exploiting their functions. "The evil of prostitution and promiscuity is that it is an act against the person whose function is thus exploited and becomes a sexual thing; and being an act against the person, it is also an act against the structure of relationship of which the person is a part. According to Howe:

> "A holy sexual relationship is one in which the interrelatedness and wholeness of function and being are preserved and honoured in thought and act. In holy love the lover 'loves, honours and cherishes' his beloved as a person... in this sense is sexual sacramental, for the act is an outward and visible sign of the mutual union between two persons in which functions serves its real purpose, which is to be instrument for the realisation of the fullness of being."

Howe continues, "It is now necessary to make very clear that sex expression needs marriage to give it meaning which in itself it does not have."

On the theology of sex, Howe affirms that there are only two sexes, man and woman, He says,

> "There is man who is not complete within himself, and female who is not complete and sufficient within herself... that is, woman was made to complete man and man to complete woman, anatomically, biologically, emotionally, mentally and spiritually."

Spiritualising the sexual urge in humans, Howe affirms again,

> "A part of the power of sex drive springs from the longing of the incomplete being for completion. The separation is intolerable, and a divided creation groans and suffers, longing for union and fulfilment."

So, sexual act is considered a sacramental act to complete humanity, to make whole the estranged creation. It is also said that the word SEX itself comes from a Latin word meaning completion or union. In this sense, sex in Christian understanding is God's gift, sacred to be expressed within the married structure. Its abuse has no place in Christian understanding. We read so much about its abuse in the developed societies. The church is faced with not only the question of homosexuality among its members but also among the clergy. So also is with the question of pre-marital sex and the question of abortion, the question of the use of condoms in the face of the pandemic, AIDS or STI. In the midst of reports of such laxity there are also reports of Western societies opting for single sex partners and restraining from pre-marital sex. A recent Forerunner report is an example;

> "YOUTH PLEDGE SEXUAL PURITY: (USA) A full page newspaper advertisement headlined: 'In defence of little virginity' has been running in hundreds of cities in the United States. It was run by Focus on the family in the Daily, USA TODAY.

This prompted many individuals, Churches and organisations to pay for running the ad in their own cities.

It has now appeared in 1000 news papers in United States, 273 in Canada, 31 school news papers and in seven other countries, meanwhile, about 500,000 teenagers are now expected to sign pledge cards to remain virgins until marriage.

> The Southern Baptists' "True Love Waits" campaign is said to be receiving wide national support and unusual media coverage.[6]

Related to such issues is the question of self-gratification that fills periodicals like Teenager (masturbation). The pastoral counselors may not see such ways of meeting sexual needs as healthy. However, the myths usually associated with masturbation as physically harmful is often dealt by physicians as harmless. The guilt feeling associated with the act is said to cause an immense harm to the mental state of the youth which the pastoral counselors can help resolve such fears realistically.

One thing that the church will always believe is that family is the ground of the society. A wholesome belief in human sexuality and thus a proper respect of love and marriage will build a sound society where each will respect oneself and the others, minimize self-indulgence and increase love and respect for the other, and for God. Sex should be used to complete the broken creation, not estrange the creation from itself and God.

Marriage is a divinely ordained union with a moral purpose. A person may choose to remain single on a moral ground too. The society should not underestimate persons who choose to remain single for God has plans also for those remaining single for good reasons. When a man and a woman decide to unite in marriage God gives them responsibilities related to married life. The spouse (and children if any) becomes the immediate reference person(s) in living a life of witness in respect of charity, honesty, sanctity and accountability of the person before God. For instance, that spouse cannot be more godly, truthful and responsible in the eye of the society than s/he can be to the spouse or children. When a couple is not assigned to have children God may have many other alternative missions for that couple to that couple. The impaired fertility is not in the wife always as believed in the villages. The impairment can be in either of the two spouses.

Christian boys and girls should determine to live respectable lives and present themselves to the spouse their best in all respects to the spouse. This is important especially in respect of their sexual relationships. In normal marriages about ten to fifteen years of longing, anticipations and expectations is consummated as the spouses unfold each other's treasure to share with the only one whom she/he loves. This is an event of celebration of joy – a joy shared not only by the two but also to which the world wishes them the best. There is no law against this legitimate joy, which is from God. Irresponsible living, impatience and selfish desire can mar this moment of highest joy, a joy made for each other by God. This happiness awaits all those persons who wait prayerfully for that great day of union – a union that triggers a new mile in the pilgrimage of life.

ENDNOTES

1. Roland Bainton, 'Christianity and Sex' in *Pastoral Psychology*, 1952, Sept.

2. Reuel Howe, 'A Pastoral Theology of Sex and Marriage' *Ibid.*

3. *Ibid.*

4. *Ibid.*

5. *Ibid.*

6. Forerunner, Bangalore, April, 1994.

CHAPTER 24

Social Education for Combating AIDS and Drug Abuse

Drug abuse and AIDS are the twin enemies of humanity today. Both are agents of slow killing that can catch us unaware. This epidemic is no longer foreigners' problems but realities in our midst that claim so many of our loved-ones. This problem affects not only the victims and the helpers but the whole community. The whole community needs to be informed for a concerted fight against this common enemy. We have been living with these ailments for some years and are now inured to its threat. Most of us are flooded with facts and information about them and so, elementary information are eliminated here in this section. What is mentioned below are some of the ways of recognising and combating the epidemic.

A. DRUG ABUSE

24:1. Drug Abuse

A drug is any substance, other than food, that produces changes in the physical or mental functioning of an individual. *Drug* abuse refers to 'Taking a drug for other than medical reasons in *amount, strength, frequency* or *manner* that damages the physical and mental functions.' Addiction is 'a state of physical or psychological dependence or both, in a person, who has taken the drug periodically or continually.'

Causes

Drugs are life-saving substances when used properly. When they are abused, they destroy life. Tragically, people abuse drug when they want to *experiment, to be one of the gang, to avoid responsibilities,* to *relieve boredom, for kicks to help human relation,* to become *more creative, to escape unhappiness,* to *reduce anxiety* and *tension*, and such other assumptions. However, drug abuse never solves problems nor brings happiness. Drug abusers fulfil the old saying, "from the frying pan into the fire". Humanity has proved by experience that an attempt to avoid life's realities by use of drugs only lands them to tragedy ! Young people can be allured by such seeming short cut to happiness only to find themselves clutched by the jaws of death !

24:2   The Drug Scene in India

Besides those illegally cultivated and processed in India, there are two main outside sources of drug supply to India: The GOLDEN CRESCENT (Iran, Afghanistan and Pakistan) on the immediate west of India, and the GOLDEN TRIANGLE, (Myanmar, Laos and Thailand), on the immediate east of India. The product from the Golden-Crescent goes through Karachi to Mumbai for further shipment to Europe and North America, and hence the chance to flow in to India. The two highest producers of Opium in the world are said to be Myanmar (60% of world total produce), and Afghanistan (following Myanmar).[1] India is engulfed by these two top world producers of opium. It is reported that Mumbai city alone has 1 lakh addicts. India, estimated to have 50-70 lakh addicts presently will have 15 millions addicts by 2000 A.D.[2] It is reported that five people die daily of addiction in India. (Some other report 30-50 millions Indian addicts by 2000 A.D.)

The North-east India has a 1600 k.m. border with Myanmar, the highest opium producer in the world. The frequent seizure of narcotics in the region justify that there is a major link between the Golden Triangle and the North-East. Consequently, Nagaland and Manipur are reported to have the highest addicts in the country. It is estimated that Manipur has 30,000 addicts and Nagaland 10,000.[3] Though the evil is very much present in other states of the North-East they are not as threatening as Manipur and Nagaland. Perhaps Mizoram will figure next to these two leading states, followed by Meghalaya and Assam. Tripura and Arunachal will have the least addicts. In 1992, a group of experts from SARRC reported that, of the 100,000 addicts in Delhi there were several thousand children. The report said, "The horrifying yet pathetic fact is that there are at least 10,000 child smack addicts in Delhi alone."[4]

24:3   Causes of Drug Addiction

The team of experts from the South Asia Association for Regional Co-operation (SAARC) identified some of the causes of drug addiction as:

- gradual slackening of parental control

- erosion of moral values

- frustrations arising out of socio-economic problems

- large scale westernisation

- affects of films and pornography

- lack of recreation

- chronic pains.[5]

Some young people take drugs hardly as an expression of revolt against traditional norms and values. However, "of the students taking to drug hardly any realize the implications which would make their life an agony and totally unproductive."

Ignorance on the part of the user, group pressure, availability, broken relationships, parental neglect and failures in life, are other causes of drugs use.

24:4   Symptoms to Recognise Drug use

Symptoms will vary depending on the kind of substance used. However, among the common signs are follows:

A.   *Change in Behaviour and Life Style*

Unexpected change in mood and attitude, secrecy about activities and whereabouts being deceptive or lying, change of friends, loss of interest in studies, with a fall in grades, selling of personal and household goods, change in food habits depending on the kind of drug used. Sleeplessness or oversleeping, loss of interest in cleanliness, indifference towards family activities, use of sun-glasses (even in the night), and such radical change of behaviour.

B.   *Changes in Physical Conditions*

Pretending to be *drunk,* slurred speech or *overemphasis* on words, *tremor, red eyes* or watering eyes, *out of focus or glassy,* complaining of *regular illness* to hide the effects of drugs, *constipation* from reduction of appetite etc. Loss of short-term *memories,* craving for *sweets,* occasional *vomits late* nights, waking up at night to have a smoke (or may leave home early with a sense of urgency if the home atmosphere is not conducive).

C. *Signs of Presence of Drugs*

Injection marks on arms and other parts of the body, blood stains on the clothes, presence of the items used in taking the drug, syringes, silver paper, small boxes and tightly rolled paper packets in the bed room, discovery of drugs from smell of drugs like cannabis, loose unused tobacco. Use of heroin can be found out by a laboratory test or the urine of the suspected person. Cigarette burns (holes in the clothing), burnt finger tips (esp. thumb and middle finger) skin rash (due to adulterated substance in making up "brown sugar"), irregular menstrual cycles in the case of women.

As mentioned above, symptoms may vary depending on the kind of substance used or even in different individuals. These few listed above are collected from a presentation by 'HOPE' (Bangalore), and from the list of Benjamin Lobo, an addict who became a counselor. Lobo and Jessica, in their book, 'The Answer to Drug Addiction' suggest even to be cautious about *Potential Addict* if we are to be vigilant for preventive readiness:

Treatment of the addict being pre-dominantly medical, the society may do well to check situations conducive to drug use as preventive measures. Lobo and Jessica identify the following conditions contributing to children's addiction:

An *overprotected child* with consequent low frustration tolerance. In India, this category may include the *eldest* or the *youngest son,* or the son born after 2 or 3 daughters. At the other extreme, neglect/or rejection of the child causes feelings of *inadequacy or inferiority* complex in the child.

Lack of proper *communication* at home, unhealthy childhood experience caused by broken homes and various other problems at home.

Irregular attendance at school, general *delinquency* during adolescence characterised by rebellion and *anti-authority* behaviour, self-indulgence in *smoking* at an early age, association with *undesirable companions,* fear of *failure* due to inability to cope with the *standards set by parents,* and unwarranted spokes by parents in the child's choice of a career that frustrates the child. (p.227).

With the above clues for identifying drug abuse in the society we may now underline what the society can do in preventing this social evil. Combating this problem is a concerted effort of the whole people, including the government.

24:5   Role of the Government

The Indian government has a New Narcotic Drugs and Psychotropic Substances Bill, 1985, prescribing a maximum punishment for drug trafficking offences to 20 years rigorous imprisonment and a fine of Rs. 2 lakhs, and a maximum punishment of 30 years rigorous imprisonment and a fine of Rs. 3 lakhs, in the case of repeat offence. The bill also has provisions for punishment in varied degrees for cultivation and processing of other drugs.

For prevention of illicit traffic in Narcotic drugs and psychotropic substances and also for combating abuse of such drugs and substances, the government of India promulgated an ordinance in July, 1988, for preventive detention of any person indulging in illicit trade or providing support to it.[7] This has some amendments in 1993.[8]

The society should voice for strict *implementation of such laws* against illicit drug dealings in the country. The government should also *publish* pamphlets for information on the various aspects of addiction. Information on drug and drug abuse should also be included in the regular *curriculum* of the schools. The government should also involve the voluntary organisations combating this evil even by financial aid. Facilities for *treatment and rehabilitation* of the addicts should be provided.

24:6   Role of Educational Institutions

The institutions should see that there is a close contact of the teachers with the students to understand their background and problems. Special care should be taken for the students from broken homes or addicted parents. The institutions should attach students Counseling Centres with the help of social workers and trained teachers. They should organize awareness programmes for teachers, students and parents. Drug peddling in the premises of the institutions should be strictly prevented.

24:7   Role of Social Welfare Organisations

As I write this section, I read in one of the dailies dated Oct.. 6, 1994 reporting that KRIPA, an NGO, which has 21 centres in the country for de-addiction and rehabilitation of drug and alcohol addicts and has counseling centres at Imphal; and Kohima, will open another counseling centre in Shillong.[9] This is encouraging. We do have in NEI, few organisations and centres dealing with this social problem. Such organisations should also produce more films and slides on addiction and its consequences to educate the mass. More forum for discussions, debates and seminars on the various aspects of addiction should be arranged.

Publication of booklets and pamphlets for a large scale education. Provide avenues for recreation, part time programmes and games for the local youth. A new de-addiction centre of 10 bed was opened at Mon Nagaland by the Army on June 3, 1996.

Local youth bodies (religious or otherwise) should co-operate to mutually help each other to eradicate the evil from the locality, even by choosing steering committee members to initiate action. Bodies like the SCM and the YMCA/YWCA/EU and local Student Unions should take active role to combat the evil.

24:8   Role of the Church

The church should understand and accept drug abuse as a pastoral problem. The attitude of the church towards the youth should be healthy, telling the truth but in love, as Paul advised (Eph.4:15). They should recognize the *psychological and developmental problems* and approach them with sympathy to these facts of life. The church should open centres for treatment and rehabilitation which are not profit oriented. Organize programmes for family enrichment, proper counselors, and awareness education. The church should have more *trained counselors*, especially the pastors. Drug addiction is a *medical problem* in which the pastors may not have the right knowledge to handle the addict. However, the pastor, with his/her healthy theology can help people find life's meaning and its moral purpose. There have been *testimonies from the recovered* addicts that they could come back to life only when they recognised *the power beyond,* God (whatever faith). A child brought up with a strong sense of *religious values* may not easily take up drugs as a solution to life's problems. The church should therefore have, greater concern in combating this evil.

24:9   Role of Parents

Almost any enquiry made for dealing with this problem would propose a heavy dose of parental role. This is because of the role they play in the formative years of the child at home. Most researchers find the age group 16-25 pro-dominant in their statistics, implying that the youth at homes are more involved. One expert maintains.

> "The best prevention of drug abuse is good parenting and the best place for preventive attitudes to develop is in the family. The child should experience unconditional love and acceptance and be encouraged to develop his or her own personality."[10]

The parents should value the child's participation in the family, recognize the child's strengths and encourage them, spend sufficient time with their children, regard the child's friends and deal with them fairly, parents should be patient enough to listen to the problems of their child. Parents should themselves do what they want their child to do.[11] They should understand their problems but be *firm* (thus saying, 'As your parent I cannot allow you to engage in harmful activities' etc.). Be supportive in helping out to find ways out from life's problems.

If, as Benjamin Labo affirms, the best way to destroy a nation is to destroy its youth, drugs have begun its invasion in our youth! And the youth are said to be 'hardly aware' of the consequences of drug taking. We must all decide individually to say 'No to drugs and say Yes to life'.

24:10 The Twelve Traditions

Our group experience suggests that the unity of the Al-Anon Family Groups depends upon our adherence to these traditions:

1. Our common welfare should come first; personal progress for the greatest number depends upon unity.

2. For our group purpose there is but one authority – a loving God as He may express Himself in our group conscience. Our leaders are but trusted servants; they do not govern.

3. The relatives of alcoholics, when gathered together for mutual aid, may call themselves an Al-Anon Family Group, provided that, as a group, they have no other affiliation. The only requirement for membership is that there may be a problem of alcoholism in a relative or friend.

4. Each group should be autonomous, except in matters affecting another group or Al-Anon or AA as a whole.

5. Each Al-Anon Family Group has but one purpose: to help families of alcoholics. We do this by practicing the twelve Steps of AA *ourselves*, by encouraging and understanding our alcoholic relatives, and by welcoming and giving comfort to families of alcoholics.

6. Our Al-Anon Family Groups ought to never endorse, finance or lend our name to any outside enterprise, lest problems of money, property and prestige divert us from our primary spiritual aim. Although a separate entity, we should always cooperate with Alcoholics Anonymous.

7. Every group ought to be fully self-supporting, declining outside contributions.

8. Al-Anon Twelfth-Step work should remain forever nonprofessional, but our service centers may employ special workers.

9. Our groups, as such, ought never be organised; but we may create service boards or committees directly responsible to those they serve.

10. The Al-Anon Family Groups have no opinion on outside issues; hence our name ought never to be drawn into public controversy.

11. Our public relations policy is based on attraction rather than promotion; we need always maintain personal anonymity at the level of press; radio, TV and films. We need to guard with special care the anoymity of all AA members.

12. Anonymity is the spiritual foundation of all our traditions, ever reminding us to place principles above personalities.

24:11 The Twelve Steps

1. We admitted we were powerless over alcohol–that our lives had become unmanageable.

2. Came to believe that a power greater than ourselves could restore us to sanity.

3. Made a decision to turn our will and our lives over to the care of God *as we understood Him.*

4. Made a searching and fearless moral inventory of ourselves.

5. Admitted to God, to ourselves and to another human being the exact nature of our wrongs.

6. Were entirely ready to have God remove all these defects of character.

7. Humbly asked Him to remove our shortcomings.

8. Made a list of all persons we had harmed, and became willing to make amends to them all.

9. Made direct amends to such people wherever possible, except when to do so would injure them or others.

10. Continued to take personal inventory and when we were wrong promptly admitted it.

11. Sought through prayer and meditation to improve our conscious contact with God *as* we understood Him, praying only for knowledge of His will for us and the power to carry that out.

12. Having had a spiritual awakening as the result of these steps, we tried to carry this message to others, and to practice these principles in all our affairs.

(Courtesy - Al-Anon's Twelve Steps & Twelve Traditions, N.Y. 1987).

24:12 Acquired Immuno Deficiency Syndrome (AIDS)

(See also appendix 2 for causative factors.)

This genocide and pandemic disease is developed from a virus called 'Human Immuno Deficiency Virus (HIV)' The first case of AIDS was detected in America in 1981, but the HIV was believed to have existed in Africa much earlier, than this. The present statistics show 14 million HIV positive patients (This includes 1 million children), in the world. Two thousand people are infected every 24 hours, and the world will have 30-40 million HIV positive patients by the year 2000 A.D.[12] It is reported that, of 3000 women contracting HIV daily and 500 women dying daily of AIDS, 70% of them are young women, of age group 15-25. Thus, higher rates of AIDS in women is reported.[13] In the US, one dies of AIDS every 14 minutes. The Sub-Saharan Africa has 8 millions HIV positive patients. Germany has about 6,500 AIDS patients of which Berlin city alone has 25,000.[14] The ninth International Conference on AIDS victim of Asia was detected in 1985.[15] UN's anti AIDS agency gives world-wide AIDS patients as 25.5 million (CL, 8-6-96).

A news write up with a headline "Declare AIDS a national Calamity" reported that India will have 5 crore HIV + patients by the year 2000 A.D., of which there will be about 50 lakhs AIDS patients. By the turn of the year 2000 India will have 40-50 million HIV patients with 10,000 dying daily and making 20,000 orphans daily. (Tel. 6.6.95)

It is reported, quoting WHO, 1999, that India will over take all African countries by 2005, "it seems like this has already happened yet the world has not realised it." This report by Lalitha gives the 2002 statistics as, World HIV+ 40 million, India 27 million which will double in 14 months.*

The founder of the Indian Health Organisation, Dr. Gilada, reports that Mumbai city, the AIDS capital of India" has 150,000 HIV patients and 15,000 full blown AIDS patients.[16] Mumbai has about 100,000 prostitutes of which 50% were found sero-positive.[17] A third of the total clientele of

---

*Leslie & Adrian eds., Called for Peace, ISPCK, Delhi, 2003.

these prostitutes are found to be students![18] A man on the average frequents these red light areas 22 times a year. Thus we can easily imagine the proliferation of the killer disease in our society. Sexual contact is said to be the highest risk of HIV infection. For, 50% of the HIV patients are found to be sex workers, 15% which are patients of Sexually Transmitted Disease (STD). In India, one most potent carrier of AIDS virus are said to be the hijras (eunuchs). India, has about 6 lakhs hijras of which 12,000 to 15,000 are in Delhi alone. These castrated males are said to engage in male prostitution, and 40% of them are found HIV positive.[19] It is generally feared that by the next couple of years India will become the worst hit AIDS country in the world! A paper published in Lancet says Mumbai is probably the most rapid generators of new HIV cases anywhere on the earth.[20] India may soon become HIV Capital, reports UN (The Stateman, Sept. 25, 1995)

Today, the world figure of the 50 million infected India is said to have 57 lakhs infected according to the report in the *Times of India, May 19, 2009.*

24:13 The North-East Indian Scene

The North-East is reported to have a quarter of the total AIDS carriers of India![21] It was reported also that Manipur may acquire the status of "AIDS capital of India."[22] According to the Centre's annual report of 1991-92, out of 1000 Indians tested, 5.2 cases of sero positive were found, and in the North-East, out of 1000 tested, 140 cases of sero positive were found. The report said that maximum numbers of sero positive cases and drug addiction were from Manipur and Nagaland.[23]

State-wise, Arunachal is presently declared AIDS free state.[24] Mizoram reported 20 HIV positive last year. Assam reported one full blown AIDS patients and 35 HIV cases last year. Meghalaya was reported "AIDS on the rise in Meghalaya" having 36 HIV cases.[25] Nagaland is reported to have 5000 intravenous drug users of which 2,500 were HIV positive and 500 full blown AIDS.[26] Dimapur town alone is reported having 700 HIV positive.[27] A total of 112 AIDS cases were also reported. Of the total AIDS cases of the NEI 91% is said to be in Manipur. Its vicinity to the Golden Triangle (Myanmar, Laos and Thailand) of drugs must be the reason for this alarming percentage. Manipur is also listed as one of the three leading AIDS cases in the country (the other two being Tamilnadu and Maharastra). The NE Sun, June 6-12, 92, reported that there were 20,000 heroin addicts in Manipur and said in every 1000 persons in the state there are 11 addicts.

As it was reported of prostitutes in Kolkata who, upon detection of having AIDS fled the place to continue their trade elsewhere in disguised names. The case of AIDS in the North-East is lurking at large, to spring to any innocent person. Few months ago a Guwahati paper reported of a professional blood donor who admitted having AIDS. Nobody is free of this pandemic. The North-east is declared "Sitting On The AIDS Bomb!" Thus it has become a community problem.

Today, of the total statistics of 2.5 million infected in the North East the number of infected people in the two leading States, Manipur and Nagaland, is figured, 29,147 people in Manipur, including 1000 children (The Sentinet, May 10, 2009), and 19,000 in Nagaland (The Times of India, May 23, 2008).

24:14 Mass Awareness for Prevention

Ways of infection : The virus is said to pass through body fluid like blood and semen (and vaginal fluid). This is why sexual contact with the infected person is to be avoided. Other infected instruments like razor, syringes, tooth brush (any poking instruments) are to be avoided or properly sterilised before use. Infected mothers also infect the foetus.

The high risk groups are said to be the IV drug users and the sex workers. In drug users, esp. the heroin addicts, the cell that fights antibody is low making them more susceptible to diseases. However, the HIV does not flow through food, water, cups, handshakes, toilet seats, insects, living or playing together as often misunderstood. It does not infect through saliva either as saliva contains proteins that check the virus. Even in AIDS patients the virus content in their saliva is found very low*

In some patients fever and throat infections come first. But symptoms vary widely over the world. In USA pneumonia is a common symptom, weight loss (slim disease) is a common symptom in Africa. In India, the common symptoms are Tubercolusis, Gastro-Intestinal.[28] Other common symptoms are prolonged sickness, persistent severe headaches, general weakness, flu or cough for more than a month, and disease of the skin and inside of the mouth. A recent report shows the mouth as manifesting symptoms for easy detection.

---

*8 out of 1000 tested reported in 1996 (clan. 22.5.96)

24:15 Preventive Measures against AIDS

It is commented that AIDS is not a medical problem as medicine has not been able to fight it. There has not been any vaccine against AIDS.* The only way to prevent it is to *Live Responsibly* with one and all in the community. Dr. Baishya, has listed five ways of living responsibly as follows:**

a)   Have sex with only one faithful partner.

b)   Use condom if you know or suspect that you or your partner is infected.

c)   Do not have sex with prostitutes (male or female) or people who go with them.

d)   Do not take an injection, except in a recognised health institution where you are sure that the instruments are sterilised.

e)   Make sure instruments for circumcision are boiled.[29]

A Zambian pamphlet on AIDS (July 1987) said the most common means of transmitting AIDS in Zambia was sexual contact, and warns us thus:

> "If you are unmarried, the key to avoiding AIDS is sexual self-control.

> If you are married, the answer is also simple: One man, one woman for life in both sense of the word 'life'."***

With regard to use of condom, the pamphlet warned: "Some people say that using a condom protects you from AIDS. But condom leaks and the protection they give is very uncertain." The UNAIDS has proposed a kind of gel to be used by the female (MMU).**** However, popularisation of condom used is the major preventive measure in permissive societies. Even 'Femidom' a protective sheath worn by the female is developed. In such societies, popularisation of condom used is demonstrated through cultural festivals, demonstrating proper condom use in amusing manners.[30] In most traditional societies of the North-East where pre-marital or extramarital sex is prohibited, homosexuality is not acceptable. Therefore condom approach may be applicable only in the cases of married partners affected

---

*   SUN, April 24, May 5, 1995.

**   Clar - May 19, 1996.

***   see infra, prevention research in progress (Appendix-I).

****   Clar 15.5.96.

by the disease. In this region, family values are still respected (as in other parts of India). A strong sense of family ties, sanctity of marriage and faithfulness to married partners are among the family values. The emergence of Christian values has reinforced these values. It is true that human nature has the tendency to abuse any good norm or value but we can still use these values as strategies in prevention of this killer disease. It has also been reported that checking the STD will cut the HIV progress by 50% (Clar 6-2-95).

More like the tribal majority of North-East India the tribal Israel had laws to maintain sanctity of life and marriage. The parents were commanded not to give their daughters to prostitution (Lev. 19:29; Dt. 23:17-18; 22:13-30). Their youngmen were admonished to avoid fleshly evils (Eccl. 11:9-10), and to avoid such enticement (Prov. 1:10). The tribal communities of the region can return to such inherent values when today, the rest of the world also teaches such sanctity and faithfulness to combat with this sexually (mostly) caused Pandemic. Such will be easier than popularisation of condom use as in other parts of the world.*

The church, with its teachings on the sanctity of marriage, forbearance and moral purpose of the whole creation can play the main role among these religious oriented communities. The church, in collaboration with the government and the non governmental organisations should organize program for public awareness of the intensity of this danger. As this pandemic sweeps over the globe, most of the people affected are found to be due to their ignorance of the intensity of these dangers. A recent report says (November '95) TV is the most important source of information on AIDS for the public in India. As this pandemic sweeps over the globe, most of the people are said to be affected due to their ignorance of its danger. Programmes should include mass education in health care, sex education in schools, teachings for responsible living, particularly to the youth. Youth organisations like the SCM should take part to organize seminars, consultations and cultural programmes with this theme. If the youth force is often used by the society including the government, the same force should also be used to fight this disease that eats away humanity. The youth can also approach the government to improve screening facilities

---

* However, Condom use is prescribed in male prisons. It is reported that homo-sexuality is found in 90% of male prisoners. "If condoms are not allowed, there are chances that "AIDS may spread inside the jail" (The weekly SUN, Oct. 1-7, 1994, p.9).

to detect the affected persons, to test blood properly before transfusion, and to check drug trafficking and flesh trade that ravage our towns.

The African communities are said to be the first causality of this dreaded disease. A Ugandian widow, Kaleeba (40), whose husband died of AIDS in 1987, founded an AIDS support organisation the same year, to train people how to take care of AIDS patients by the community itself. She says, the aim of the organisation is to improve the quality of their lives, not to stop people from dying. There the families are encouraged to take care of their own people. She says, "If AIDS took everything else out of this country, one thing we must not allow AIDS to which snatch away is 'community togetherness'. The family spirit must survive at all costs.[31]

Having taken all precautionary steps to prevent the disease, we should also consider how to live together with AIDS patients when some of us are attacked, as it will. A new art which we have to learn is the art of living together with these terminal patients: to accept them and to encourage them to die in dignity.

The church should lead in this living together with the 'poor', the afflicted with Christ-like spirit of love and care. The church need not be judgemental towards the AIDS patients as reported in some cases. This epidemic does not respect human spirituality. It can attack the innocent as well as the holy person. I would like to quote the warning from the Uganda's Health Minister, JS J.C.S. Makambi:

> "We in Africa did not have the warning or the wealth of knowledge now available on how to control the disease .... Let what has happened to us not happen to you or anybody."[32]

24:16 Taking Care of People Living with HIV/AIDS

This section summarizes some key general social support messages that are important to ensure that nutrition education is effective for both people with HIV/AIDS and their carers.

Taking Care of Yourself – Advice for the Person with HIV/AIDS

Nutrition education has a place alongside other advice and support directed at promoting well-being and positive living. General recommendations for taking care of yourself are given below:

- The body needs extra rest. Try to sleep for eight hours every night. Rest whenever you are tired.

- Try not to worry too much. Stress can harm the immune system. Relax more. Relax with people you love, your family, your children and your friends. Do things you enjoy, e.g. listen to music or read a newspaper or a book.

- Be kind to yourself. Try to keep a positive attitude. Feeling good is part of being healthy.

- Take light exercise. Choose a form of exercise that you enjoy.

- Find support and get good advice. Ask for advice from health workers. Many medical problems can be treated.

- Ask for help and accept help when it is offered.

- Stop smoking. It damages the lungs and many other parts of the body and makes it easier for infections to attack your body.

- Alcohol is harmful to the body, especially the liver. It increases vulnerability to infection and destroys vitamins in the body, under the influence of alcohol you may forget to practise safe sex.

- Avoid unnecessary medicines. They often have unwanted side-effects and can interfere with food and nutrition. If you do take medicines, read the instructions carefully.

Caring for a Person with HIV/AIDS

The carer looking after a person with HIV/AIDS may be a member of the family or, if the person lives alone, a neighbour, relative or friend. It is not easy to care for a person with HIV/AIDS and whoever grows, prepares, cooks food and serves it to a person with HIV/AIDS needs support. The task involves meeting the needs of the sick person and balancing these with the needs of other members of the family. Too much help may be overprotective and takes away the dignity, independence and self-respect of the person with HIV/AIDS while too little help may not provide the support that is needed to ensure that the person eats well and has the strength to resist infection.

24:17 Recommendations for Carers

- Spend time with the person living with HIV/AIDS. Discuss the food they need to maintain and gain weigh and manage their illness. Get to know what kind of food they like and do not like. Involve them in planning their meals.

- Keep an eye on their weight. If possible, weigh them regularly and keep a record. Look out for any unexpected weight loss and take action.

- Check the medicines they are taking. Read the instructions to find out when they need to be taken, what food to be avoided and any side-effects.

- Be encouraging and loving. If people want to have food of their choice at any time of the day, try to get it for them. They may suddenly stop liking a food, refuse what has been prepared and want something different. They are not trying to be difficult. These sudden changes in taste are a result of their illness.

- Be firm about the importance of eating and encourage them to eat frequently, but do not force them to eat. Giving them too much food at one time may cause them to refuse.

- Keep a watchful eye. Look around to see if the house is clean, that there are no hygiene problems and there is enough food.

- If the sick person lives alone, invite them to join your family for a meal. Encourage others in the community to visit them and invite them out.

Carers will have their own concerns and worries, fear of the future, for their families and for their own health. It is important that they take care of themselves, get enough rest and have the appropriate information and support to carry out their difficult task. The important messages given below cannot be emphasised enough.

- HIV/AIDS is not spread by food or water.

- HIV/AIDS cannot be spread by sharing food, dishes or cooking utensils such as cups, plates, knives and forks with a person who is HIV positive.

- HIV/AIDS cannot be spread by touching another person, hugging, shaking hands or holding other people in a normal way. There is no need to avoid body contact with a HIV positive person.

(Courtesy of FAO-2002, Living Well with HIV/AIDS, for the materials of this page)

While the dominant route is sexual, 80% above anywhere, Assam is reported the highest frequency of unprotected sex in the NEI States. Manipur is termed the 'hot bed' or the 'epicentre' of AIDS in the region.

Nagaland is ranked the 6th among AIDS populated States in the country.[33] In Nagaland the virus is reported moving toward the rural population. Rural people rarely know the danger of the virus or the need of safe sex. When infected they can neither afford the drugs to sustain themselves, nor is such facility within their reach even if they can afford to buy. Nutrition and sanitation in these rural areas are very poor too.

Science keeps us hoping. Though AIDS cure has not been reported some improved means of handling the disease or by treating the opportunistic infections, by keeping the nutritional level of the infected stable are reported. Powerful drugs like ART or HAART have been in use. HIV/AIDS vaccine is promised and being tested. Even in India such a test is promised by the end of this year.[34] Such drugs that may sustain and prolong the life of the infected are not available for all in India. Hence it is reported that the Americans live with the virus longer than Indians. All these survey is to conclude with the refrain, *science has so far been negative though HIV is positive.* This again is to assume the conquest of the virus is either distant or impossible to science. We now turn more toward what may be considered psycho-socio-religious means of sustaining as an ally to the ongoing search by the science.

24:18 Psycho-social Implications of the Infected and the Affected

Resounding the case of the lepers in the Old Testament stories the people living with HIV/AIDS (PLWHA) today are stigmatised by the society, even using terms like *'new lepers.'* The loved ones of the infected feel the same stigma as they are often looked at with fear and hate, unfortunately. They are made to feel ashamed, victimised, isolated, and even divinely punished. The spouses of the infected, especially the wives, feel cheated by their spouses. Millions of children whose parents had AIDS cannot reflect or respond but are made orphans. They are refused acceptance in the society, refused admittance in educational and recreational centers.

An overwhelming percentage of the PLWHA are reported to be youth in their age levels of 15-25. Their self-esteem, their sense of competition, consciousness in public appearance, capability, brilliancy, vision for life mission and physiological drives are all in ascending scale at this time. The moment they are diagnosed HIV+these entire aspirations come down suddenly to the lowest ebb. However, their physical needs, the need to give and receive love, their emotional susceptibility and vulnerability remain the same even after the infection. Klaus Wendler[35], in his study of the psychological impact on the infected suggests that the diagnosis makes a strong negative impact, causing despair and discouragement. Then the patient regresses psychologically to earlier stages of life which were more comfortable and gets in to denial of the reality by mental defenses saying s/he does not have AIDS, or that it can be cured. Then the patient acknowledges the reality and goes through the suffering and pain, even agreeing to continue the treatment utilising the energy and time still available with him/her. Finally, the patient accepts the reality of death and prepares for it and settles the rites of exodus with the loved ones.

The carers need to know their need of physical touch, loneliness, frustrations and resentments, including hostility to God and the doctors. They cannot bear the society's stigmatisation. Human sexuality plays such an important part in personality that its reciprocity with loved ones releases physical and emotional tensions and brings reassurance of one's importance as a person deserving love and affection. Above all, the carers should remember that their physical presence with the sufferer with the attitude of acceptance, attention, and affection, reaffirming the patient as valuable and likeable, listening patiently and reflecting to their emotional expression become important part of the caring. Klaus Wendler's advice is, "while AIDS cannot be treated, one can always care for the person until the very end." (JPC, March '89, *op.cit.*). The least we can as carers do is to help them die in respectful and affectionate manner.

24:19 Care in the Light of the Traditional Pastoral Functions

Seward Hiltner, a leading pastoral theologian from the Princeton Theological Seminary conceptualised the pastoral function under three heads: *Healing task, Sustaining task,* and *Guiding task.*[36] Later, Clebsh and Jaekle, added one more vital task as *Reconciling task* of the Pastor.[37] Still later, H.J. Clinebell, felt *Nurturing task* as another vital task of the pastoral ministry.[38] These functions are underlined here to see how the present challenge of AIDS care can be facilitated by the Church in general and the pastors in particular, assuming these tasks. Each of these is briefly examined keeping in mind the topic on AIDS care, but the first two only are examined in more detail for want of time and space in this paper.

Healing: Taking the person and the society as an organism, a functioning whole, Hiltner understood healing as the process of restoring functional wholeness that has been impaired as to direction and/schedule (PPT-p.90). Disease and illness suggest that certain direction-impairing processes are at work and that these must be deprived of force if healing is to take place. Recent drugs that prevent the virus from further reproducing can be an example.

When the disease process is arrested the healing process becomes dominant. The factors that create brokenness that requires healing, says Hiltner, are of four broad types, *Defect, invasion, distortion,* and *decision.* In the light of these conditions of brokenness the HIV can make a person broken by defect (inborn defect in the person including the lack of immune system), invasion (the virus invading the person from external agencies), distortion (by human misunderstanding and misjudging, unjust distribution of facilities, discrimination etc.) and decision (by the person's deliberate decision to adopt harmful behavior).

When two Church historians, Clebsh and Jaekle, studied the functions of Pastoral care from the historical perspectives from the early church to date they found that the church at times used a variety of instruments in healing ministry including, anointing, Saints and relics, charismatic healing, exorcism and magico-medicine. They also found that pastoral healing has been aimed to overcome some impairment by restoring a person to wholeness and by leading that person to advance beyond his/her previous condition, that is, healing had a forward gain over the condition prevailing before illness.[39] Healing of the physical wound is an area of the physician and so the pastor may have very little capability to effect healing in literal sense. Christian healing, however, should certainly be effective beyond the grave. When healing is either impossible or distant, the pastoral carer takes another mode of care, Sustaining care.

24:20 Sustaining Care

Sustaining care emphasizes on *standing by.* Sustaining ministry takes place where change is impossible at least for the moment. It is the ministry of support and encouragement when the situation is irreparable. Bereavement care is an example of sustaining care and so also the ministry to the PLWHA whose situation the pastor cannot reverse. In sustaining care even comfort is not always effective and silent companionship may do better in such situations. Later on, says Hiltner, the crisis pass or assimilate and emotion down when consolation can be relevant. The emphasis in sustaining care is on the suffering of this present time, and, not on any degree of glory which shall be revealed later (cf: Rom. 8:18). Clebsh and Jaekle found sustaining care most relevant in the early church where the church's frontiers were hostile, persecution, invasion, martyrdom that made the trend of human destiny in the hand of God appear moving downward. Sustaining care made the believers re-affirm that in spite of these destructive situations human fulfillment lay beyond such destruction. These scholars found that during these turbulent early centuries pastoral sustaining took four forms: preservation, consolation, consolidation, and redemption.

Preservation – It sought to help a suffering person suffer as little loss as possible. The ministry of holding the line against other threats, or further loss, or excessive retreat. Bereavement, receiving a life threatening medical report can be examples. A word, a glance, a word, a touch and a gesture are useful methods of caring in such a situation.

Consolation – It sought to offer the hope that actual losses could not nullify the person's opportunity to achieve his/her destiny under God. The caretakers should know when words of consolation benefit the sufferer most. Hymns and scriptures, prayers and sacraments, if used appropriately, can benefit much. Inappropriate use of religious resources can harden the sufferer's heart toward God.

Consolidation – It sought to help gather the remaining resources available to the sufferer to build a platform from which to face up to a deprived life. A PLWHA may decide to live the remaining few years for the best benefit of the family and the loved ones. Not all things of life tumble down at any loss. One can embrace the loss, 'face up to it' and build up strength again.

Redemption – It is the stage of embracing the loss and to utilize whatever is left of us by the loss. The available time is redeemed, in biblical sense (Eph. 5:16) and lived in quality. Like in consolidation above, the PLWHA can make best use of the time available with him/her and become a benefactor for many, even by advocating AIDS prevention and becoming a member of the social worker in AIDS care. John Milton, the great poet is said to have written three epics after he became completely blind. Ashok Pillai of Delhi, a PLWHA who had lived 11 years with the virus was said to be the first to spread the message that HIV was not just about dying, he said, "it is about making the best use of one's limited years" (The Times of India, April 20, 2002).

24:21 Guiding, Reconciling and Nurturing Care

Guiding, Reconciling, and Nurturing Care will also contribute important modes of ministry to the PLWHA and the affected persons around them. Guiding will include educational, preventive measures, physical arrangement and assistance. However, Hiltner made sure that pastoral guiding is not a directive guiding. Even the choice of therapy or use of means to heal can be left to the patient once the spectrum of available resources are informed to the person in need. The choice is left to the person.

Reconciling ministry will also play an important role, especially with the PLWHA and the family and the society, including reconciliation with God. Reconciling with oneself as a person and with the loved ones. Dying after reconciling with one another and reassurances of love and acceptance is different from dying with bitterness. Nurturing will have an important role in ministry to the PLWHA and the affected. Nurturing not only the body for healthy living but also the spirit with the spiritual food befitting the destiny with which God gave us life and to whom our souls will finally find rest. Empowering, is perhaps the most current role the Pastoral Carers need to assume. This will conscientize, enable support the neglected section of the society to claim their rights and stand on their feet.

Unlike the Greek philosophical concept of apathetic theology (that is, God cannot feel or suffer). Christian theology affirms the pathos of God (God capable of being affected by outside influences and feelings). The pathos of God is manifested in the divine compassion revealed in Jesus.[40] A compassionate Christian caretaker is therefore, one who exemplifies a deeply felt sense of solidarity with suffering persons transcending class and culture. Compassion is the cardinal virtue of the pastoral tradition, the indispensable quality that motivates and deepens all charitable, healing, and caring acts into events of moral and spiritual significance (Ezhanikatt, cited above). Pastoral ministry is a ministry of caring for human needs. It requires compassion, more than just sympathy in words. A case method study of pastoral theology from the global perspective concluded with a note on AIDS, thus, *"Although AIDS is an affliction with global implications, ministry to persons with the virus (or with AIDS) is highly personal, calling for deep compassion and often sacrificial love and caring."*

24:22 Some Alternative Caring Paradigm

1. *Kaleeba takes AIDS back to the Community:* Kaleeba was left a young widow after her husband died of AIDS in Uganda in 1987. Her life then was dedicated to saving humans from this cruel killer. She said, "Our principal message is faithfulness, abstinence, then condom, in that order." She found that the infected came to know their fate only when they were so told in the hospitals. Her AIDS Support Organisation (TASO) aimed to reverse this order and take the PLWHA back to the community. For it was a part of the African culture to care and support the sick by the family, much like the tribals of this region. Kaleeba, taking the patients back to community declared, *"If AIDS took everything out of this country, one thing we must not allow AIDS to snatch away is community togetherness. The family spirit must survive at all cost."*[41]

2. *Heal lives if you can't cure cancer:* A group of doctors in Kolkata seeing they could not cure the terminally ill fathers decided to raise money from among themselves and began to support those children whose parents died of cancer.[42]

3. *AIDS can't be cured, care is our immediate priority* (D.E. Messer)[43]: Messer exclaimed that there is no time even to ask whose sin causes the infection. There is no time even to ask whether God loves and cares for the PLWHA. Jesus is already at work with the PLWHA. Franklin Graham is quoted to have said, "When the history of the 21st century is written, may it be said of Christians that we show the love of Christ by leading the way in defeating HIV/AIDS."[44]

4. *AIDS can't be cured but AIDS can be treated:* Health and Family Welfare Minister, A. Ramados exclaimed this reflecting on the last International AIDS conference in Bangkok. (Nagaland Post, July 15, 2004).

5. *Bush, Atal or Gate can't stop AIDS, people on the street can:* This remark by G.N. Sibley, US Consulate General, while visiting Guwahati, is another cry to take AIDS prevention back to the common people on the street as against flood of money that won't stop AIDS and the command of the politicians which often remains only in papers. (The Sentinel, 14.12.02)

Researchers from London reported having engineered and tested a killer, T-Cell receptor that is able to recognize all of the different disguises that HIV used to evade detection. They said the disease could be a history within a decade (Times of India, Nov. 11, 2008). Again, a researchers couple, Gain and Eddy Arnolds, reported from London, that they have edged closer in developing a vaccine to guard against HIV infection by targeting a vulnerable piece of the virus (The Sentinel, March 13, 2009). In India, another weapon is developed called 'a prick-finger test' for HIV that can produce result in 20 minutes. India plans to test 22 million every year with this kith (Times of India, July 4, 2008).

24:23 Conclusion

The task of the church is healing. Healing is a concise word for all that the church does as co-worker with God in making humankind whole again. To reconcile the erring humankind to Himself has been God's mission since the Fall of humankind. Jesus was sent by God to heal the wounded souls of humankind. He was wounded so that his wounds should heal the infirmities of humankind. He is often called a wounded healer. He healed humanity without removing their pain, death and finitude, that is, heals humanity without removing sickness and death from their human sickness. He added meaning to human sickness, death and finitude. A person is healed from those life realities by going through them not by a miraculous removal of those human realities.

Counseling cannot remove human finitude. It can only help people to recognize strength and wisdom to face life's realities more meaningfully. Seward Hiltner, talking of the Pastoral task spoke of healing, but also sustaining even when healing is not possible.[45]

Wayne E. Oates talks of the Pastoral Counselors' task as "healing sometimes, remedy often, but comforting always."[46]

This implies that healing does not always mean removal of the impairment. Healing continues to take place even beyond death. That is one can die as a healed person. This understanding of healing ismore meaningful to the present day pandemic diseases like AIDS. This writer has read several times about AIDS patients testifying that they are ready to die as healed persons.

Jesus is the model healer who bore the pain and death to be victorious over them. It was also vicarious death so that his wounds should heal those he cared and died for. The prophet Isaiah put it thus;

> "Surely he has borne our griefs and carried our sorrows,..... he was wounded for our transgression... upon him was that chastisement that made us whole..." (53:4-5)

The healed and restored person is to glorify God. The Hebrews were liberated to serve God, not to live a licenscious life. Those people healed by Jesus went glorifying and testifying God. For, healing is to get back to the good relationship with God that leads to an abundant and joyful living. (See also appendix-1)

ENDNOTES

1. North-East Times (NET) Oct. 1991.

2. Sentinel, 1-4-92 (also Observer, 4-11-92.

3. NE Sun, 7-5-93 (also NET. 8-10-92).

4. Health Action, Nov. 1988, p.23.

5. Observer, 14-11-92.

6. Sentinel, 1-4-92.

7. Sentinel, 24-10-92.

8. Assam Tribune, 18-8-93.

9. Eastern Clarion, 6-10-94.

10. NE Times, 14-9-92.

11. *Ibid.*

12. Assam Tribune, 4-7-93.

13. NET, 30-7-93, TEL. 22-5-95.

14. NET 4-7-93.

15. Newsfront, 23-7-93.

16. NET 15-2-94.

17. NET 6-6-93.

18. NET 15-2-94.

19. Clarion 14-3-94.

20. Clarion 2-5-93.

21. Sentinel, 30-6-92.

22. India Today, Nov. 92.

23. Clarion, 2-5-93.

24. Clarion 17-9-94.

25. Newsfront, 28-4-93.

26. Clarion, May 2 & Dec. 3, 1992.

27. NET 29-10-92.

28. NET 3-11-92.

29. *Ibid.*

30. NET 4-7-93.

31. NET 6-6-93.

32. Assam Tribune, 4-7-93.

33. The Asian Age, Guwahati, Oct. 29, 2003 and Dec. 26, 2002.

34. The Easteen Clarion, Jorhat, Nov. 6, 2000 and Nagaland Post, July 24, 2004.

35. "Ministry to patients with AIDS: A Spiritual challenge" Journal of Pastoral Care, March 1987.

36. *Preface to Pastoral Theology,* (Abingdon, Nashville, 1958).

37. *Pastoral Care in Historical Perspectives* (Prentice Hall Inc. Englewood Cliffs, NJ 1964).

38. *Basic Types of Pastoral Care and Counseling* (Abingdon, Nashville, 1984).

39. *Pastoral care in historical perspectives,* p.33.

40. J.Moltman, *The Crucified God,* p.267.

    #Henry Wilson et.al. (eds.) *Pastoral Theology from a Global Perspective* (Orbis book, Mary Knoll, NY 1996).

41. North-East Times, Guwahati, June 6, 1993.

42. Times of India, Delhi, August 7, 2004.

43. NCCIR March 2002.

44. R.L. Hnuni, "HIV/AIDS: Biblical Perspectives" presented during Bangalore, Sept. 2003, cited above.

45. Preface to Pastoral Theology.

46. Pastoral Counseling.

CHAPTER 25

A Model of
Effective Counseling*

The purpose of this introductory book is to meet the urgent need of the students of pastoral care as well as the general pastoral ministry. Thus, the process of the pastoral interview in advanced form as the following model may not be easily grasped by students of introductory course. The following process of the interview does not mean this is a rigid framework to be followed in all circumstances. As the Counselor has to follow the agenda of the Counselee the course of the dialogue may turn up quite different from this structure. This section may be read along with Chapter 19 'Conditions for Healing Relationship'.

The following conceptual model presents three aspects of effective counseling – the phases of the process, the goals of both, the counselor and the counsele in each phase and the skills required to be utilised by the counselor for the achievement of the goals in each phase. The model is developmental in that it potrays the developments in the process, and implies the development by the counselee of the potentials required to cope with the problematic in living successfully. The model presents a pre-helping phase and three stages of the process of counseling.

PRE-HELPING (Expressing-Attending)

This phase refers primarily to the counselor. The counselee may initiate the process by asking to speak with the counselor. On the other hand, the counselor may pick up in a conversation, distress signals from a person,

---

*This Outline model is from a handout given by Carlos Welch in a counseling Workshop, Bangalore, 1986.

such as, a sigh, a disturbed look in the eyes, statements like, "I just don't understand...', "It's just becoming too much", "Why is this happening to me?", etc. On becoming aware of such expressions, the counselor focuses attention on the person and indicates willingness to listen.

Counselor's Goal: Attending

To attend to the other, both physically and psychologically: to focus awareness on the verbal and non-verbal expressions of the other.

Counselor's Skills: Listening Attentively

The Counselor, by his/her posture, as counselor, now focuses attention on the questions: What is this person communicating about him/herself? About his/her feelings? About his/her thinking? About his/her behaviour? About difficulties in living?

STAGE I : Self Exploration - Responding

While attending to a congregation member, or another person, the pastoral person becomes aware that the other has expressed something personally significant. He/she responds in a way that *helps the counselee explore his/her behaviour* (feelings: attitudes: what he/she does, fails to do: what is destructive or constructive in his/her living. etc.)

Counselor's Goal: Responding Accurately

To respond to the other with empathy, genuineness and respect: to establish rapport (a trusting, collaborative working relationship): to respond with the most accurate understanding of what the **counsellee** has expressed so as to facilitate the counselee's self exploration.

Counselor's Skills

Empathic Understanding-the counselor responds to the counselee in a way that shows he/she has listened and that he/she understands what the counselee is expressing about himself and what he/she is feeling. In some sense, the counselor sees the counselee's world from the counselee's frame of reference. It is not enough to understand: the counselor communicates his/her empathic understanding.

Genuineness - The counselor is open, spontaneous in his/her responding. At this time, he/she is a human being to the person before him/her. The roles of priest, pastor, teacher, administrator, etc., are transcended and the counselor is transparent in his/her warmth and concern.

Concreteness - When the **counsellee** rambles or speaks in generalities, the counselor grounds the helping process in concrete feelings and concrete behaviour. The counselor communicates in ways that models focussing on specifics.

The skills of stage I are crucial. If the helper does not have them, she/he simply cannot help, for the skills of stages II and III are built on them. The ways in which empathic understanding, respect and genuineness are expressed may change somewhat as the counselor moves deeper into the helping process, but the need for these skills continues throughout the process.

Counselee's Goal: **Self Exploration**

To explore his/her experiences, behaviour, and feelings relevant to the problem in his/her life: to tell the story of emotionally stressful events: to explore the ways in which he/she is living ineffectively.

Utilising the responses of the counsel\or, the counselee expands his/her awareness of him/herself. In the process, he/she *clarifies issues*, begins to recognize patterns in behaviour and becomes conscious of feelings in relation to failures, needs and goals. While not an end in itself, self exploration is necessary to reach self understanding, which is the foundation for change reflected in action.

STAGE II : **Integrative Understanding/Dynamic Self Understanding**

As the person receiving help explores the various problem areas of his/her life. He/she gives away enough data that is useful to the degree that *it can be pieced together* to reveal behavioural patterns in his/her life. He/she begins to understand him/herself in ways that were not apparent before. He/she begins to *own responsibility from his/her* thoughts, feelings and actions. He/she experiences insight.

Counselor's Goal : Integrative Understanding.

To understand and fit together the data produced by the counselee: to see and help the other identify behavioural themes: to help other see the "larger picture".

Counselor's Skills : All the skills of Stage I

Facilitative Self-Disclosure: The helper shares his/her own experiences to the extent that it will actually help the counselee understand him/herself. The counselor is free and spontaneous in volunteering personal information about him/herself, provided this communication is constructive in facilitating the client to deeper self understanding.

Immediacy of Relationship : The helper is willing to explore his/her own relationship to the **counsellee** ("You-me" talk), to explore the here-and-now of counselor-**counsellee** interaction to the degree that it helps the counselee get a better understanding of him/herself, of his/her interpersonal style and of how he/she is utilising the helping process.

Confrontation : The counselor speaks specifically about discrepancies, distortions and inconsistencies in the counselee's life and in his/her interactions within the helping relationship itself to the degree that it helps the **counselee** develop self-understanding that leads to constructive behavioural change.

Counselee's goal : Dynamic Self Understanding

To develop understanding that sees the need for change, for action: learning the skill of putting together the larger picture for him/herself: identifying resources, especially unused resources.

Ideally, as stage II progresses, the counselee sees more and more clearly the necessity for action on his/her part. He/She might well be fearful of change and may doubt that he/she has the resources necessary for change. These fears and doubts must be dealt with if he/she is to act. Sometimes he/she needs to be supported to act first in order to learn that his/her fears and doubts are baseless. The dynamic self understanding sought in stage II may be defined as insight that leads to action programmes.

STAGE III : Acting Action - Fecilitating

Effective counseling leads ultimately to changes in behaviour. The procrastinator meets deadlines comfortably: persons in conflict work through to resolution: passive persons take initiative etc. In this final stage, the counselor and counselee work together in such a way that the counselee experiences satisfaction in living effectively.

Counselor's goal : Facilitating action

To collaborate with the counselee in working out specific action programmes: to stimulate the counselee to act on his/her new understanding of him/herself: to explore with the counselee a wide variety of alternatives for engaging in constructive behavioural change: to give support to and direction to action programmes.

Counselor's Skill

ALL THE SKILLS OF STAGE I.

ALL THE SKILLS OF STAGE II.

Developing action programmes - Utilising problem clarifying and problem solving approaches, decision making processes, programme planning models, training in interpersonal skills.

Counselor's Goal: Acting

This may mean stopping self endangering activity, like absenteeism. This may mean starting on some programme of growth, i.e., a physical fitness programme. This may mean developing new attitudes, such as, a sense of self worth through the conscious monitoring of accomplishments. Someone may decide to "talk things over with the boss." If so, the learning of communication skills may be a pre-requisite programme. The results of effective counseling are revealed in action, or, changes in behaviour.

In most cases, the counselor and the counselee collaborate in both the elaboration of action plans and the working through of problems that may arise as the programmes are pursued. If action programmes require prior skills training, the counselor may train the counselee him/her self, or refer him/her to someone also. If a referral is made, it is important that the helper maintains contact with the counselee and supports him/her through the skills training programme.

POST COUNSELING: Celebration

The satisfaction and fulfilment experienced by the counselor and counselee as effective counseling results in effective living by the counselee, spontaneously leads to celebration. Awkward efforts at expressing appreciation on the part of the counselee are best met over a cup of tea, as the transition is made to discontinuing the "counseling" relationship amidst the other relationships and roles of pastor and parishioner, teacher and student, etc.

APPENDIX 1

On the Road to Conquest of AIDS

The following are some news captions and reports from the ongoing research to conquer this dreaded pandemic: AIDS. Perhaps some of these attempts have been further developed, if not proved abortive by today. This is just a list of daily news items remembered by the present writer.

1. A vaccine against AIDS tested on monkeys found successful. Result of its efficacy on human awaited. (March '96).

2. A test conducted by transplanting baboon's marrow on AIDS patient. Its result awaited. (March '96)

3. Use of HIV-2, a weaker virus than the HIV-I as vaccine on the manner cow-pox used to immunize small-pox, is attempted. Prostitutes infected with HIV-2 found 70% less chance of getting the HIV-1. Further, its presence (HIV-2) may prolong the incubation period by 50%, say 25 years as against 10 years now before the HIV-1 is developed. (June '95)

4. Acupuncture may cure AIDS, Cancer (March '95)

5. Aspirin may sound HIV's death knoll (Feb. '95)

6. Heat therapy for AIDS patients? (March '95) (More for India)

7. Indian developed AIDS test kit cheapest (June '95)

8. Urine therapy cure AIDS (March '95)

9. Ayurvedic compound brings hope to AIDS (April '95)

10. Sidha Medical System claims AIDS cure (Nov. '95)

11. 'Super' anti-AIDS vaccine on the anvil, a 'super antigen' that will prevent developing AIDS in the HIV infected.

12. New gene therapy approach has infinite power and may help treat AIDS (The Hindu 26.12.02)

13. Protein may help fight against AIDS (TOI - Sept.'02).

14. A cocktail of HAART (highly active anti-retroviral therapy) can keep HIV from spreading (Sent. 21.10.03).

15. India's first candidate for AIDS vaccine to be tested by the end of 2003 (Sent. 13.10.03).

16. Better sanitation, better nutrition, people's acceptance and care of the infected, and above all the person's will to live can prolong life even after infection. However, on the conquest of the virus the medical science is still negative though HIV is Positive.

   Of late, *The Times of India* has been making the public aware of the killer disease how to prevent it and also how science is revealing possibilities of its conquest in few years.

The following are among them:

17. That people in Pakistan who considered AIDS as taboo and hushed from open talk now consider it as a problem affecting the country. The people see religious preachers as influential and the preacher of Islam, Hinduism and Christianity, including the teacher of Seminaries in the country are engaged to make the people aware of the Pandemic.[1]

18. That Chennai based Indian researchers are heading to prove indigenously developed AIDS vaccine to be successful.[2]

19. That both US and UK scientists are hoping to conquer this pandemic and making it a history within a decade.[3]

ENDNOTES

1. *The Times of India*, December 27, 2008.

2. *The Times of India*, August 2008.

3. *The Times of India*, November 2008.

APPENDIX 2

AIDS
Causative Factors Reported Recently

1. The belief for about twenty years that the HIV was first transmitted to humans by chimpanzees is revolutionised by a new discovery HIV-like virus in monkeys. This virus is named Simian Immunodeficiency Virus (SIV) discovered in the spot-nose monkeys. Humans got the virus by eating the infected meat of the spot-nose monkeys. (reported by the Sentinel, April 2002 quoting *Down to Earth).*

2. In some communities the myth of AIDS cure by raping a virgin is still strong. In India women are made potential causes as their ability to negotiate. Violence against women and coerced sex in India are causes to infecting women with the virus every few minutes. (Sentinel, Aug. 2002).

3. War condition facilitates spread of AIDS. For, soldiers committing the crime of rape will not pause to wear condom. The wounded soldier does not have time to test the donated blood to be transfused, either. (July '95)

4. Dead bodies can transmit AIDS when the bereaved members hug or kiss the love one who died of AIDS. (April '95)

5. Some AIDS patients get married by mutual agreement. Three such couples were reported in India in June 1995. But the situation is grave when some partners know they are infected before marriage and 'deceive their brides by not disclosing to them'. A patient revealed at a clinic:

"In our community after the husband's death, the wife commits *sati* (suicide). I have AIDS. Why should not I die after marriage along with my wife." (June '95)

6. Spreading AIDS in an act of revenge. A 28 year old man from Luco, Spain was reported saying, "I like infecting other people" as a revenge after he was tested having the HIV. (April '96).

APPENDIX 3

SCRIPTURE
Text for use in Counseling

Avoid random reading of the passages. Read them well beforehand and meditate upon them before you present them appropriately. Use these only where relevant.

Anxiety and worry:	Ps. 43:5, Mt. 31-33; Phil. 4:6-7, 19:1 Pet. 5:7.
Bereavement & loss:	Deut 31:8; Ps. 27:10; Ps. 119:50; 91; 2 Cor. 6:10.
Comfort & blessing:	Ps. 23:4; Lam. 3:22-23; Mt. 5:4 Mt. 11:28-30; Jn. 14:16-18; Rom. 15:4; 2 Cor. 1:3-4; 2 Thess 2:16-17.
Developing confidence:	Ps. 27:3; Prov. 3:26; 14:26; Is. 30:15; Gal. 6:9; Eph. 3:11-12; Phil 1:6; 4:13; Heb. 10:35; 1 Pet. 2:9.
Protection from danger:	Ps. 23:4; 32:7; 34:7; 17; 19; 91:1-2; 11; 121:7-8.
Fear of death:	Ps. 23:4; 116:15; Lam. 3:32-33; Rom 14:8; 2 Cor. 5:1; Phil 1:21; Thess 5:9-10; 2 Tim. 4:7-8; Rev. 21:4.
Discipline through difficulties:	Rom. 8:28; 2 Cor. 4:17; Heb. 5:8; 12:7; 11; Rev. 3:19.
Disappointment:	Josh 1:9; Ps. 27:14; 43:5; Jn. 14:1; 27:16-33; Heb. 4:16; 1 Jn. 4:15.
Development of faith	Rom. 4:3; 10:17; Eph 2:8-9; Heb 11:6; 12:2a; Jas 1:3; 5-6; 1 Pet 1:7.

Fear:	Ps. 27:1; 56:11; Prov. 3:25-26; Is 51:12; Jn. 14:27; Rom 8:31; 2 Tim. 1:7; Jn 4:18.
Forgiveness of sin:	Ps. 32:5:1-19; 103:3; Prov. 28:13; Is. 1:18; 55:7; Jas 5:15-16; 1 Jn. 1:9.
Forgiving others:	Mt. 5:44-47; 6:12; 14; Mk. 11:25; Eph. 4:32; Col. 3:13.
Friends & friendship:	Prov. 18:24; Mt. 22:39; Jn 13:35; 15:13-14; Gal. 6:1; 10.
Growing spiritually:	Eph. 3:17-19; Col. 1:9-11; 3:16; 1 Tim 4:15; 2 Tim 2:15; 1 Pet 2:2; 2 Pet. 1:5-8; 3:18.
Guidance:	Ps. 32:8; Is. 30:21; 58:11; Lk. 1:79; Jn. 16:13; Jas. 1:5.
Help & care:	2 Chron 16:9a: Ps. 34: 7, 37:23-34; 91:4; Is. 50:9; 54:17; Heb. 4:16:13-5-6; 1 Pet. 5:7.
Living the Christian life:	Ps. 119:11; Jn. 15:7; 2 Cor. 5:17; Col 2:6; 1 Pet 2:2; 1 Jn. 1:7
Loneliness:	Ps. 23:27:10; Is 41:10; Mt. 28:20b; Heb. 13:5,6.
The love of God:	Jn. 3:16; 15:9; Rom 5:8; 8:38-39; 1 Jn. 3:1.
Obedience :	1 Sam. 15:22; Ps 111:10; 119:2; Mt. 6:24; Jn. 14:15; 21; Jas 2:10; 1 Jn. 3:22.
Overcoming temptation	Is. 41:10; Mt. 26:41; 1 Cor. 10:13; Phil 1:6; 2 Thess 3:3; 2 Pet 2:9.
Peace of mind:	Is. 26:3; Jn. 14:27; 16:33; Rom. 5:1; Phil 4:7; Col. 3:15.
Persecution:	Mt. 5:10-12; 10:22; Acts 5:41; 9:16; Rom 8:17; 2 Tim 3:12; Heb. 11:25; 1 Pet. 2:20.
Praise & gratitude:	1 Sam. 12:24; Ps. 34:1; 51:15; 69:30; 107:8; 139:14; Eph. 5:20; Heb. 13:15.
Provision:	Ps. 34:10; 37:3-4; 84:11, Is. 58:11; Mt. 6:33; Rom. 8:32; 2 Cor. 8:9; Phil. 4:19; 1 Tim. 6:17.
Return of Christ:	Mt. 24:30-31; 36; Lk. 21:36; Acts 1:11; 1 Thess 4:16-18; Tit. 2:13; 1 Jn. 3:2-3; Rev. 1:7.

Sickness & infirmity:	Ps. 41:3; 103:3; Mt. 4:23; Jn. 11:4; Jas. 5:15-16.
Sin :	Is. 53:6; 59:1-2; Jn. 8:34; Rom. 3:23; 6:23; Gal. 6:7-8.
Sorrow:	Prov. 10:22; Is. 53:4; Jn. 16:22; 2 Cor. 6:10; 1 Thess. 4:13; Rev. 21:4.
Strength :	Deut. 33:25; Ps. 27:14; 28:7; Is. 40:29-31; 2 Cor. 12:9; Phil 4:13.
Suffering:	Rom 8:18; 2 Cor. 1:5-7; Phil 1:29; 3:8; 10; 2 Tim. 2:12; 1 Pet. 2:19; 4:12-13; 16; 5:10.
Temptation:	1 Cor. 10:12-13; 12-13; Heb. 2:18; Jas. 1:2-3, 12-14; 1 Pet. 1:6; 2 Pet. 2:9; Jude 1:24.
Trust:	Ps. 5:11; 18:2; 37:5; Prov 3:5:6; Is. 12:2.
Victory :	2 Chron 32:8; Rom 8:37; 1 Cor. 15:57; 2 Cor. 2:14; 1 Jn. 5:4; Rev. 3:5; 21:7.
Witnessing:	Ps 66:16; Mk. 5:19; Lk. 24:47-48; Acts 1:8; 4:20.

Glossary

This section is included to acquaint the reader with the common expressions found in counseling literatures and conversations. This is not to pretend that pastoral carers are trained to use psychiatric jargons fluently. These terms are available in plenty in pastoral care literatures and this inclusion will save the busy pastors' time by avoiding search for dictionaries of psychology. These terms are drawn from two psychiatric glossaries and modified where necessary.*

Abnormal Behaviour : A pattern of behaviour considered to be outside the limits generally set for a given time, place and culture. An abnormal people cannot respond appropriately to stimuli.

Abreaction : Release of repressed emotion and ideation, especially during psychoanalytic therapy (see Catharsis)

Alcoholic Anonymous : A lay organisation with branches in many large cities, organised for the purpose of treating alcoholic addicts by personal, religious and social rehabilitation.

Ambivalence : Incompatibility of simultaneous attitudes, generally unconscious, with regard to alternative possibilities of action, e.g., mixed love and hate for the same person.

---

*A psychiatric Glossary : American Psychiatric Association, 1957, and *Principles of Dynamic Psychiatry*, J.H. Masseraman, W.B. Saunders, London, 1946.

Amnesia	:	Loss of memory; inability to recall certain specific events following certain traumatic experiences.
Anima	:	The inner 'being' in Jungian concept as against the outer characteristics of the personality.
Anxiety	:	A state of apprehensive tension experienced in circumstances of direct or symbolic danger. When anxiety is persistent it is called Worry. When worry is intense it becomes Panic.
Attitude	:	A readiness to react in accordance with referential patterns predetermined by individual experience.
Addiction	:	Strong emotional and physiological dependence upon alcohol or a drug which has progressed beyond voluntary control.
Amentia	:	Absence of intellect. The basis of amentia is usually organic and due to a developmental lack of adequate brain tissue.
Auto-Erotism	:	Securing or attempting to secure sensual gratification from one's self. This is a characteristic of an early stage of emotional development.
Behaviorism	:	A system of psychology that studies the behaviour of human beings (Watson) and excludes consciousness and other subjective and conative considerations as irrelevant.
Birth Trauma	:	The deprivation of womb security at birth (Rankian theory), constituting a 'psychic' shock which leaves an unconscious but ineradicable anxiety.
Bestiality	:	Sexual relation between human and animal.
Catastrophic Reaction	:	Severe disintegration of behaviour under excessive stress, especially in patients whose adaptive capacities are impaired by cerebral injury.
Catharsis	:	The partial dissipation of the morbid, residue of a repressed traumatic experience by the

therapeutic verbalisation or acting out, accompanied by affective discharge. It is the process of releasing an emotional pent-up (bottled up emotion).

Censor	:	In psychoanalytic theory, that function of the Ego or Super-Ego that bars dangerous impulses or ideas from consciousness, or distorts and disguises them by displacement, reversal and symbolisation, as in dreams.
Collective Unconscious	:	In Jungian theory, a portion of the unconscious common to all human kind; also called racial unconscious. A given race may have a distinct collective unconscious, so also to all living things.
Complex, Inferiority	:	Unconscious feeling of inferiority or in adequacy stemming from excessive disciplinary subordination or physical inadequacy (organ inferiority) in childhood, for which the individual may try to *overcompensate* by excessive ambitiousness, aggressiveness, domination, or special accomplishment to erase the handicap.
Complex, Electra	:	Denotes the incestuous attachment of the female child to her father (from the Greek myth of Electra's love for her father and her revenge on her mother).
Complex, Oedipus	:	The erotic attachment of the child to the parent of opposite sex, repressed because of the fear of castration (Freud) by the jealous parent.
Confidential Respect	:	This is a very important element of caring and counseling relationship. Students are so familiar with the word 'confidence' that they always take for granted and do not learn its meaning in healing relationship. It has nothing to do with the confidence of the counselee or the counselor. Confidentiality, or confidential respect refers to the rule of respecting confidential information. More specifically, the counselor keeps secret whatever the counselee communicates at

personal conversations in a trust relationship. Confidential respect is a quality in a disciplined person in areas of profession and human relationships Confidentiality is required quality in person living and working together, beginning from the couple's conversation to the resolutions of the Board of Deacons to the physicians's chamber, and to the staff of national security. The counselors do not reveal any information given by the counselee during session without permission from the informant or counselee.

Criminality	:	A social, anti-social or illegal conduct which is in accordance with the conscious standards and intent of the individual.
Defence Mechanism	:	A process by which the EGO partially satisfies the unconscious instinctive drives of the *Id* by behaviour that conforms with the self-regulative demands of the SUPER EGO. Repression, Rationalisation, Projection and Compensation, are among the mechanisms.
Dementia	:	Deteroration of perceptive, integrative and manipulative capacities due to organic disease of the brain.
Denial	:	An unconscious defence whereby the patient refuses to recognize or accept unwelcome connotation or concepts. The material denied may be a thought, wish, need, or external reality factors. What is consciously intolerable is simply disowned by the protectively automatic and unconscious denial of its existence.
Depression	:	A state characterised effectively by maintained dejection in mood, ideologically by gloomy ruminations or foreboding, and physiologically by the depressive syndrome. Psychiatrically, a morbid sadness, dejection or melancholy; to be differentiated from grief which is realistic and proportioned to what has been lost. Depression may vary in depth from neurosis to psychosis.

Diagnosis	:	The determination of the nature and intensity of a morbid process or processes.
Dipsomania	:	Morbid addiction to alcoholic drinks. Recurrent bouts of extreme drunkenness between periods of sobriety.
Displacement	:	The transfer of symbolic meaning or value from one object or concept to another : e.g., a mother may cherish a pet excessively after her child's death. An emotion is transferred or "displaced" from its original object to a more acceptable substitute object (an employee kicks the dog instead of this boss).
Dynamics	:	The determination of how an emotional or a behaviour pattern develops; the mechanisms of the development of emotional reactions, especially intrapsychic defence mechanisms.
Electroshock Therapy	:	A form of treating psychiatric disorders by passing an electric current through the brain, usually with the induction of convulsion and coma.
Ellipsis	:	The omission of words, phrases, or thoughts from their context, due to unconscious repression or organic impairment.
Emotion	:	A subjective feeling (of which one may or may not be aware), such as fear, anger, grief, joy or love.
Empathy	:	The objective recognition of the significance of another's behaviour, as distinguished from *sympathy*. Empathy denotes a deeper understanding, of the feelings, emotions, and behaviour of another person, and their meaning and significance.
Eros	:	From the God of Passion in Greek mythology; an instinct related to love of self or others. In psychoanalytic theory, every person has two instincts: *eros* and *thanatos*, one for love and preservation and the other for destruction and death.

Erotomania	:	Excessive preoccupation with erotic fantasies and activities; usually used with reference to morbidly increased heterosexuality.
Euphoria	:	An exaggerated sense of well-being, usually accompanied by discontentment, carefree hyperactivity. The sense of well being is not consonant with apparent stimuli or events, usually of psychologic origin, but also seen in organic brain disease and toxic states.
Euthanasia	:	The induction of death, particularly in the incurably ill, by rapid and painless methods.
Exhibitionism	:	Erotic pleasure in exposing the body, with or without concomitant desire to stimulate a sex partner. Usually a "showing off" of the male genitals to females for sexual gratification.
Fantasy	:	Imagined scenes or occurrences.
Fear	:	Emotional response to consciously recognised and external sources of danger, to be distinguishedfrom anxiety.
Fetishism	:	Process of attachment of special meaning to an inanimate object (or fetish) which serves, usually unconsciously, as a substitute for the original object or person. The substitute object is often a neurotic source of sexual stimulation or gratification. In sexology, a fetish is an object charged with special sentimental or erotic interests.
Fornication	:	Extramarital coitus.
Free Association	:	In psychoanalytic therapy, unselected verbalisation by the patient of whatever comes to mind. The therapist asks the patient to express or describe all thoughts, sensations and emotions as they occur during the therapy.
Gerontophilia	:	Fascination with old people (paedophilia refers to fascination with children)

Gestalt Psychology : A German school of psychology which places emphasis on a total perceptual configuration and the interrelations of its component parts (see Gestalt therapy in this book).

Grandiosity : Delusions of being wealthy, famous, powerful, omniscient etc.

Guilt : Conscious or unconscious dread of loss of love or retributive punishment for impulses or deeds forbidden in earlier experiences.

Grief : A normal, appropriate emotional response to an external and consciously recognised loss; self-limiting and gradually subsiding within a reasonable time (to be distinguished from depression).

Homesexuality : Erotic interest or relations between individuals of the same sex. Lesbianism is the homosexual love between women.

Hydrotherapy : Treatment of disease by various types of baths or by internal administration of water.

Hallucination : A false sensual perception in the absence of an actual external stimulus. Hallucination can be of emotional or chemical (drug, alcohol etc.) origin, and may occur in any of the five senses.

Hamartophobia : Morbid dread of sinning.

Hedonism : The doctrine that all behaviour is, or should be, directed toward securing a maximum balance of pleasure, and avoiding displeasure as far as possible.

Hypnosis : A trance-like passive state produced by reiterated suggestions that makes the subject manifest increased receptivity to suggestions and directions (Mesmerism was an earlier term for hypnosis).

Hysteria : An illness resulting from an emotional conflict and generally characterised by immaturity, impulsiveness, attention-seeking and the use of mental mechanisms of conversion and

		dissociation. Manifestations are hysterical blindness, paralysis or convulsions.
Idiosyncrasy	:	A delimited behaviour pattern in one individual considered peculiar by another but not sufficiently so to be called neurotic or psychotic.
Illusion	:	A misinterpretation of a sensory percept; usually correctable by closer or supplementary examination of the stimulus which induced the illusion.
Impotence	:	Impaired ability to erect the penis for intercourse, due to neurotic inhibition or by organic disease.
Incest	:	Culturally prohibited sexual relations between members of a family, as between father and daughter, or brother and sister.
Inhibition	:	Unconscious interference with or restriction of instinctual drives. The internal checking or restrain of a conation, affect, thought or act.
Insanity	:	A vague legal term variously connoting inability "to distinguish right and wrong", a mental state in which the person is unable to care for oneself or constitute a danger to others.
Inversion	:	Assumption of feminine sexual role by men, or a masculine one by women.
Id	:	All the unconsciously determined instincts or libidinal strivings constituting the conative portion of the personality.
Latency period	:	The period between five and puberty when libidinal drives (oral, anal, genital) recede from direct expression because of the progressive formation of Ego Defences.
Libido	:	The energy associated with the instincts of the Id. Sex drive included life force.
Lunacy/Lunatic	:	Obsolete legal terms for insanity or psychotic.
Mania	:	A mental illness marked by heightened excitability, acceleration of thought, speech, and

		bodily motion, and by elation and grandiosity of mood. It is a morbid preoccupation with some impulse, idea or activity, e.g., dipsomania (of drink), kleptomania (of stealing) etc.
Masochism	:	In sexology, erotic desire derived from physical pain. The pain may be inflicted by oneself or by others. It may be consciously sought or unconsciously 'arranged' or invited.
McNaghten Rule	:	(From McNaghten who murdered England's Prime Minister's secretary). This rule implies that the criminal is not guilty if s/he was labouring under such a defect of reason, from disease of the mind, as not to know the nature and quality of the mind, as not to know the nature and quality of the act one was doing, or if he did know, that he did not know he was doing what was doing.
Narcissism/Narcism	:	(From Narcissus who fell in love with his reflected image) Self love. Refers also to the self-interest in children which is normal but is pathogenic in adult.
Neurosis	:	A behaviour disorder characterised by anxiety, phobias, obsessions or compulsions, etc. caused by unresolved unconscious conflicts. Neurosis is one of the two major categories of emotional illness, the other being the psychoses. Neurosis is with minimal loss of contact with reality. Neurotic illness represents the attempted resolution of unconscious emotional conflicts in a manner that handicaps the effectiveness of a person in living. There are types of neuroses classified according to the particular symptoms which predominate.
Nonverbal communications	:	A good listening requires more than just two ears. It is often said that a person communicates his/her inner state only 30% verbally and communicates 70% non-verbally. This would mean telephonic counseling is lesser effective than face to face counseling so far as the counselor's grasping of the gravity of the

problem is concerned. Even in telephonic conversation the counselor would gather information through the pace, tone, the Para-Language, and the quality and the structure language of the speaker. The other aspects of non-verbal communications include: posture, eyes contact, facial expressions, dresses, distancing, kind of perfume used, gestures, moist palm, dry throat, time management, palpitations, insomnia, and frequent body movement. All these behaviors of the counselee communicate along with or without verbal communications. A counselor, listening to the mere words only of the counselee will therefore miss the point.

Obsession	:	A persistent conscious desire or ideas, recognised as being more or less irrational by the subject which usually impels compulsive acts on pain of anxiety if they are not performed.
Onanism	:	Coitus interrupted for extravaginal ejaculation, as in the biblical story of Onan (Gen. 38:4-10).
Orgasm	:	The height of erotic pleasure, just preceding detumescence and relaxation. It generally refers to erotic sensation centred in the genitals, but orgastic sensations in the mouth, breasts, anus or even skin (as in masturbatory - equivalent scratches) have been described.
Panic	:	Extreme anxiety, with blind flight or marked disorganisation of behaviour.
Phobia	:	(From greek word 'phobos' meaning fear). It is a repressed fear transferred to a particular object or event, the resulting fear or terror of which is called 'Phobia'. Most people have one or more phobias, usually of mouse, snakes, insects or other objects or situations. But in some individuals such fears are so intense as to interfere with their normal living, restricting their freedom or requiring the constant presence of another person. All phobias are unreasonable fear resulting from varieties of disguised or

converted emotional apprehensions. Examples, *ergasiophobia* = morbid dread of activity, *zoophobia* = morbid fear of animals, *nyctophobia* = of night, *hydrophobia* = of water etc.

Pleasure Principle : The psychoanalytic concept that humans, instinctally seek to avoid pain and discomfort and strive for gratification and pleasure. In personality development theories the pleasure principle antedates and subsequently comes in conflict with the reality principle. The tendency to seek release from the libidinal tensions.

Psychosis : A severe emotional illness in which there is a departure from normal pattern of thinking, feeling and acting. It is commonly characterised by loss of contact with reality, distortion of perception, regressive behaviour and attitudes, diminished desire of elementary impulses and desires, abnormal mental content including delusions and hallucinations. Many of such patients require commitment to a mental hospital. This is one of the two major categories of mental illness, the other being *neurosis*.

Psychosomatic Medicine: *Psychosomatic* refers to the constant and inseparable interaction of the mind (psyche) and the body (soma). The study, theory and application of dynamics of total behaviour (biodynamics) in relation to the practice of medicine and its several specialties.

Psychotherapy : The generic term for any type of treatment which is based primarily upon verbal and non-verbal communication with the patient in distinction to the use of drug, surgery, or physical measures such as electro or insulin shock, hydro-therapy and others. Most physicians regard intensive psychotherapy as a medical function. Psychotherapy is also the science and the art of influencing behaviour so as to make it more individual, and more compatible with social norms.

Rapport	:	An inter-personal relationship in which each participant feels a non-competitive sharing or compatibility of desires and goals.
Reality Principle	:	In Freudian theory, the concept that the pleasure principle in personality development in infancy is normally modified by the inescapable demands and requirements of external reality. The process by which this compromise is affected is called "reality testing".
Regression	:	The resumption under stress, of earlier and experientially more satisfactory modes of behaviour. In psychoanalytic theory it is the return to infantile phases of libidinal organisation. Such behaviour is also seen is severely psychotic patients.
Sadism	:	Pleasure, often directly erotic, in inflicting pain or other suffering on human beings or animals. This is the reverse of *masochism*.
Schizophrenia	:	Various types of severe emotional disorder of psychotic depth characteristically marked by a retreat from reality with delusion formations, hallucinations, emotional disharmony, and regressive behaviour. Formerly, this was called *dimentia praecos*.
Sympathy	:	A compatibility of desire or affect between two persons, distinguished from *empathy*. Sympathy is an expression of compassion for another's grief or loss.
Telepathy	:	The communication of thoughts from one person to another without the intervention of physical means. Not yet generally accepted as scientifically valid (cf: extrasensory perception).
Transference	:	The unconscious attachment to others of feelings and attitudes which were originally associated with important figures (parents, siblings etc.) in one's early life. More specifically, the unconscious attitude of the patient toward the analyst and the role in which the latter is

fantasised e.g. maternal, rivalrous, erotic. etc., (cf: countertransference).

Trauma : A physical or psychological injury which is disruptive to the optimal adaptations of the organism.

Unconscious : (Freudian) that part of the mind or mental functioning the content of which is only rarely subject to awareness. It is a repository for data which has never been conscious, or which may have become conscious briefly and was then repressed. In Freudian theory, it is the portion of the personality which is in contact with the *id*, and the function of which are not available to direct awareness.

Voyeurism : Erotic pleasure in clandestine peeping. A compulsive interest in watching or looking at others, particularly at genitals. It is roughly synonymous with "Peeping Tom". This behaviour is found mostly in males.

Word Salad : A mixture of words and phrases which lack comprehensive meaning or logical coherence, commonly seen in schizophrenic.